PENGUIN BUSINESS
EXPROVEMENT

Innovation practitioner **Hersh Haladker** is the founder of InstillMotion, an innovation lab and consulting firm that has worked with several Fortune 500 companies, across a variety of industries, to enable the exprovement of unique business challenges. With a career spanning over sixteen years, and a background in innovation design from the Royal College of Art, innovation engineering from Imperial College London and innovation entrepreneurship from Imperial College Business School, his unique solutions stem from the three-pronged perspective of creativity, feasibility and good business sense. He is a Fellow of Design London, and through InstillMotion Labs, has developed several novel innovations that have been granted patents.

Raghunath Mashelkar is India's preeminent research and innovation leader. He has been the director general of Council of Scientific and Industrial Research (CSIR), the president of Indian National Science Academy, the chairman of National Innovation Foundation and the president of Global Research Alliance. He has served on the board of directors of leading companies, from Reliance to Tata Motors to Hindustan Unilever. He has won over sixty national and international awards and medals, besides being honoured with forty-five honorary doctorates from universities around the world. He was a member of the Science Advisory Committee formed by successive governments for around thirty years. The President of India has honoured him with the Padma Shri, the Padma Bhushan and the Padma Vibhushan, three of the country's highest civilian honours.

ALSO BY RAGHUNATH MASHELKAR

From Leapfrogging to Pole-Vaulting
Reinventing India
Timeless Inspirator: Reliving Gandhi

ADVANCE PRAISE FOR THE BOOK

'Dr Mashelkar has always provided the vision to achieve innovation-led exponential growth for India. This new Haladker-Mashelkar book gives a fascinating new path to achieving disruptive game-changing innovation. Life is generally about continuous improvement, but here we see the "how" of creating the magic of exponential improvement, not just incremental, by drawing parallels between seemingly unrelated industries.'

—**Mukesh D. Ambani,**
chairman and managing director, Reliance Industries

'This richly illustrated, inspiring book shows how the unexpected connection is more powerful than the obvious. Businesses can achieve exponential, not just incremental improvement if they adopt the new insightful innovation strategies emanating from this book.'

—**Anand Mahindra,**
chairman, Mahindra Group

'The book shows that ideas could easily flow from anywhere. The magic lies in creating connections of the seemingly unconnectable. A powerful new paradigm for innovation-led exponential growth.'

—**Narayana Murthy,**
founder, Infosys

'"Thinking out of the box", recognizing unseen relations and being prepared for what you did not expect are key to basic discoveries as well as to innovative applications. This book presents an extensive collection of striking illustrations of the power of such a mindset to drive growth and open new horizons to companies. It will be of great benefit to all those wishing to practise a successful entrepreneurial spirit.'

—**Jean-Marie Lehn,**
Nobel laureate

'Whether your goal is to produce the next blockbuster or to save the planet, *Exprovement* will guide you to greater achievement. Human ingenuity is an inexhaustible resource; *Exprovement* explains how to mine it for maximum effect.'

—**Alan Finkel,**
former chief scientist, Australia

'Ramesh Mashelkar is at his innovative best when he partners with young innovator, Hersh Haladker, to conceptualize the power of converging parallels. An inspiring read for every start-up entrepreneur who wants a breakthrough idea.'

—**Kiran Mazumdar-Shaw,**
founder, Biocon

'Exprovement is a new terminology. It is not about small incremental micro improvements of 10 per cent but about large macro impacts of ten times. The authors have provided a rich repository of live case studies on how breakthroughs in products, processes and technologies emerge by linking simple observations from completely diverse fields. This book gives us a new paradigm for game-changing breakthrough innovations using the power of lateral thinking, and also not just the "what" of it but the "how" of it.'

—Sam Pitroda,
former adviser to Prime Minister of India

'*Exprovement*, a new book by Haladker and Mashelkar, India's two deep and disruptive thinkers is electrifying. It provides entirely new strategic insights to young innovators and organizational leaders for achieving spectacular growth and market leadership. How much I wish that I had this book with me during the not-so-successful battles for the needed policy reforms.'

—Vijay Kelkar,
former chairman, the Finance Commission of India

'A novel concept of "exponential improvement", deeply explored by the eminent and distinguished scientist Raghunath Mashelker (FRS) and innovation specialist, Harsh Haladker, has created an exciting and free-flowing, narrative. This book is replete with novel concepts to excite the emerging generation as well as the experienced.'

—Ashok Ganguly,
former chairman, Hindustan Lever

'If you wish to go from the known to the unknown, from the seen to the unseen, and from the felt to the yet unfelt, then this is the book that will help you get there. From repurposing to redesigning to rethinking the entire spectrum of new product and service design is just one aspect of the book. It tries to achieve much more, it helps you overcome the habit of getting satisfied with small improvements, it propels you to think of transformational change in your organizations and also in your own life.'

—Prof. Anil Gupta,
founder, Honey Bee Network

'Did you know that the roller ball pen inspired the computer mouse in the 1960s? Or that the house window wipe triggered the first car wiper in the early 1900s? Or that the variable response human eye inspired the intermittent car wiper in the 1950s? All these represent the grand principle of obliquity. Learn more about these in this fascinating book.'

—R. Gopalakrishnan,
former executive Director, Tata Sons

'Through a diversity of real-life examples ranging from healthcare to architecture to space exploration to gastronomy, the authors show how exponential improvement can be achieved by drawing parallels from remotely different sectors of industry. A must-read for all those seeking breakthrough innovations.'

—William Haseltine,
chairman, Access Healthcare

'Dr Mashelkar, innovation guru and a doyen of Indian science, globally recognized for popularizing concepts like Gandhian engineering, pole-vaulting and more-from-less-for-more (MLM), has now created a new concept: exprovement. Co-authored with innovator Hersh Haladker, *Exprovement: Exponential Improvement through Converging Parallels*, provides amazing examples of exprovement in a variety of fields, taking us from astronomy to gastronomy, from children's toys to space. The insights of the authors add a method to serendipity and innovation, creating a guidebook or manual for all dreaming to be innovators and organizations that want to be innovative. This should be compulsory reading for youngsters with dreams of new products, policymakers seeking to promote innovation and indeed for anyone who enjoys the intellectual challenge of a book that makes one think, taking you from the amazement of "wow!" to a now-I-know "aha".'

—Kiran Karnik,
former president, NASSCOM

'*Exprovement* is a book to help unlock limitless potential. It is a penetrating investigation into how individuals and organizations have drawn parallels to help them deliver exponential improvement. Right from how a football club improved its odds of winning by transforming players into human microprocessors, to how space scientists developed a novel landing solution by taking inspiration from a baby toy, the book offers practical insights on how to develop such an exprovement mindset—the tools, the attitude and the skills required. It is a value-add read for any industry leader or individual looking to go beyond the incremental approach.'

—Harsh Mariwala,
chairman, Marico

'This book provides pragmatic advice and insights for organizations to look at *Exprovement*, far beyond aspiring for change or improvement. Through a well-structured multidimensional approach and concepts, comparative cases and drawings from different sectors, this book can identify new opportunities. It provides a road map, a cogent and impactful reminder of how important it is to think beyond boundaries and imagine a result that we have not yet experienced as visionaries and entrepreneurs. In the ever-changing technological situation, strategic innovative thinking has become the core of a business to generate new revenues and unlock the new value of customers.'

—G.M. Rao,
chairman, GMR Group

'Fifteen stories that draw parallels from very different industries making it a great go-to book for one and all. I can see exprovement becoming a part of corporate vocabulary.'

—Richard Rekhy,
former CEO, KPMG

'Raghunath Mashelkar, the diehard champion of disruptive innovations has written yet another, utterly delightful book. With co-author Hersh Haladker, the book is peppered with many amazing and often contemporary stories of innovation that arose not from tinkering with adjacencies, but from the most unexpected places. Who would have thought that a pizza box can lead to better cancer detection? Or a baby toy leads to safer lunar landing. Their paradigm is called exprovement, which is not incremental but radical and exponential growth by seeking and stumbling onto the most startling connections. Their stories illustrate a profound insight into pattern recognition or problem-solving, about an approach to innovation, that only the nimblest minds can master. Mashelkar's unique contribution lies in making abstract concepts simple using the most evocative metaphors. His convex lens analogy is wonderfully apt, which says parallel and apparently unconnected ideas converge to a sharp focal point when they pass through the lens. A book that is both exhilarating and insightful and a must-read for all those seeking to shake up things for the better.'

—Ajit Ranade,
vice chancellor, Gokhale Institute of Politics and Economics

EXPROVEMENT™

Exponential Improvement Through Converging Parallels

HERSH HALADKER
RAGHUNATH MASHELKAR

A very special thank you to Gitanjali Singh Cherian, whose meticulous research and skill in crafting an engaging narrative contributed to elevating the outcome of this book.

BUSINESS

An imprint of Penguin Random House

PENGUIN BUSINESS

USA | Canada | UK | Ireland | Australia
New Zealand | India | South Africa | China

Penguin Business is part of the Penguin Random House group of companies
whose addresses can be found at global.penguinrandomhouse.com

Published by Penguin Random House India Pvt. Ltd
4th Floor, Capital Tower 1, MG Road,
Gurugram 122 002, Haryana, India

First published in Penguin Business by Penguin Random House India 2023

Credit for cover design: Ramesh Talada
A big thank you to Omkar Patil and Amya Madan for their contribution to the book.

10 9 8 7 6 5 4 3 2 1

ISBN 9780143461821

Typeset in Adobe Caslon Pro by Manipal Technologies Limited, Manipal

www.penguin.co.in

Hersh Haladker's dedication

'To my grandmother, who taught me to fearlessly explore my curiosity and nurtured within me a maker's mindset.'

*

Raghunath Mashelkar's dedication

'To my mother, who is no more but continues to be everywhere for me.'

The unexpected connection
is more powerful
than the one that is obvious.

—Heraclitus

Contents

Introduction

How does one inspire growth in a way that has never been thought of before?

In a world where the next big idea could be waiting around the corner, most of us tend to seek inspiration from the ecosystem with which we are familiar and well acquainted.

For example, a person working in the automotive industry generally analyses automotive companies to find innovative solutions; a person working at a soft drink company would generally study processes within the food and beverage industry, and so on.

But what if a person from the automotive industry draws a parallel with a process followed in the food and beverage industry?

What if that parallel is able to give them the leverage to begin with a clean slate—a new perspective that addresses problems or inspires growth, in ways they had never thought of before?

The clean slate is NOT about beginning from scratch.
It is about beginning with a NEW PERSPECTIVE.

This new perspective gives an organization the opportunity to shed some of the baggage that is either redundant or comes in the way of its continued growth, while taking cognizance of newly relevant circumstances—for example, the impact of 'failed' products, unexpected political changes, a global pandemic, market saturation, climate change, evolving customer wants and other such elements.

Through the real-life examples covered in this book, readers will begin to understand that this new perspective—the perspective of *exprovement* that allows companies to start on a new footing—can be gained by looking for parallels outside of one's industry.

Readers will also gain insight into how the application of parallels to their own organization could create exponential improvement, breakthroughs, new solutions, new markets and even entirely new industries in some cases.

This book in fact, is the result of the coming together of two parallel perspectives from two diverse backgrounds that share a common goal—that of encouraging an exprovement mindset amongst today's organizational leaders.

Dr Raghunath Mashelkar, who is a globally decorated scientist and a transformative science leader, has held board positions at several leading companies and has been one of the eminent leaders of the innovation movement in India. He brings in the 'big-picture' perspective of breakthrough innovation and radical organizational transformation in a fast-changing world.

Hersh Haladker, credited with developing innovative products and processes and fostering a culture of innovation at several organizations across many industries, brings in the 'maker' mindset of a practitioner— one who imagines ways to transform macro-level ideas into practical and effective solutions.

The authors of this book celebrate the concept that diversity of perspectives is the key to extraordinary breakthroughs and have come together to conceptualize, develop and share the idea of exprovement.

Before beginning this book, it is important to keep two things in mind:

1. **Parallels for exprovement can be drawn with practically anything—it doesn't necessarily have to be with another industry.** You will see examples where parallels have been drawn with operations, technology and products from entirely different industries, abstract ideas, nature, the human body, areas of

study, mindsets, toys, sports and so much more! The possibilities are endless!

2. **A 'clean slate' can mean different things for different companies.**
For some companies it can mean deciding to modify and re-introduce a product that failed in one industry into another, entirely different industry. For example, Play-Doh started out as a wallpaper cleaning product that removed coal residue but lost its market appeal with the declining use of coal furnaces in the 1950s. By drawing a parallel with the idea that one Cincinnati school teacher had, which was to use the product in arts and crafts classes, the company pivoted, decided to make the product more colourful and went on to become hugely successful in the children's toys industry.[1]

For some organizations it could mean drawing a parallel with ways of operation or technology from another industry and integrating those into one's own industry. For example, in 1913, Ford drew a parallel between its car manufacturing assembly line and that of the slaughterhouse/meat-packing industry, where various meat parts were sequentially removed by workers from a moving line. By modifying the conveyor belt concept that brought parts to workers, rather than workers moving to the parts, Ford was able to reduce the time it took to build a car from more than 12 hours to 1 hour and 33 minutes![2, 3]

For others, a clean slate could mean drawing a parallel with an untapped need (to create a new product/service or reimagine one's own product) discovered by paying close attention to what the market has to say. For example, YouTube started out as a dating website for users to upload videos in lieu of their dating profile. But when users began to upload videos of whatever they felt like, the founders realized that there was a market for a platform where user-generated content (UGC) could be uploaded, which gave rise to YouTube as we know it today.[4]

The defining moments for successful companies like the three mentioned above—that maintained their relevance in evolving marketplaces and which eventually led to their unparalleled success—began with them drawing a parallel with an idea or need that was born in an entirely different place from the original business idea.

The possibilities of what a clean slate could mean, thus, are as endless as the possibilities for drawing parallels!

The last chapter outlines the ways in which one can begin to develop an 'exprovement mindset', with tips, thoughts and practical tools that serve as a guide.

Covering areas as diverse as healthcare, architecture, eldercare, space exploration, sports team management and gastronomy, to name just a few, the scope of exprovement isn't by any means limited to just a few industries or areas of study—the cases explored in the book will highlight how the concept of exprovement by drawing parallels can be applied to any organization.

1

Exprovement

REDESIGN THE BICYCLE OR RETHINK HUMAN-POWERED MOBILITY?

Bicycles have been around since the early 1800s. The first bicycle, said to have been invented by Karl von Drais, had a frame made of wood, two wooden wheels with iron rims, leather-covered tires and no pedals.

A person using the 'swiftwalker' as it was known, walked straddling the cycle, lifting their feet off the ground during descents.[1]

Nowadays, bicycles have disc brakes, shock absorbers, lightweight frames, wheel options to suit a variety of terrains and several other features that make their design and operation quite different from that of the initial version.

Today, if a bicycle manufacturing company wants to explore directions for growth, there is a wide spectrum to consider, from redesigning its current bicycle model by incorporating newer technology, to reimagining and developing an entirely new way for human beings to transport themselves.

While both ends of the spectrum have the potential to result in a novel solution, the solution that entails a redesign is likely to be an IMPROVEMENT of what already exists, while the solution that involves rethinking human-powered mobility is likely to be something more disruptive in nature—something that brings about an entirely new manner of human mobility; a radical improvement or EXPROVEMENT.

Redesigning the bicycle is a solution that works in the existing context of how things are, but rethinking human-powered mobility requires a new context to be established, and therefore would be an exponential improvement, or exprovement.

Organizations can meet their growth objectives in both ways. However, if the aspiration is to create disruption, organizations must invest in exprovements. The process and outcomes may not always be pretty or even desirable, but it is imperative to stay ahead of the curve, as all exprovement efforts will be worth it in the long run.

To adopt an exprovement mindset, organizations must recognize and understand the difference between improvement and exprovement.

Redesigning a bicycle and rethinking human-powered mobility call for drastically different approaches. The outcome therefore will also be drastically different, and sometimes, unexpected.

A team working on redesigning the bicycle has an existing perception of what a bicycle is, what it can do, what it is used for and what it is made up of—wheels, pedals, a seat, a handlebar etc.— i.e., they would work within the current context of what a bicycle is and does. So, the outcome is likely to be a better and improved version of the bicycle, such as better aerodynamics, better shock absorption etc.

A team working on rethinking human-powered mobility starts with a clean slate where the context needs to be reworked and re-established. Keeping their goal in mind, they would probably focus on understanding physical movement that can generate momentum and/or look at ways in which a person can be propelled. The outcome, which may or may not involve a bicycle or even a vehicle that we recognize, is more likely to be an exprovement—one that achieves a goal, but in a new context.

Improvements (which usually result from design thinking and behavioural economics) help an organization 'leapfrog', while exprovements (which usually result from disruption and innovation) help an organization 'pole vault'.

Leaders need to be clear about which they want to achieve and accordingly choose an approach that aligns with their goal.

This book focuses on how exprovement can be enabled.

THE DELTA

Every leader is driven by a vision for their organization. The vision of 'what could be', which is tempered by the reality of 'what is'.

What leaders work towards every day is bridging the gap between 'what is' and 'what could be'—we refer to this gap as the delta.

The delta is **what** drives change in organizations.

Why do organizations want to bridge the delta? Because of their desire to improve or exprove something—either their offerings, their relevance, their bottom line, their public image etc.

Coming to **how** organizations can bridge the delta, it can be done through either improvement or exprovement.

While improvement is incremental, exprovement is an exponentially improved outcome to an existing or foreseeable challenge, accomplished by creating something that is currently not part of the ecosystem within which the problem exists.

Improvement and exprovement can both bridge the delta based on 'what could be', but they each have a different approach, and so result in a different outcome.

Two major factors determine the outcome:

1. Which part of an organization is involved in bridging this delta
2. What is the degree of change expected

Both are correlated and can be better explained through the context of the delta graph.

The Delta Graph

The delta graph describes the what, why and how of change and progress within an organization using familiar business terms and shows how business objectives, which originate in different parts of an organization, result in different degrees of change within the organization itself.

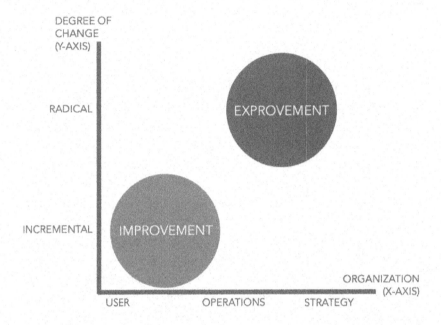

In the delta graph, the x-axis represents the part of the organization where the change lies—either at the user, operations or strategy level. The y-axis represents the extent of change—whether it is an incremental or radical change.

Users and operations seldom have the ability to influence radical views and actions, thereby resulting in improvements. The strategy level usually has the ability to drive radical initiatives, thereby resulting in exprovements.

While improvement usually happens as a result of change in the part on the left side of the x-axis, exprovement happens as a result of change in the part towards the right side of it. So, improvements tend to happen in the areas of operations and users, whereas exprovements are more strategic and are driven by the top management of the organization.

As a corollary, if the degree of change expected or desired is smaller (improvement), the approach needs to focus on the user and operations levels, and if the change expected is radical (exprovement) the approach needs to focus on the strategic level, often involving major changes.

Therefore, it becomes critical to have a well-defined 'what could be', or to ask the right question with reference to the desired outcome.

A Delta in Flux

An important factor that hugely influences the bridging of the delta is change—demographic, political, technological and environmental change to name just a few—which constantly alters where an organization sees themselves and where they would like to position themselves.

Simultaneously, the scenario and context of the organization itself keeps evolving, in terms of its capabilities, customers, consumers, competition, etc.

As a result, organizations are constantly chasing the delta in not just one, but many contexts, including, but not limited to:

- The delta between other organizations and themselves
- The delta between new markets and the ones they currently serve
- The delta between new technology and what they currently employ

HOW TO APPROACH EXPROVEMENT

Ask The Right Question

Exprovement begins with asking the right question; with taking a step back and understanding the level of impact one wishes to make to be able to pole-vault forward.

The road to exprovement begins with big picture thinking. Once one has decided to go down this path, it becomes imperative to ask big picture or macroscopic questions.

In the automotive industry if one asks the question 'What can we do to improve the fuel efficiency of a car?' one is likely to come up with a more efficient way of burning fuel, and thereby **improve** efficiency by a small percentage.

Whereas, if the question asked is 'How can we achieve minimal running cost of an automobile?' one is likely to look at alternative fuels such as electricity or fuel cells, and thereby **exprove** the running cost by an exponential amount.

It is also important to enable an environment that allows free exploration, imagination and creativity, in order for an exprovement to materialize.

Here is an example of the kind of leadership mindset that sets the stage for exprovement.[2, 3]

A lead design engineer places a small rectangular wooden block on the table at the research lab at his company and explains that he wants the team to make a cassette player that matches the dimensions of the block of wood. He says nothing more and leaves the technicians to freely explore what they can come up with.

The engineers eventually came up with the Sony Walkman, an exprovement when it was launched in 1979, which made it possible for the first time for people to listen to music on the go through wired headphones.

This approach to exprovement was effective for several reasons:

- The lead engineer, Nobutoshi Kihara, gave his team a constraint that provided just the right number of guidelines but didn't confine their imagination and creativity to a rigid playing field. For example, he did not say 'Make me the smallest tape recorder you can'. They would probably still be working on it, trying to solve the additional problems that would have accompanied such a tight constraint.
- He did not say 'Make something new and revolutionary that will let people play music wherever they want', though this was actually what happened in the end! Instead, he had an **idea** of the goal he wanted to achieve, and by leaving the playing field regarding **how** to achieve it wide open, he gave his team the freedom to explore wherever their imagination took them.
- He knew what size he wanted the device to be—this was his starting point—and he knew what his end goal was (a portable tape player), but he left his team to figure out how to bridge the delta between the two.

Thus, a leadership mindset that is able to identify the correct target board (a partial vision of the final outcome) but leave the dart-throwing to the enablers is far more likely to hit the bullseye of exprovement than if they were to lay down a list of specific constraints.

Look for Parallels in Unrelated Areas

Beginning with identifying relevant practices from an unrelated industry or field and correlating them for application in the industry one is trying to achieve exprovement in will lead to a point where the parallels meet, which is where exprovement happens.

Drawing parallels refers to finding ways in which two or more seemingly distinct contexts are similar, while the degree of distinctness in the contexts is what determines the degree of change or exprovement.

Does one draw a parallel between a football team and a hockey team or the strategies of a football team and the making of a microprocessor?

While the first parallel is likely to result in an improvement because it remains in a similar context, the second is more likely to result in an exprovement due to how drastically different the contexts are.

Here are four examples of parallels that can be drawn:

Drawing Parallels With Nature

Biomimicry (mimicking nature) has many great examples of drawing parallels to achieve exprovement.

For example, researchers have modelled a lightweight hammer after how momentum is transferred from the body to the head of a woodpecker when it pecks wood.

The hammer has a rotating crank, which is connected by means of a rod to the casing, so that the motor plus its mounting oscillates about a central pin, and the motion is transferred to the hammer head by parallel springs—in essence modelling the hammer after how the bird's head, body, vertebrae and neck tendons work in tandem.

The researchers put forth that this hammer had several advantages over the conventional design: 'It was originally conceived for use in space exploration, where it has no net inertia until it comes into contact with an object, and even then the force delivered can be tuned. It could also be used where working space is at a premium, such as dentistry or surgery, or to remove flash from castings.'[4]

Drawing Parallels Between Similar Products For a Unique Application

Back in 1957, two engineers set out to make an alternative to traditional wallpaper, their aim being to create a machine that would produce a type of plastic wallpaper with a paper backing. Their prototype involved sealing two shower curtains together, trapping air bubbles in between.

However, when their invention didn't catch on as per its intended use, they explored using the new 'wallpaper' as a material for greenhouse insulation. It turned out that there were materials that were far better insulators than their invention. But one of the things that came out of these experiments and failed applications was the realization, or rather the confirmation, that the wallpaper did have some insulating properties.

Nearly three years after the plastic wallpaper was invented, Frederick W. Bowers, on hearing that IBM was looking for a packaging material to protect their new 1401 computer during shipment, realized that the moderately insulating plastic wallpaper with its trapped air bubbles would be the ideal solution.

This is the story of how Bubble Wrap, a product developed by Alfred Fielding and Marc Chavannes for an entirely different purpose, eventually came to be a product that revolutionized the shipping industry and was instrumental in the success of e-commerce, offering protection to billions of products shipped across the globe.

Plastic wallpaper and Bubble Wrap as products are not that different from each other. But their application and purpose are. This shows how sometimes an intended improvement in one industry can end up being an exprovement in another if one's mindset is kept alert and open to drawing parallels to find applications.[5]

Drawing Parallels Between Diverse Products for Unique Application

A chance observation by a hair salon owner nearly thirty-five years ago sparked the idea for our next example of exprovement.

Phil McCrory was watching a TV news report on the Exxon Valdez oil spill in 1989 when he noticed that the fur of an otter who was a victim of this environmental disaster had soaked up a lot of oil—so much so that the water surrounding its body was completely free of petroleum!

McCrory's inquisitive mind got thinking, and drawing a parallel with all the waste hair that was collected at his salon every day, he decided to experiment.

He gathered a bunch of hair clippings, stuffed them into a pair of his wife's pantyhose (so they would be contained, yet remain absorbent) and put the spongy device into a children's wading pool filled with a mixture of water and motor oil.

His intuition had been correct—within minutes the hair-pantyhose 'sponge' absorbed the oil from the water, turning it crystal clear!

After confirming the findings of his home experiment via external validation from Texas A&M University that his invention really did work and could be applied in a larger context, he was able to secure a patent for his idea of using human hair to absorb oil spills, which was closely followed by a patent for an oil absorbing mat.

McCrory's idea went on to be manufactured and sold by World Response Group as OttiMat, which has also been tested by NASA and has been used in clean-up efforts of oil spill disasters such as a 2,50,000-litre fuel oil spill in the San Francisco Bay in 2007 and the 2010 Gulf of Mexico oil spill. World Response Group also started manufacturing SmartGrow (based on McCrory's other patent), a hair mat used to fertilize plants.

This is an example of an exprovement developed by drawing parallels between two completely unrelated products (one of them a waste by-product) to create a new impactful application in a completely new context. Further, and to quote McCrory's own words, 'This is environmentally safe, it has no chemicals, it's 100 per cent hair. You don't get any greener than hair!'[6]

Drawing Parallels Between Unrelated Industries for a Unique Application

An example of this form of exprovement is a case cited when eBay founder Pierre Omidyar was talking to consultants, trying to find a way to get fresh produce from farmers to consumers in Hawaii before the produce perished. Approximately one-third of the produce was getting spoiled before it reached its destination.

As a prime example of an exprovement-inclined mindset, Omidyar asked, 'What about the post office? Doesn't the post office go to everybody's house six times a week? Why don't we just mail the head of lettuce?'

He was quickly able to draw a parallel between the post office—an organization that was already well established with a network of individuals that went to people's houses six times a week—as the type of solution that could potentially solve the perishable produce problem.

It is the kind of mindset that would think of connecting the completely unrelated industries of fresh produce and postal services that is likely to develop (most probably after some iterations) an exprovement.[7]

THE LIMITLESS POTENTIAL OF DRAWING PARALLELS

When one thinks of drawing parallels, what makes it even more exciting is that further parallels can be drawn from the first one, leading to more exprovements and improvements.

Take the example of stainless steel, which since its discovery over a century ago, has gone through a journey of transformation, with its application being diversified across various industries.

'In 1913, Harry Brearley of Sheffield, UK discovered 'rustless' steel. Although there had been many prior attempts, Brearley has been credited with inventing the first true stainless steel, which had a 12.8% chromium content. He had added chromium to molten iron to produce a metal that did not rust. Chromium is a key ingredient, as it provides the resistance to corrosion. After this discovery, Sheffield itself became synonymous with steel and metallurgy.

Brearley stumbled upon this discovery while trying to solve the problem of erosion of the internal surfaces of gun barrels for the British army during the onset of the First World War.'[8]

Since 1913, stainless steel has gone through many iterations, which have helped it find applications in a variety of forms and products in numerous unrelated and diverse industries.[9, 10] Some of these include:

- Storage containers for nitric acid, because of its ability to resist corrosion
- In the construction industry
- In the automobile industry
- In the beverage industry as a safe and hygienic fermenting vessel
- As kitchen sinks that have a long life
- As cutlery we use every day
- As safe, non-toxic surgical instruments
- In washing machines

The list of applications of stainless steel is a long one; too long to completely be laid out in this book, but looking at how the exprovement of stainless steel could find parallel applications across several industries is what has led to the material's high demand globally, with its market size being valued at $111.45 billion in 2022.[11]

TYPES OF IMPROVEMENT AND EXPROVEMENT

Exprovements usually happen through disruption or innovation, while improvements usually happen via progress or change enabled by design thinking or behavioural economics.

Disruption

Disruption refers to creating the next big context. For example, this could be in terms of finding a new application for a product or service or modifying it to have value in an entirely new market. This approach is the most strategic and requires the organization to make radical and bold changes.

It involves setting a large goal with no constraints. At first the goals may seem far-fetched; some might even be subject to ridicule, but eventually, they become accepted as the new path forward.

For instance, in the seventies or the eighties the idea of nearly everyone on the planet owning a cell phone was unimaginable. Today, it's a reality. Till a few years ago, the idea of a driverless car was dismissed as unrealistic. Today, we are sitting on the cusp of it becoming a reality.

Since current operations and sometimes even users have little to do with the disruption itself, it makes disruption a more strategic undertaking. Disruption can take place in a few different areas:

1. Disrupting the market: bringing in a new product or service
2. Disrupting operations: bringing in new technology that makes a process or product vastly better.
3. Disrupting the way of doing things: adopting a new business model.

Going back to asking the right questions for the desired outcome, questions to achieve disruption could look like:

•   Can companies run without any employees?
•   Can airports be made modular?
•   How do we make a universal currency?

Innovation

Innovation refers to creating something that fits into a futuristic context via the application of new or emerging technology. This approach is also strategic and requires the organization to make bigger-risk changes.

Innovation is about seamlessly adapting to fit into the changing context and about creating solutions that lie within the bounds of the next or emerging context of the organization.

Innovation typically falls into one of the following three categories:

1. Innovation within the same market
2. Innovation with the same technology
3. Innovation with a new business model

Questions that could inspire innovation could sound like:

- How can banking fit into the upcoming context of blockchain?
- How do we make a universal currency that's virtual?

Design Thinking

Design thinking happens by making the current offering more desirable, viable and feasible in the current context of its usage by making design changes to a system, process or product.

This approach is user-centric and requires the organization to make bigger, but not radical changes.

Design thinking is about creating great experiences for all stakeholders and their needs within the current context. The process starts off by gaining an in-depth understanding of the user's experience in the current context.

Questions that could lead to improving the experience for the user could sound like:

- Can coding be made more intuitive?
- How do we facilitate transactions with a virtual universal currency?

Behavioural Economics

Behavioural economics uses a psychological approach to make a current offering more acceptable to consumers. This approach is user-centric and requires the organization to make smaller, incremental changes.

Questions that could prompt behavioural economics-inspired improvements could sound like:

- How can we make air conditioning acceptable in winters?
- How do we make transactions with a virtual universal currency acceptable?

Thus, behavioural economics is about influencing decision-making to get a favourable outcome by changing perception.

For example:

- 'Buy 1, Get 1 Free' deals have been known to get a better response than '50 per cent off'.
- 'Hate To Lose' puts a different spin on things than 'Love to Win'.

This approach needs a deep understanding of consumers and their behaviour and involves encouraging a change in perception to make something more acceptable.

The improvement involves making small, low-cost changes to enable favourable decision-making, thereby increasing acceptability of an existing offering. Behavioural economics therefore works closely with a company's operations and very closely with its users.

To highlight the difference, looking at the transportation industry, a basic improvement (via design thinking) would be rearranging seats to reduce overcrowding.

But taking a path parallel to the insect world while developing self-driving cars and incorporating the principle of how locusts move without colliding into each other, on the other hand, is an exprovement that could potentially cause disruption to the transportation industry.

Both provide solutions to the problem, but to very different degrees and with very different potential for impact. Each of the four ways of bridging the delta as mentioned above thus calls for a different approach.

LEARNING BY EXAMPLE

Each of the case studies that follows this chapter goes into detail to explore the parallels that have been drawn or could have been drawn to achieve exprovement.

The book's aim is to encourage organizations to develop new context for their offerings; to create exponential improvement (exprovement) rather than merely incremental improvement.

Citing case studies from around the world and using various industries as examples, we have attempted to showcase unexpected instances where exprovement has been achieved:

- Can a top professional football club exprove by taking a path parallel to that of innovation in the electronics industry?
- Could the fruit juice industry present the agricultural industry with a parallel path to exprovement that could mitigate problems caused by global warming?
- Can technology from the video gaming industry offer the physiotherapy industry a parallel path to exprovement?
- Can an innovation in the labelling industry lead to an exprovement in the medical world that has the potential to save millions of lives?
- How does technology developed in the late 1800s for the electric industry present a parallel path to unleashing the potential of the human brain in ways we've never seen before?

By bringing focus to real-life examples such as these, where exprovement has already been achieved, breaking down the science behind exprovement and offering practicable tools and processes, the book aims to serve as a guide for leaders, enabling them to develop and accomplish their own radical business vision—the need of the hour in today's dynamic and unpredictable business playing field.

2

How to Make a Footballer as Efficient as a Microprocessor

2 May 2016 is a day that anyone who claims to be a diehard football fan will remember—even if Leicester City is not their favourite team. For what Leicester City Football Club (LCFC) achieved that day made sporting history—they were crowned the English Premier League (EPL) Champions.

What made this event remarkable?

The fact that absolutely nothing leading up to the season seemed to point to their doing well in the league, let alone being crowned champions:

- In the 2014–2015 season they were nearly relegated from the EPL, just sliding through by winning seven of their last nine matches.
- Prior to this win, Leicester City's best performance of its 132-year existence was being ranked second, way back in 1929!
- The club's newly appointed sixty-four-year-old manager had just been fired as the manager of the Greek national team, had never won a top division title and was touted as most likely to be the first manager of the season to lose his job.
- Leicester City began the 2015-16 season with the pitiful odds of a 5000-1 chance of winning the title. To put things in perspective, William Hill gave better chances to finding Elvis Presley alive, at 2000-1!

So how *did* Leicester City pull off one of the biggest upsets in premier league football history?

A NEW PERSPECTIVE

While theories vary from the bizarre (that King Richard III was a LCFC fan and his reburial at Leicester Cathedral, after his remains were found under a car park, was the reason) to the divine (that the blessing of the pitch and handing out of lucky charms by the Buddhist monks that were invited by the club's Thai chairman were the reason), the real reason had everything to do with great team management, player scouting and recruitment.

And ultimately, a new perspective to achieving the team's goals.

Claudio Ranieri, the team's manager who had been called 'uninspiring' by some before the start of the season, brought cohesiveness to the team. He used his well-known sense of humour to diffuse tense situations and keep players relaxed, and fostered a feeling of empathy within the team.

But the lesser known, and perhaps defining ingredient of Ranieri's successful formula was his adoption of scientific methods. Together with the club's sports science and medicine team, Ranieri developed routines based on science and integrated these into the team's regular practice and recovery schedules, which ultimately brought about exprovement and unexpected, unparalleled success that the team had never experienced before.

Don't Maximize; Optimize

The Leicester City team's strategy for the 2015–2016 season was speed and counter-attack. Fast counter-attacking requires more sprints, which usually leads to a high incidence of injuries. Here Ranieri brought in a new perspective, which was that reducing these injuries had to become as important a goal as improving the player's performance.

So the team had to be able to perform sprints on a regular basis, *without* their bodies breaking down.

Soccer, like many sports, is an injury-prone game. To give a point of reference, at the end of December 2019, over 200 EPL players had injuries, and about 50 per cent of these were either knee, hamstring or ankle related injuries.[1]

These statistics back up several studies conducted on soccer players between 1996 and 2012, which revealed that in each case at least 50 per cent of the players' injuries were non-contact in nature, with one study revealing that 65 per cent were lower limb injuries.[2] Another study on the prevention of muscle injuries found that muscle injuries represent about 30 per cent of all time-loss injuries in men's professional football and that muscle indirect injuries and overuse injuries are more common (about 96 per cent in soccer) than direct injuries (contusions).[3]

This brings us to the obvious conclusion that if the incidence of players' muscle injuries came down, they would be able to play more, would take less time off for recovery and would be in better overall health. Given its high rate of occurrence in professional football, focusing on solving this problem becomes crucial. This realization paved the way for bringing about a new approach to what could potentially ensure the success of the team.

If You Can't Measure It, You Can't Improve It

Leaning heavily on its sports science team, the new methodology employed at LCFC consisted of measuring, recording and analysing data at various points:

1. Hamstring Muscle

The muscle vital to achieving faster and consistent sprints on the field is the hamstring muscle. The team used a device from the sports science industry, called the NordBord, which combines advanced sensors, real-time data and cloud analytics to measure hamstring strength.

Using force cells to measure the force being applied by the athlete using the device, data is transmitted via a USB cable to a computer or tablet. Being able to track and record data allows footballers and coaches to monitor and compare a player's hamstring strength over a period of time, post injury, between left and right legs and with other team players as well—all valuable information to help understand where improvements can be made.

2. Player Movement

Ranieri's team also used the Catapult GPS vest—a sports science innovation that can obtain valuable data on the players' every movement, such as distance run, changes in direction, intensity, acceleration and deceleration.[4, 5]

3. Pitch Density

The density of the pitch was also measured daily, and the type and duration of the players' training session was altered based on the information.

4. Subjective Data

Besides the objective data, players were also required to fill out daily questionnaires on things like how well they had slept and how their bodies felt post practice. This important subjective data helped fine-tune training sessions and allow for adequate recovery time when needed.

LCFC also began to use a cryotherapy ice chamber for injury recovery—this proved vital in helping Jaime Vardy recover much quicker than expected from a hip injury. Bags of ice were also used to massage players, helping to speed up their recovery.

Further, the club began to include a forty-eight-hour recovery process after games, something uncommon amongst sporting clubs.

The new methods employed were all in line with conserving the players' performance at optimum levels, rather than exploiting them to their breaking point.

A WINNING FORMULA

Did the new methodology pay off for Leicester City?

- Jaime Vardy's Premier League top speed record of 35.44 km per hour during that season says it did.
- The fact that Leicester had the fewest injuries, used fewer players than any other EPL team and had the most number of counter-attack goals and shots that season says it did.
- Then of course, there is 2 May 2016!

Ranieri's willingness to look beyond his own skill set led him to bring together the efforts of a multidisciplinary team made up of expertise from the fields of sports, science, technology and medicine, which led to exprovement in the form of the unexpectedly successful result that Leicester City achieved.

The team's outstanding performance certainly made the case for employing science and technology in the sporting world to improve performance, prevent injury and accelerate recovery time.

The fact that Ranieri's winning team had the least number of injuries of the season and used the least number of players when compared to other EPL teams emphasizes the point that, when it comes to exprovement, a change in perspective can make all the difference.

DOES A PARALLEL PATH TO EXPROVEMENT EXIST?

Our analysis of Ranieri's strategy is that he focused on optimizing rather than maximizing the players' output. In other words, he made them stop before they reached breaking point so that whenever they were playing in a match, they were playing at their best—not at suboptimal level—and their bodies were not 'breaking down' from overuse.

This could only be achieved by measuring what was happening with the players' muscles, and employing sports science technology allowed him to do this.

To test our theory of whether he might have been able to arrive at this strategy by examining parallel industries, we explored several industries where efficiency and saving or optimizing resources are of primary importance to success. These included studying things such as:

- how fuel efficiency in cars is achieved
- how misers manage their money
- how birds conserve energy while flying in a certain formation

One industry that stood out as a parallel to Ranieri's strategy was the microprocessor industry.

- It is an industry built around the idea of doing more by using less (energy).
- It is an industry that is highly data-driven—it measures the quantity of resources that would be required for a certain task and then optimizes them.
- It uses tools, including, ironically, those that cool the microprocessor (a direct parallel to the cryotherapy chamber used by Ranieri) and prevent these high-performance components from breaking down, in spite of the pressure they are under.

So in essence, Ranieri turned his players into human microprocessors— high performance units that gave a peak output when required, without breaking down.

PEAK PERFORMANCE IN SPORTS—WHAT NEXT?

Indirect and muscle overuse injuries, such as those experienced by football players, are preventable. The problem lies in the fact that it is often difficult to judge exactly when the player is getting to the point of overuse.

What if there were a way to incorporate Ranieri's perspective and methodologies into something that could easily be used by sportspeople to let them know how their muscles were performing, to achieve the same results that Ranieri did—i.e., optimized player output?

This is where Finnish company Myontec could play a vital, game-changing role.

Myontec's patented intelligent clothing technology brings electromyography (EMG) to the sporting field in the form of garments that can measure and record muscle activity. There are no cables or ports involved. A user just has to slip on a Myontec garment, which has electrodes embedded in it, and vital muscle activity and performance data are recorded, interpreted and transferred to a smartphone or tablet via an app. Most importantly, this happens in real time.

The exprovement of Myontec's MBody garments eliminates post facto data analysis, bulky equipment and the need for cables, bringing EMG straight on to the sports field in a user-friendly format.

Telling an elite sportsperson, their coach and physiotherapist exactly what is happening with their muscles while they are training, playing a match or undergoing recovery treatment post injury is invaluable.

While EMG itself is a disruptive technology and has the potential to add huge value to several industries, the experience of undergoing an EMG is not the most pleasant as it involves either attaching electrodes to the skin, which sometimes cause small spasms as the electric current passes through, or inserting needle electrodes into muscles, which can be painful.

By exproving—creating a whole new context for how technology (EMG) from a parallel industry (healthcare) can be used in the professional sports industry—Myontec has enhanced the potential of EMG. Myontec garments are comfortable, require no cumbersome attachments, and via the accompanying app, allow for easy access to the information they capture. Further, by making the garment similar in look to any other sportswear, Myontec uses improvement in the form of behavioural economics (building on an already defined context, i.e., clothing) to make the garment more acceptable and appealing to the user.

The detail into which the analysis can go is remarkable. It is able to monitor muscle load, muscle balance and muscle ratio.

Scan the QR code to see what Myontec can do for sportspeople:

Myontec's CEO Janne Pylväs sheds light on how MBody can also help with post-injury rehabilitation:

'A coach can speed up the process just because they know which muscles to work and strengthen.

We can show football teams muscle load, but also show threshold levels when you are changing from anaerobic or aerobic.

'Football teams are using it mostly for muscle load, because we have the ability to see whether cramp is coming. Muscles get tense and if you can see if the left hamstring is more tense than the right we are alerting the teams and the coaches and they can see that in real-time.'

Going further, the technology can even help prevent career-threatening injuries.

'We see who's had an ACL operation, but we can also see who's going to be next with a similar injury. That's something coaches, athletes and doctors don't even know.'[6]

Myontec's products carry the potential to bring exprovement to the entire sporting world. We are looking at a future where the Cristiano Ronaldos and Rafael Nadals of the world will be able to tell—accurately and in real time—exactly what is happening with their muscles at any given time.

BEYOND PROFESSIONAL SPORTS—IMPROVING PERFORMANCE IN EVERYDAY LIFE

How far could Myontec's EMG exprovement be taken to improve the health and wellness of people other than professional sportspersons?

An exprovement can either be used in its original form for applications other than its original intended one, or it can be improved or exproved upon even further—i.e., upgraded or converted to another version—for application in other industries as well. Examples of both scenarios are given below:

Fitness

To begin with, Myontec's smart clothing could find a place in the everyday life of anyone who exercises, as the technology gets even better and more affordable. The most popular wearable tech devices used by the common man today are activity tracking devices. However, these do not always provide accurate information. Since most of these devices use an accelerometer to sense movement, things like swinging your arms around while staying stationary, or moving while keeping your arms in one position (e.g., while cycling) can lead to inaccurate data recording. Myontec's technology enables devices to be embedded into compression exercise clothing, thus allowing for accurate, surface-level, non-invasive monitoring. Given that accuracy matters greatly to people who own a wearable device[7], Myontec sports shorts, T-shirts, socks and other garments could find a role in the everyday life of the common man who exercises.

Manufacturing

In the manufacturing industry, Myontec can add value to occupational health and safety.

At Delete, a Finnish company where most of its approximately 900 employees engage in physically demanding work, Myontec's technology has allowed for the company to monitor and gather data on workers' muscle load, with the aim to 'prevent work-related injuries and musculoskeletal damage, to recognize injury risks and reduce sick leave and incapacity.'[8]

In the future, we could see companies with physically demanding work environments employ clothing like MBody to improve the working conditions and overall health and safety of their employees.

Design and Engineering

According to Myontec's website, its ErgoAnalysis technology can be used to design ergonomic hand tools and improve a work environment by detecting good working postures and proper joint angles that use less muscle load. Besides ideal muscle load, this has the potential to reduce pain and eliminate unhealthy, extreme body positions. Besides tools, the technology can even be used in the design of ergonomically optimal cabins, seats or even gloves.[9]

In the long run, this means improved employee health, reduced sick leave, improved productivity, better HR policies based on reliable information, and better prioritization of company investments.

Physiotherapy

Building on exproving by integrating conductors, sensors and electrodes into the weave of textiles, the world of e-textiles such as those manufactured by Myontec is exploding in ways like never before. One of the areas that has great potential is the medical world. Clothing such as MBody can be used, for example, to improve physiotherapy results in those recovering from an injury or to monitor muscle activity of the elderly to help prevent as muscle atrophy.

Given the fact that human beings are in contact with textiles for up to 98 per cent of their lives,[10] e-textiles are poised to bring exprovement at the very least to the fields of sports, wellness and health.

WHAT NEXT FOR SMART CLOTHING?

Besides integrating EMG into fabric, a host of other technologies is beginning to find its way into the garments we wear every day, making the future of smart clothing very exciting. Here are two examples:

Neonatology and Paediatric Diagnostics

At the time of writing this book, Aalto University in Finland was conducting research on developing another exprovement—soft baby clothing that can diagnose and monitor neurological disorders in premature babies via embedded textile electrodes, a baby hat that performs the job of an EEG, and AI diagnostic sleepsuits that monitor babies' movements and help in early detection and rehabilitation of motor skill problems.

The improvement in this case would be to develop fabric that is capable of integrating the technology yet is comfortable enough to be used on the delicate skin of babies.

Here too, as the technology becomes more mainstream and affordable, it could find its way into the everyday clothing of babies and children, giving parents valuable information about their child in the same way their smart watch does today.

Temperature Measurement

Ushering in further exprovement in smart clothing, researchers at the Harvard John A. Paulson School of Engineering and Applied Sciences (SEAS) have developed a soft, stretchable, self-powered thermometer that can be integrated into stretchable electronics and soft robots.

'We have developed soft temperature sensors with high sensitivity and quick response time, opening new possibilities to create new human–machine interfaces and soft robots in healthcare, engineering, and entertainment,' said Zhigang Suo, Allen E. and Marilyn M. Puckett, professor of mechanics and materials at SEAS.[11]

Developing sensors that are pliable, not rigid like earlier ones, means that the sensors will be able to twist and stretch along with the device they are integrated into or the wearer of the device, paving the way for the next generation of smart clothing, soft robotics and biocompatible medical devices.

DEVELOPING AN EXPROVEMENT OUTLOOK

What are some of the types of questions that LCFC could have asked to find exprovement solutions in unrelated industries?

- What can one do to make a team at the bottom of the league *win?*

Setting a large goal—not just one of incrementally improving performance—can set the ball rolling while exploring parallel industries for solutions.

- With what unrelated industry, product or process can a parallel be drawn, where efficiency is vital to success?
- Which other industry, product or process already exists that intermittently needs peak performance?
- How is fuel efficiency in cars achieved?

Reserve, KERS (kinetic energy restoration system), auto off when not in use—can any of these be applied to improve the efficiency of players?

- How do misers manage their money? How do they decide what to spend on and what not to?
- How do birds conserve energy while flying in a certain formation?

3

What's the Link between
Babies and Space Exploration?

When you picture something that has been designed by NASA, what generally comes to mind is an object that is sleek and looks like it's at least five generations before its time.

You'd be in for a surprise then if you chanced upon the organization's Super Ball Bot, an all-in-one landing and mobility platform whose design could play an important role in NASA's exploratory missions.[1] This bot looks more like an unwieldy mass of entangled spiders trying to make their way across a surface than a sophisticated robotic system.

FROM SENSORY EXPLORATION TO SPACE EXPLORATION

Why would NASA design something like this and where did the inspiration to do so come from?

A couple of NASA engineers were tossing around a baby toy meant for 'sensory exploration' when inspiration struck. As Adrian Agogino threw the toy up in the air, Vytas SunSpiral noticed how well the toy absorbed impact on landing and realized that its design could be a good one for another type of landing—a planetary surface landing![2, 3]

The toy in question, commonly known as a Skwish[4], is made of rods and cables connected together in a spherical shape, but the rods don't connect to rods and the cables don't connect to other cables. 'A child can hit themselves over the head with it and they won't get hurt.'[5]

When the toy is thrown on to the ground (or a baby hits themselves on the head with it) it compresses a bit, but then bounces back up—i.e., it absorbs energy while hitting the surface, which it then distributes while bouncing back, resulting in the toy not breaking.

As Agogino observed, 'That happens to be great for what we want.'[6] Drawing a parallel with how the toy reacted on impact, they set about designing a new kind of robot for planetary surface landing missions.

Scan the QR code to watch a video that helps understand the potential of the Super Ball Bot:

A POWER-PACKED, FLEXIBLE SOLUTION

The two space engineers realized that the scientific principle they were observing was tensegrity, a term coined by Buckminster Fuller, who studied the relationship between tension and structural integrity.[7]

Tensegrity structures like the space robot are excellent at distributing forces, or in other words, absorbing impact. Since there is no rigid connection between any of its structural components, the collapsible system becomes extraordinarily resilient to external forces, which get absorbed across the entire structure, instead of causing stress at certain points that could lead to damage or breakage. This means that the mass of the structure can be drastically reduced without compromising its strength, thus also making it easier to pack and unpack.

'Super Ball Bot also features tunable stiffness. By increasing or decreasing the tension on the cable network, the bot can transform from a nearly rigid structure to a squishy and compliant pile of interconnected sticks. Those sticks are the muscles of the robot, containing motors that wind and unwind the cables. And by making the right cables the right lengths at the right times, the sticks can make the robot move.'[8]

The easily manipulated bot can also fit into tight spaces and can house a device capable of collecting data as it is manoeuvred across the surface of a planet.

The Super Ball Bot could be very useful in exploration missions such as those to Saturn's moon, Titan, which has fascinated astrobiologists due to its similarities to Earth, including the fact that it is the only other known planetary body to have liquid on its surface.[9] However, landing through the thick atmosphere of Titan and navigating its varied terrain, which includes solid ground, slushy surfaces and sea, is no easy task. A case in point was in 2005, when the European Space Agency's Huygens probe parachuted down on to Titan's surface but had difficulty moving around and was only able to return data for around ninety minutes in the hostile environment.[10]

The Super Ball Bot could lead to exprovement by overcoming problems in a new way, with a new approach, inspired by a completely unrelated industry, as detailed by the NASA Innovative Advanced Concepts (NIAC) Program, in the following ways:

'Small, lightweight and low-cost missions will become increasingly important to NASA's exploration goals for our solar system. Ideally teams of dozens or even hundreds of small, collapsible robots, weighing only a few kilograms a piece, will be conveniently packed during launch and would reliably separate and unpack at their destination. Such teams will allow rapid, reliable in-situ exploration of hazardous destinations such as Titan, where imprecise terrain knowledge and unstable precipitation cycles make single-robot exploration problematic. Unfortunately, landing many lightweight conventional robots is difficult with conventional technology. Current robot designs are delicate, requiring combinations of devices such as parachutes, retrorockets and impact balloons to minimize impact forces and to place a robot in a proper orientation. Instead we propose to develop a radically different robot based on a "tensegrity", built purely upon tensile and compression elements. These robots can be light-weight, absorb strong impact, are redundant against single-point failures, can recover from different landing orientations and are easy to collapse and un-collapse. We believe tensegrity robot technology can play a critical role in future planetary exploration.'[11]

TOY-INSPIRED SPACE RESEARCH

If you think drawing parallels between how toys work and designing space equipment based on them is a one-off thing it's not!

One of the reasons why toys are a great place to look for exprovement is because they are often not constrained by having to work under a set of given conditions. NASA engineers know that their designs must work in space; toy designers on the other hand, especially those designing fantasy space vehicles, are not bound by the actual physics of space. Their imagination can conjure up anything it wants.

Here are a few more instances when playthings provided the answers:

Lunar Rover Design

George Barris, who was an auto customizer and built many custom cars for Hollywood, including K.I.T.T. for the show *Knight Rider*, the TV Batmobile and the Munster Koach, was once approached by NASA engineer Robert Yowell, who was intrigued by Barris's 1971 design of a model fantasy toy lunar rover called Moonscope, which had wheel and suspension systems that were far ahead of its time.[12, 13]

Modular Design

In 2003, the interchangeability of LEGO bricks served as inspiration when the US Air Force Research Laboratory's Space Vehicles Directorate was tasked with bringing electronic components to spacecraft.

Designing interchangeable parts with standardized ports meant that sections of an instrument could easily be removed or changed if something got damaged or if the device had to be put to a slightly different use, without having to redesign the entire instrument. This modular design would not only save time, material and money, but would also allow for a device to be transported far more easily, in parts that could be assembled once in space.[14]

Studying Fluids in Space

In 2021, it was reported that NASA was going to send the very popular child's plaything 'slime' to the International Space Station to study how a non-water fluid behaves in microgravity.[15]

'Astronauts aboard the station will play games with it, toss slime-filled balloons, make slime bubbles and even spray each other with slime in order to understand how a fluid, which isn't water, behaves.'[16]

Spacecraft Landings

A toy was the inspiration behind designing a device for yet another important part of space missions—spacecraft landings. When spacecraft land, they do so at very high speeds of Mach 10 or more, and friction causes the surface of the vehicles to heat up to very high temperatures—over 1400°C. Heat shields, which do basically what their name suggests—protect an object from overheating—come to the rescue by slowing down the spacecraft. However, heat shields work well in Earth's atmosphere, which is dense, but on planets that have thinner atmospheres, such as Mars, the aerodynamics of landings are much more difficult.

NASA's Hypersonic Inflatable Aerodynamic Decelerator (HIAD), an inflatable heat shield, was designed to overcome landing problems in such scenarios, and the inspiration came from a baby's stackable ring toy! Being inflatable, the shield can be opened to a much larger size. When tested in 2012, the HIAD was about 0.5 metres when packed, but 3 metres wide when deployed.[17, 18]

From the first crewless Viking mission in the 1970s to NASA's most recent Curiosity rover launched in 2011, engineers have used the same heat shield technology to land on Mars—rigid aeroshell heat shields. This has limited what can be done on Mars missions in many ways. For one, a hard aeroshell can only be as big as the diameter of a rocket's nose cone, which holds the lander. If the aeroshell were larger, the load that the rocket carries could be higher too. Till now space scientists have only been able to land around 1.5 tons on the surface of Mars. But using the new inflatable shield design inspired by a completely unrelated industry could allow a landing of between 20 to 40 tons!

The system, which is composed of a stack of inner-tube-like rings strapped together, is made of synthetic material that is fifteen times stronger than steel and can withstand temperatures of over 1500 degrees Celsius.

On NASA's latest Low-Earth Orbit Flight Test of an Inflatable Decelerator (LOFTID) mission to Mars in November 2022, the heat shield was expected to slow the vehicle down from over twenty-five times the speed of sound to under 990 kmph, with a plan to deploy 'higher up in Mars' atmosphere, expanding NASA's touchdown options throughout the Martian southern highlands.' Previous missions had been able to land only in the planet's northern lowlands, below the base elevation level. The mission was reported by NASA to have been a "huge success."[19]

Another impact of the exprovement is that it could save a lot of money as it could help recover spent boosters for reuse, which is 'a notoriously expensive aspect of space travel.' According to Barb Egan, the civil space programme director of United Launch Alliance, 'the business hopes to one day use it for its Vulcan heavy-lift rocket, whose thrusters make up about 60 per cent of each launch cost.'[20]

Scan to read more about this exciting mission:

TOY-INSPIRED PARALLELS ACROSS INDUSTRIES

It's not just NASA and the how-to's of space missions that have been inspired by toys. Several diverse industries have also found innovation and exprovement solutions in toys.

Biomolecular Engineering

Microfluidics, often referred to as lab-on-a-chip, involves manipulating or precisely controlling tiny amounts of fluids using channels that measure from tens to hundreds of micrometres. Besides several applications, microfluidics is used in medical diagnosis, for example, to determine whether a tumour is spreading by drawing just a teaspoon of a cancer patient's blood instead of conducting a biopsy; the technology also allows for extremely precise liquid administration of drugs and is used for reconfigurable DNA chips.[21, 22, 23, 24]

Researchers at Johns Hopkins University's Department of Chemical and Biomolecular Engineering have made use of the easy reconfigurability of LEGO and the design of a Pachinko game machine to conduct experiments to better understand the underlying mechanisms of microfluidic devices.

'. . . the researchers covered a large Lego board with cylindrical Lego pegs and placed the board vertically in a fish tank filled with glycerol, a viscous liquid. They dropped various-size ball bearings into the tank and watched the balls' trajectories around the pegs . . . Researchers rotated the board to see how different angles affected the results and dropped hundreds of balls to obtain the statistics they needed.'[25]

In this way, by combining the design properties of two toys/games, they were able to conduct particle separation experiments for a mere $350, including $50 worth of LEGO, when generally researchers would use that value of chemicals in just a single day.

Landmine Detonation

According to the United Nations Institute for Disarmament Research, casualties due to mines and war residue explosives in 2020 climbed to 7073 up from the 5853 recorded in 2019.[26]

In most places, the most common method for clearing landmines is manual detonations by mine-clearing experts—a time-consuming and expensive undertaking—'in some cases it costs thousands of dollars to clear just a single mine.'[27]

A former Afghani refugee, inspired by the little rolling objects he and his friends would race across fields with, as children growing up in Afghanistan, developed, in 2013, a low-cost, entirely biodegradable detonating device that would roll across a field, detonating landmines, while being powered by the wind's force remotely, i.e., without needing a person to physically detonate the landmine.

The exprovement, known as the Mine Kafon Ball, resembles a giant hi-tech tumbleweed, is capable of safely detonating up to four mines in a single journey[28] and contains a basic GPS tracking device able to record the area it has 'cleared' by its tumbling path.

'The core sphere that contains the GPS system is high enough from the ground to avoid damage from most anti-personnel mines,' explains inventor Hassani.

'The lengths of the spikes are based on the height of an adult's leg—because the kinds of mines that it is designed to clear are those that will take a leg off below the waist of an adult.

'So, as it moves the spikes get blown off, but the centre stays intact,' explains Hassani. 'It can withstand up to four explosions before it loses too many of its legs to carry on.'[29]

Today, Hassani's exprovement has incorporated further improvements, including making use of emerging technology like robotics and multi-sensors to evolve into the Mine Kafon Drone System (MKDS), which can map, detect and detonate landmines.

Learn more about the MKDS by scanning the QR code:

Nanoelectronics

In 2006, physicist Jeremy Levy was introduced by German researchers Dr Jochen Mannhart and Stefan Thiel to a new kind of microchip they had been working on that comprised two insulating layers, which when put together created a conducting interface. Even more interesting was the fact that the conducting state could be changed to an insulating state and back again by connecting it to a battery. It could also be made to remain in the conducting state by cutting off the power supply, i.e., removing the battery.

Levy was immediately reminded of the Etch a Sketch toy he used to play with as a child, in which lines are 'drawn' by the toy's stylus scraping aluminium powder from the underside of a glass screen. He wondered if a similar approach could be applied to the chip he had just been made privy to, to draw and erase nanowires—connectors for the transportation of electrons, extensively used in nanoelectronics or devices that use components that are only a few nanometres in size such as supercapacitors, flexible wearable devices and OLED displays.

Inspired by the Etch A Sketch, Levy and his colleagues developed a nanoscale transistor that, like the toy, used two layers—in this case insulating material—but instead of scraping, used an atomic force microscope's sharp tip to apply a positive voltage on the material's surface, which resulted in it drawing conducting lines between the insulating layers.

This enabled making wires that were just 2 nanometres wide, with the added advantage of the conducting lines being able to be selectively erased by applying negative voltage.

The single-electron transistor was about 1000 times smaller in area than silicon-based transistors used in electronic devices, adding significant potential to the semiconductor industry, which is always looking for ways to shrink components further.[30, 31,32, 33]

Robotics

Amongst the various applications of soft robotics, which is 'the subset of robotics that focuses on technologies that more closely resemble the physical characteristics of living organisms'[34], of great interest is their use in medical and surgical applications, including prosthetic limbs and minimally invasive surgeries.

One of the main setbacks in these applications has been the ability to achieve speed, due to use of fluidic actuators (the part that helps achieve movement).

Researchers at Harvard, who were inspired by how a pop-up popper toy works, have been able to overcome this barrier and create a high-speed soft robot actuator, resulting in a soft robot capable of hopping.

'Shell buckling, the mechanical effect that makes a toy popper pop, is used to create an actuator which is effectively two toy poppers joined together at the base. As air is pumped into the assembly, the thinner outer cap expands and the thicker inner cap quickly buckles and collapses—propelling the actuator into the air just like the toy popper.'[35]

According to Professor Katia Bertoldi, senior author of the study, 'This actuator is a building block that could be integrated into a fully soft robotic system to give soft robots that can already crawl, walk and swim the ability to jump. By incorporating our jumper into these designs, these robots could navigate safely through uncharted landscapes.'[36]

Blood Testing

Several types of blood tests, including testing for malaria and tuberculosis, are conducted by spinning a test tube containing a blood sample at very high speeds in a centrifuge. But a centrifuge is an expensive piece of equipment—often unaffordable for the communities that are hit hardest by such diseases. In the search for a cheaper alternative, engineers and scientists experimented with things like salad spinners, but couldn't find anything that could spin quite as fast, till bioengineers at Stanford University began to see a parallel between spinning toys and what they needed.

Inspired by spinning toys, Manu Prakash, an assistant professor of bioengineering at Stanford, 'began brainstorming design ideas with Saad Bhamla, a postdoctoral research fellow in his lab. After weeks of exploring ways to convert human energy into spinning forces, they began focusing on toys invented before the industrial age—yo-yos, tops and whirligigs.

"'One night I was playing with a button and string, and out of curiosity, I set up a high-speed camera to see how fast a button whirligig would spin. I couldn't believe my eyes," said Bhamla, when he discovered that the whirring button was rotating at 10,000 to 15,000 rpms.'[37]

They went on to develop a 'paperfuge', modelled on a button whirligig, which could successfully conduct several types of blood tests, didn't require electricity and cost less than 20 cents, but it could only hold a miniscule amount of liquid. Two years later, in 2019, however, a related team developed a 3D printed version of the paperfuge, which was able to hold 2 ml of fluid and cost less than $1, creating exprovement in the form of a cheap, easily transportable disease detection device that could positively impact the lives of millions.[38]

THE FUTURE OF DRAWING PARALLELS WITH TOYS

While individual toys could continue to provide one-off exprovement ideas across industries, looking at the future, one of the main areas that has a lot of potential for using toys as a parallel is prototyping, simulation and learning.

A great example is the Fischertechnik construction toy sets, which have, since 1965, been fascinating the young and the old, those who are engineers and those who are not, with channel-and-groove design engineering modelling kits that can be assembled into practically any shape.

With the addition of accessories, such as power motors, gears and power sources, models can be made mobile, while the integration of 'electrical and electronic components such as microswitches, magnetic-sensing reed switches and photocells, which sense position and provide input to motors,' help simulate robotic movement.[39]

Besides being an object to play with, Fischertechnik sets have been used not only to inculcate an interest in engineering in young people but to teach older students as well, in areas such as construction, engineering, mechanics, physics, robotics and even renewable energy (the H2 Fuel Cell Car kit), to cite a few examples.

Today, the company's Industry 4.0 and IoT simulation kits are being used to train people and simulate SmartFactory scenarios of the future—where production and intelligent networked systems will combine to enable self-organized industrial production.[40]

Prototyping and simulation for planning, testing and developing industrial processes and factories in such scenarios can save a lot of time and money, and help to anticipate problems during simulation, before they arise in real time.

Here are some examples of companies that have used Fischertechnik's model/simulation kits:

- With the help of the company's IoT simulation, 'Objektkultur Software GmbH was able to show how a factory equipped with IoT can be quickly and securely integrated into the existing IT and controlled in the cloud.'[41]

- Accso—Accelerated Solutions GmbH—used a Fischertechnik assembly line model to simulate quality control in the production process as part of the project Anomaly Detection in Images.[42]
- The BMW Group has used a Fischertechnik factory model to conduct a virtual test run to optimize the project planning and commissioning phase as well as increase the start up quality of one of its factories.[43]

DEVELOPING AN EXPROVEMENT OUTLOOK

What are some of the types of questions that could lead to finding exprovement solutions from the toy industry?

- If toys are a great parallel for space tech at NASA, what exprovements can they inspire in the industry I work in?
- If a Skwish toy's structure facilitates soft landing, can aeroplane wheels be made with a similar design?
- If NASA is considered an organization that deals in futuristic technology, can drawing parallels with toys help predict the future, or even be a part of it?
- Can toy sets such as Fischertechnik and LEGO Technic help come up with the next exprovement for manufacturing?
- Can a toy from which an exprovement parallel is drawn, become the first proof of concept of the exprovement?

4

How Would an Insect
Build a Commercial Complex?

'The challenge was to build a building which was as comfortable as an air-conditioned building . . . without air conditioning.'[1]

How does an architect faced with such a task find a solution? A solution to an unusual request, for no less than a 30,000-square-metre building.[2] A solution that calls for exprovement.

For Zimbabwean architect Mick Pearce, who was approached by Old Mutual Investment Group in 1991 with this bold request, inspiration lay not in another industry, but in another realm—nature.

Pearce looked for ways in which plants and animals regulate heat and stay cool in hot climates using just the natural environment.

' . . . that led me to look at animals in nature, and how they make their houses. That inspired me . . . if animals can do that . . . then there's got to be a way of doing it if we copy that system. That led me to this new approach to architecture which we call biomimicry—it's copying natural processes.'[3]

LEARNING FROM LITTLE THINGS

He found the solution to exprovement by drawing a parallel with how termites in Zimbabwe build their nests. These creatures, the largest of which are no more than an inch in size, have evolved to naturally adapt their homes to the same climatic conditions (where temperatures can change by up to 10°C between day and night) in which the new building was to be constructed. Some of these mounds are nine metres tall—skyscrapers to each one of the millions of tiny termites that live inside them.[4]

Termite nests are porous and structured to allow good ventilation, which is essential to maintaining ideal temperature and humidity levels, without which these soft-cuticled creatures could easily get dehydrated.

A termite mound's double-layered architecture provided the ideal parallel to what Pearce required. Their 'dense core provides strength and stability, while a porous shell surrounding the core allows ventilation'.[5]

Inspired by the termite mounds, Mick Pearce, working with the Arup company, began to design the Eastgate Centre, a passive energy residential and office complex commissioned in Harare.

His design makes use of the large variation between day and night temperatures in Zimbabwe, in the same way that termites do. The structure, like a termite's nest, has variations in wall thickness, hooded windows, light-coloured paints and external shading.

'Imagining the mounds as air conditioners, Pearce drew up plans for a masonry-insulated building of large, open spaces shot through with elaborate ductwork and clusters of tall heat-exchanging chimneys. The ducts would channel air through the building, while the chimneys would siphon heat from the bustling occupants and machinery during the day, venting it up and out to cool the building after dark. To get the design and engineering just right, Pearce ultimately became a bit like a termite himself, descending from his lofty architect's perch to personally labor at the construction site, helping to cast and install some of the masonry blocks with his own two hands.'[6]

The cool night air naturally dissipates the heat that has been generated inside the building during the day, cools the entire building down and it is also captured and stored in the concrete structure itself, which serves as a thermal store.

The floors of the building have a hollow space beneath them, in which teeth-shaped concrete structures retain the cool air.

The following morning, by switching on fans, air blows over the cooled concrete structures, effectively pushing cooled air into the building—thus creating a natural air conditioning system. A labyrinth of circulation pipes and ventilation chimneys keep the interior temperature of the complex between 21.1 and 25 degree Celsius at all times.[7]

The jagged facade of the Eastgate complex is another representation of biomimetic design. Inspired by the cactus plant—well known for thriving in warm climates—the building's frontage is modelled after the prickly surface of a cactus' leaves, which helps dissipate heat more effectively during the night, when temperatures are relatively cooler.

Five years after Mick Pearce was approached to design the Eastgate Centre, it opened its doors to the public.

WHAT TERMITE-INSPIRED ARCHITECTURE COULD MEAN FOR THE WORLD

'The Eastgate Centre debuted in 1996, achieving world-renown for its pioneering "biomimetic" design that regulated its temperature at a fraction of the cost and energy of conventional buildings of comparable size.'[8]

Does It Work?

The first question on everyone's mind of course would be, does it actually work? Was Mick Pearce's bold and big project able to produce the same effect as that found in termite mounds?

A data logger installed by the engineers of the project—Ove Arup & Partners—has been, since 1996, providing continuous air temperature recordings at critical positions of the building, including 'the outside air temperature, the concrete structural temperature, and the room temperatures at different levels within the rooms.'[9]

The data revealed that Eastgate consumes less than 50 per cent of the energy used in conventionally air-conditioned buildings, while achieving very satisfactory conditions for all but two out of the fifty-two weeks in a year.[10]

According to a *Construction Review* article, the building's 'ventilation costs one-tenth that of a comparable air-conditioned building and it uses 35 per cent less energy than six conventional buildings in Harare.

In the first five years alone the building saved its tenants $3.5 million in energy costs.'[11]

A *New York Times* article of 2019 also reported that the Eastgate Centre uses 90 per cent less energy than a similar sized building next door.[12]

In a nutshell, Eastgate proved that building design that was a direct parallel to termite nest design could help maintain satisfactory air temperatures at a fraction of the cost of conventional methods, ease dependence on traditional sources of energy and cut down emissions released by the same—an exprovement in the architecture industry at the time.

What Does It Mean For Other Buildings?

Given that buildings account for a huge percentage of total energy demand—40 to 45 per cent in the EU[13] and 40 per cent in the USA[14]—and are responsible for around 39 per cent of global CO_2 emissions, they have an important role to play in bringing down electricity consumption and emissions caused by the same, and as a corollary, a responsibility to find greener energy solutions.

In some urban settings, such as New York City, commercial buildings account for up to 75 per cent of energy consumption. One staggering comparison was that, in 2009, the Empire State Building consumed as much energy in one day as 40,000 single family homes!

This prompted a $31.1 million deep energy retrofit project of the iconic building in 2009-10, which in the last decade or so has led to a reduction of the structure's emissions by 40 per cent (with a further 40 per cent reduction expected by 2030) and a saving of $4 million annually on electricity expenses.[15]

While retrofitting or demolition may be the only route for old buildings, now that systems like Pearce's have proved to be effective, new commercial buildings would do well to integrate similar methodology into their designs and help to drastically cut down CO_2 emissions and electricity consumption worldwide—especially since this deals with the problem at the source by taking advantage of naturally occurring phenomena in its design.

When Eastgate was completed in 1996, it cost $35 million to construct.[16] Ten to twelve years on, the retrofit of the Empire State Building cost nearly the same. The building sizes may be different, and due to inflation, this isn't an apples-to-apples comparison, but it does drive home the point that retrofits or 'design corrections' are a far more expensive proposition. And we haven't even talked about the cost to the environment from the Empire State Building's eighty years of emissions prior to the retrofit.

Is It Replicable?

The Zimbabwean building is undoubtedly a success, but is it replicable? Can it bring exprovement in other parts of the world as well?

About a decade after the Eastgate Centre was completed, Mick Pearce worked as the principal architect on another nature-inspired building on the other side of the globe—Council House 2 (CH2) in Melbourne, Australia. Besides several other eco-friendly design integrations, the heating, ventilating and cooling (HVAC) system was also designed based on how termite mounds maintain a steady temperature inside, irrespective of outside temperatures. The building uses natural convection, ventilation stacks, thermal mass, phase change material and water for cooling.[17]

For example, some termites dig right down to the water table to bring up moist mud, which they use to build the mound. When the moisture evaporates from the mud, it cools the interior of the structure, bringing the temperature down. Mirroring this evaporative cooling system, CH2 even makes use of the city's sewage water system to tap water via the basement of the building. This water goes through a three-stage filtration process and either becomes a part of the backup air conditioning systems or is used to flush the building's toilets, while simultaneously recycling a part of Melbourne's waste water.[18]

Several other nature-inspired systems also make up the design of CH2. For example, the inspiration for the facade was drawn from the way skin functions. 'The façade is composed of an epidermis (outer skin) and dermis (inner skin). The 'dermis' of the building consists of the outside zone to house the stairs, lifts, ducts, balconies, sunscreens and foliage with the inner line defining the extent of the 'fire compartment'. The dermis was designed with lightweight construction using a steel frame. The epidermis provides the micro-environment including the primary sun and glare control for the building while creating a semi enclosed micro-environment.'[19]

Here are some of the successes of Council House that prove its effectiveness:'

'Melbourne Council House 2 (CH2) is a multi-award winning and inspirational building that has reduced CO_2 emissions by 87%, electricity consumption by 82%, gas by 87% and water by 72%. The building purges stale air at night and pulls in 100% fresh air during the day. The building exterior moves with the sun to reflect and collect heat, and turns sewage into usable water. The building has improved staff effectiveness by 4.9%.'[20]

Looking at just the successes of the Eastgate Centre and Council House 2, the replicability and potential impact of termite and nature inspired buildings in general is undeniable.

'If these termite mound inspired designs were built on a smaller scale in the average family home, the savings would reach high into the billions. If these designs were in place around the world, carbon emissions would lower substantially, contributing to the worldwide effort of stopping global warming.'[21]

WHAT OTHER ARCHITECTURAL PROBLEMS COULD NATURE HOLD THE ANSWERS TO?

While Mick Pearce drew his inspiration for green air conditioning from termites, several systems and creatures existing in the natural world have served as inspiration for designing better construction solutions over the years.

In fact, architect Michael Pawlyn states in his article, 'How biomimicry can be applied to architecture', published in the *Financial Times*, that early examples of biomimetic architecture are found in the work of the Renaissance architect Filippo Brunelleschi who, after studying the strength of eggshells, designed a thinner, lighter dome for his cathedral in Florence, completed in 1436.[22]

Here are some more recent examples of path-breaking biomimicry-related exprovements in architecture:

Improved Structural Support

One of the problems faced by skyscrapers and bridges is that the rigid, inflexible materials (mostly concrete and steel) they are made of tend to crack or break easily during a natural disaster like an earthquake, resulting in damage to the structure, expensive repairs or worse—destruction of the building.

Scientists have recently found a potential solution by drawing a parallel to the structure of a Venus' flower basket—a marine sponge usually found below depths of 500 metres in the Pacific Ocean.

The structure is similar to the diagonal lattice architecture developed for bridges more than two centuries ago, but researchers at Harvard SEAS set out to test which design was actually better. The results revealed that the one made by nature had a higher strength-to-weight ratio, meaning that its architecture 'could withstand heavier loads without buckling, improving its overall structural strength by at least 20 per cent.'[23] This flexible, marine-sponge-inspired design when replicated could mean safer and taller buildings and safer and longer bridges that don't require additional material.[24]

Lightweight Construction Material

Human bones, which are made up of equal parts of calcium and collagen, serve as a model based on which software for lightweight construction material can be developed, as scientist, author and co-founder of the Biomimicry Institute, Janine Benyus, explains in an interview with the American Society of Landscape Architecture,—'"One of the major optimising technologies for buildings right now is a software called OptiStruct, which is based on a bone algorithm," she said. "The technology mimics how bones lay down material where it's needed along lines of stress and take the material away from where it's not needed. These bone algorithms are now seen in bridge and building beams, and they were used to lightweight Airbus' new rib and wing assembly by 40%.'"[25]

Nature-derived Raw Material

As a material that creates the majority of the world's bridges, roads, dams and construction in general, concrete releases a large amount of CO_2 each year and is the highest consumed product on earth besides water. While the other components of concrete (mainly stone and sand) release hardly any CO_2, the cement component of the mix does, and is the sole reason why the concrete industry makes up 8 per cent of overall global emissions.[26]

In nature, oceans absorb large amounts of carbon dioxide from the atmosphere, some of which is then extracted and turned into solid calcium carbonate by coral reefs.[27]

Scientists have been able to successfully mimic how coral reefs form calcium carbonate through a process developed by Wolf Hilbertz and Tom Goreau, which captures carbon dioxide and dissolves it in saltwater, resulting in a construction material called Biorock, which has a compressive strength similar to the concrete used for pavements, grows rapidly, strengthens with age and is self-repairing whilst power is applied.[28]

By drawing a parallel with how coral reefs are formed, the technology just described allows for buildings to be 'grown', rather than 'constructed', in a far more sustainable manner.

One of the most ambitious and exciting Biorock projects is Exploration Architecture's Biorock Pavilion, which is a 'concept for an amphitheatre-like event space that could be grown underwater.

'The form of the building is based on that of a seashell, as well as mathematical forms. The basis of the pavilion would be a skeletal structure comprised of a network of very thin steel rods, which would be immersed in a solution of minerals. An electric current would then be run through the steel skeleton, allowing the remainder of the pavilion to be 'grown' as the minerals calcify atop the base structure.'[29]

According to Michael Pawlyn, founder of Exploration Architecture, the process would produce a structure similar to reinforced concrete and use 'an absolute minimum of material to grow a whole building.'[30]

Self-Healing Buildings

The global self-healing concrete market size in 2021 was $34.10 billion, driven largely by the rising demand for durable and sustainable infrastructure, and an increased focus on reducing carbon emissions generated by construction activity.[31]

Several types of self-healing concrete have been developed over the last decade or so that have drawn their inspiration from nature.

For example, in 2011, microbiologist Henk Jonkers from the Delft University of Technology began testing a bio-inspired concrete he had developed on a lifeguard station that was prone to wind and water damage. Three years on, the structure had remained watertight, using concrete that was inspired by the way human bones heal themselves when broken.

Jonkers' innovation works by embedding concrete with 'capsules of limestone-producing bacteria, either Bacillus pseudofirmus or Sporosarcina pasteurii, along with calcium lactate. When the concrete cracks, air and moisture trigger the bacteria to begin munching on the calcium lactate. They convert the calcium lactate to calcite, an ingredient in limestone, thus sealing off the cracks.

This innovation could solve a longstanding problem with concrete, the world's most common construction material. Concrete often develops micro-cracks during the construction process, explains Jonkers. These tiny cracks don't immediately affect the building's structural integrity, but they can lead to leakage problems. Leakage can eventually corrode the concrete's steel reinforcements, which can ultimately cause a collapse. With the self-healing technology, cracks can be sealed immediately, staving off future leakage and pricey damage down the road. The bacteria can lie dormant for as long as 200 years, well beyond the lifespan of most modern buildings.'[32]

More recently, scientists at Worcester Polytechnic Institute have found a way to speed up the way self-healing concrete works by drawing inspiration from how the human body processes carbon dioxide.

Nima Rahbar, an associate professor of civil and environmental engineering at Worcester Polytechnic, realized that there was a parallel to be drawn from the speed with which carbon dioxide is transported from cells to blood vessels when we inhale oxygen and exhale carbon dioxide while breathing.

Building on this inspiration, biochemist collaborator Suzanna Scarlata's suggestion of adding carbonic anhydrase—the same enzyme that transfers carbon dioxide in the bloodstream—to the concrete powder resulted in the material converting carbon dioxide in the atmosphere into calcium carbonate crystals.

'Whenever a tiny crack forms, the calcium carbonate fills it in. A millimetre-scale crack can be filled within a day, preventing larger cracks from forming. A similar process can also be used on cracks in traditional concrete. "We spray a solution that is composed of enzyme, water and calcium," Rahbar says. "We then can blow CO2 and fill the cracks in minutes, or use ambient CO2 that will take longer to heal the cracks."[33]

CAN BIOMIMICRY RESULT IN EXPROVEMENT IN OTHER INDUSTRIES TOO?

Besides architecture, nature has over the years inspired many innovations and exprovements in a variety of industries.

You may have heard about how Velcro was inspired by an engineer noticing how burrs stuck to him and his dog when they were out for a walk. Or how the fact that many animals are able to hide in plain sight of their predators inspired the use of camouflage in the military. Here are a few more examples across industries of bio-inspired solutions.

Traffic Management

If you've ever observed a colony or even a row of ants, you would have noticed that they never seem to be caught in a 'traffic jam', despite working in a large group that's always on the move.

By drawing a parallel with how ants manage their own version of 'gridlock', Ozan Tonguz, a telecommunications researcher from Carnegie Mellon, developed an algorithm that makes traffic management in the human world more efficient. Instead of using traffic lights, the system uses GPS devices attached to each individual vehicle.

'The algorithm uses information collected from GPS devices, short-range communicators and other sensors to manage whether a driver sees a green, yellow or red light on her windshield.

In simulations, the algorithm managed the flow of cars in a way similar to how insects manage themselves'[34]—which is to allow the bigger group (or car) to move first—the results were that traffic drive time was reduced by 40 to 60 per cent, which also means that carbon emissions would be reduced thanks to the quicker commute.[35]

Underwater Adhesives

Mussels are able to cling tightly to surfaces underwater by secreting a mix of oppositely charged adhesive proteins[36]—inspiration for developing underwater adhesives or adhesives that are able to work in wet environments. Companies like Mussel Polymers Inc. manufacture products for the dental industry—adhesives for fittings, crowns, implants etc.; for the defence industry—adhesives for mission-critical military ships and vehicles; and the electronics industry—adhesives for circuit boards, solar panels and batteries.[37]

Mussel-inspired hydrogels have found useful application in the healing of wounds. For example, 'Korean scientists at Pohang University of Science and Technology (POSTECH) have developed a light-activated, mussel protein-based bio-adhesive (LAMBA) that works on the same principles as mussels attaching to underwater surfaces and insects maintaining structural balance and flexibility. The glue not only closes an open wound on a wet bleeding site within less than *60* seconds but also effectively facilitates the healing process without inflammation or a scar.'[38]

Single-pass Water Filtration

In 2021, Swedish company Aquammodate developed a water filtration system inspired by diatoms, which are single-celled organisms found in oceans and waterways,[39] and aquaporins, which are channel proteins that form pores in the membrane of biological cells.[40] 'The company's energy-efficient and selective technology produces high purity grade water in a single filter pass, desalination at any scale, and removes industrial pollutants and contaminants such as arsenic, microplastics and pharmaceutical residues.'[41]

High Strength Fibre

The silk of a spider is one of the strongest biological materials in the world. Spintex Engineering has mimicked the precision of a spider's spinnerets to produce artificial spider silk for use in textiles, apparel, aerospace and automotive industries. The start-up's process works at room temperature, is 1000 times more energy-efficient than the production of synthetic plastic fibres, has only water as a by-product and uses no hazardous chemicals.[42]

A PARALLEL WORLD OF ENDLESS INSPIRATION

... WHERE GETTING IT WRONG CAN MEAN GETTING IT RIGHT

While biomimicry has indeed helped find the solution to many problems in several industries, some of them leading to exprovement, it is interesting to note that the premise on which Mick Pearce built the Eastgate Centre was actually flawed.

'At the time of the building's design, researchers had proposed that termite mounds maintained stable internal climates by having a physical structure that enables passive internal airflow.'[43]

Subsequent research, particularly by American scientist Scott Turner, led to the understanding that 'the mounds didn't regulate temperature so much as push oxygen and carbon dioxide in to and out of the nest. This mixing of air was powered not by the colony's internal heat but by external air pressure: The termites built their mounds tall to catch the wind, not to promote convection. A mound's porous, permeable outer surface allowed air to suffuse into and through the colony, rather like the alveoli in a human lung. The mounds weren't crude air conditioners so much as a wildly complicated external respiratory system.'[44]

In spite of this flawed understanding, the Eastgate Centre was still a success because Pearce inadvertently mimicked the design so well, though his reasoning was in hindsight based on the wrong assumption.

Pearce's mantra of form following process[45], i.e., understanding *how* one is building it and *who* it is being built for, as opposed to the principle that form follows function, has led him to successfully integrate biomimicry into several of his projects.

... AND WHERE THE 'WHY' IS JUST AS IMPORTANT AS THE 'HOW'

There are other approaches to biomimicry as well that serve other functions.

'Where Pearce interpreted the termite mound directly in terms of functional units familiar to humans, other researchers use insect architecture primarily to gain insight into its inscrutable residents. "You don't have to even see the animal in order to have an excellent record of its behaviour, you just examine the structure and figure out how it was built,"' says John Wenzel, an entomologist and expert on wasp nests at the Carnegie Museum of Natural History in Pennsylvania.[46]

Digging deeper into the 'why' and not just the 'how' by observation and research can lead to many interesting and unexpected insights. Wenzel himself experienced this while studying paper wasps build nests as a student at the University of Kansas in the 1980s.

While observing the wasps lay down row after row of hexagonal paper cells, he would occasionally see a worker wasp place a pentagon instead, which he initially put down to be a 'mistake' on the part of the creature.

Later he realized that the placement of the pentagons was neither random nor a mistake. They were being placed at points of likely structural stress to add support where subsequent layers of the nest would be built with curvature—a valuable lesson in why understanding the 'why' of anomalies in nature is important in biomimicry.

Another school of thought is that 'most of today's biomimicry barely mimics biology at all. It would be better described as an expression of "biophilia", an instinctive human tendency to seek connections with other living things. To engineer and entrepreneur Rupert Soar, true biomimicry is more of a process than a product—"Architects are still looking at this in terms of designing specific structures, shapes, and forms for specific functions," Soar says. "But in nature that's not how we see solutions and innovations emerge! We just see organisms following very simple sets of rules, algorithms playing out again and again as related to some objective."[47]

But all the various approaches to biomimicry share one thing in common—the belief and proof that nature can often provide the answer to exprovement where humans cannot.

DEVELOPING AN EXPROVEMENT OUTLOOK

What are some of the types of questions that could have led an architect to find exprovement solutions in nature?

- What, in humans or animals, is able to maintain the same temperature despite the influences of external conditions? For example: blood
- What parallels can be drawn from how animals/humans maintain body temperature?
- What are some of the natural phenomena where one observes a change in temperature? For example: shade, breeze, humidity
- What parallels can be drawn from materials that interact with heat? For example: stone, water, a vacuum
- What parallels can be drawn from the shelters of animals/insects/birds? For example: nests, caves, etc.
- Can heat generated inside a building be utilized for something, instead of finding ways to get rid of it?

5

What Does Formula One
Have in Common with Clean Teeth?

If you've ever had to deal with a punctured tyre while on the road, you know how this annoying setback can cause delays in the schedule you had planned for the day, leaving you with the feeling that you've 'lost' the race against time.

Imagine yourself in a car race, where a punctured tyre seems like the thing that could put you out of the race entirely.

Not so if it's a Formula One race.

During the 2008 Monaco Grand Prix when Lewis Hamilton hit a barrier in heavy rain, it left him with a punctured tyre and the commentators lamenting Monaco's notoriously difficult circuit with great animation, as Hamilton was forced to make a pit stop.

In contrast, if you were to instead listen to team McLaren's internal feed while the same incident was happening, you would hear information and a few short instructions being calmly communicated between the team and Hamilton, and then silence until Hamilton emerges from the pit stop nine seconds later.

While an average pit stop in a race takes two to three seconds, even in this less-than-favourable situation, it took the team less than ten seconds to make the switch to a different tactic, which, besides changing tyres, involved making alterations to car components and fuelling up.

Hamilton went on to win the race that day, and the drivers' championship as well.

It is from incidents like this on the Formula One track that McLaren's Geoff McGrath was able to draw a parallel with improving the efficiency of a production line at GlaxoSmithKline (GSK) back in 2011.

THE TWO-SECOND ANALOGY

If you're wondering what someone from a racing car company was doing at a pharmaceutical company, McGrath used to head McLaren Applied Technologies (MAT; now Mclaren Applied Limited*), a spinoff of McLaren that applies Formula One's high-performance culture and working methods to other businesses.

When team MAT collaborated with GSK in 2011 to figure out how they could reduce production cycle time at GSK's toothpaste factory in Maidenhead, England, they discovered that 'a production-line bottleneck was occurring during the so-called changeover: transition periods when factory workers needed to switch products on the line from one toothpaste brand to another. This meant changing and cleaning the tubes, rearranging the tools in the line and a number of other procedures that halted production.'[1]

For McGrath, the parallel with a Formula One pit stop was obvious:

'If we can change four tyres on a Formula One car in two seconds, why does it take us two hours to do a changeover in the toothpaste factory?'[2]

The GSK and McLaren teams worked together to apply processes and procedures used at Formula One races to the factory's production line. They asked questions such as whether the tooling was standardized and if the changeover team was specially picked or was just made up of whoever happened to be available at the time the switchover to a different toothpaste cycle was being made; they made a computer model of the production line—similar to what is done for Formula One races; they even put the shop floor workers in McLaren overalls and instead of telling them what to do, let them play around with the system to figure out what needed to change.

The result was that by drawing a parallel with how the McLaren Formula One team develops a predetermined plan for any possible scenario during a race (the reason they immediately knew what to do when Hamilton had the punctured tyre), the team at the toothpaste factory 'developed a seven-step process that began before the changeover, mirroring McLaren's cycle of simulation, pre-planning, debriefing and continuous improvement. Changeover times fell by 60 per cent, dropping from an average of 39 minutes to 15, equating to an extra 20 million tubes by the end of the year.'[3]

The pit stop analogy also led to a change in perception. As Shaun Glover, engineer at GlaxoSmithKline, put it, 'We used to see changeovers as down time; McLaren sees pit stops as an opportunity to win the race.'[4]

THE BENEFITS OF A PIT-STOP-INSPIRED PRODUCTION CYCLE

While increased productivity is one positive impact of using Formula One-developed processes to improve cycle times, there are several other related positive outcomes that a company can benefit from, some of which are:

- Being able to produce more in a given time period could result in less raw material inventory and fewer man hours (lower labour costs), which directly impacts profit margins.
- Improved customer satisfaction could result from having a shorter time to market. In the services sector especially, a rapid turnaround time is vital to improving customer responsiveness, satisfaction and delight.
- Being able to rapidly churn out products, especially high-technology ones, gives companies a competitive advantage in terms of the ability to provide innovative solutions and meet launch dates sooner. An inability to do so runs the risk of rendering cutting edge R&D departments obsolete, if production cycles are not able to keep pace.
- The cost savings gained by a higher product output and a leaner manufacturing cycle also provides opportunities to experiment with new products. Companies with lower cycle times can turn their attention to developing prototypes or samples for consumers, allowing them to develop new and innovative products.[5, 6]

FORMULA ONE: TURBO-CHARGING EXPROVEMENT IN SEVERAL INDUSTRIES

The GSK exprovement isn't a one-off example of Formula 1 inspiring parallels in other industries, and neither is McLaren the only racing company to have collaborated on them. Here are a few more instances of Formula 1-inspired exprovement across industries:

Process/Protocol Optimization

'A 2005 study found that nearly 70% of preventable hospital mishaps occurred because of communication problems, and other studies have shown that at least half of such breakdowns occur during handoffs. To cite an example, in 1995, one man in Florida had the wrong leg amputated after a flubbed handoff.

"If you transfer a patient to the ICU after surgery and the ventilator isn't ready, you're really riding on the edge of patient safety," says Allan Goldman, head of the pediatric intensive care unit at Great Ormond Street Hospital for Children in London, and a chief architect of the hospital's collaboration with Ferrari.'[7]

By drawing a parallel between the role of a pit stop crew's 'lollipop man' and the supervisor who is in charge of transferring post-operative patients to the intensive care unit, Ferrari and the hospital were able to exprove the latter's safety protocol, leading to a reduction in error rates from 30 per cent to 10 per cent.[8, 9]

In a similar collaboration in 2016, the pit stop procedures used by the Williams Formula One mechanics (Williams holds the record for the fastest Formula One pit stop at 1.92 seconds, which they achieved at the 2016 European Grand Prix[10]) helped speed up the neonatal resuscitation process at Cardiff's University Hospital of Wales.[11, 12]

"'There is a growing amount of evidence to support a systematic approach to resuscitative care which is time-critical and dependent upon optimal team dynamics and clear communication," said the hospital's specialist registrar Rachel Hayward.

"Analogous with the requirements of an effective pit stop we have worked with the Williams team to implement Formula One techniques and processes to augment neonatal resuscitative care."[13]

With some of the neonatal team visiting the Williams factory to see how pit stops were carried out and some of the Williams employees visiting the hospital to observe procedures there, the teams were able to implement impactful changes, including 'ensuring that equipment could be located without delay, mapping out floorspace, using more hand signals rather than verbal communication and video analysis in post-resuscitation "debriefs".'[14]

Sustainable Refrigeration

Williams Advanced Engineering (WAE), a technology and engineering services business that is a part of the Williams Formula One group, in collaboration with Aerofoil Energy developed a component for the Sainsbury's chain of supermarkets in England a few years ago that helps make the chain's store fridges more sustainable.

The component was initially developed for Formula One cars, to divert air over and around the vehicle, enabling improved aerodynamics and performance. By drawing a direct parallel to how aerofoils control the direction of airflow in Formula One cars, WAE and Aerofoil Energy developed a device that helps keep the cold air from open-door supermarket fridges close to the fridge, preventing it from escaping into the aisles, thus making them more energy efficient.[15, 16, 17, 18]

'The device is basically a thin strip of aluminium and plastic shaped like a wing that is attached to the front of the cabinet shelves.'[19]

As explained by Craig Wilson, CEO at WAE, 'The aerofoil acts like the rear wing of an Formula One car and guides the air to create an air curtain.'[20]

As reported in 2020, with its 4,00,000[th] aerofoil installation, Sainsbury's said it had seen a 15 per cent reduction in energy consumption (a potential annual saving of nearly GBP 10 million[21]). In addition, each year, aerofoil-equipped fridges in Sainsbury's deliver carbon savings of 8,783 tonnes of carbon dioxide emissions.[22]

An added benefit—customers no longer have to brave freezing aisles as they choose their chilled products!

'By looking outside of our industry, and borrowing technology from an industry that is renowned for its speed and efficiency, we are accelerating how we are reducing the impact on the environment, whilst making shopping in Sainsbury's stores a more comfortable experience,' said Paul Crewe, Head of Sustainability at Sainsbury's, in 2017.[23]

Health Parameter Monitoring

Another parallel McGrath was able to draw during his time at MAT was that 'if we can measure the health and condition of an engine, why can't we measure the health and condition of a person?'[24]

McLaren had previously tested monitoring sensors on rugby players to predict when they would peak and when they were likely to run the risk of injury.

Now, using the sensor and engine analogy, McLaren and GSK tested a ten-pence-sized device to exprove the measurement of a stroke patient's health and response to medication.

One of the ways to do this is to measure the patient's mobility. GSK was using a system—making a patient walk between two chairs placed ten metres apart, to see how many steps and how long it took them—that was not delivering results.

According to Julian Jenkins, vice president of project planning and management at GSK, 'I don't know how long it takes for me to walk ten metres, let alone a stroke patient. It was flawed.'[25]

But using McLaren's sensing device, twenty parameters—including gait, cadence and stride frequency—could be measured.

'When I saw the first patient's data I was astonished,' Jenkins says. 'Within seconds, I could tell that the patient was very sick. There's no test that we could have done before that would reach the same conclusion.'[26]

Air Traffic Management

McLaren's data and predictive analysis technology has been used to improve air traffic control at Heathrow airport.[27]

'Simulation software created to monitor the location, position and speed of every car on the circuit was redeveloped to perform a similar function for aircraft. The resulting Decision Insight platform enables air traffic controllers to optimize the flow of air and ground traffic, thereby reducing delays and jet engine emissions. Result: happier customers, less polluted air and an improved bottom-line for airlines, thanks to savings on fuel costs.'[28]

Auditing and Advisory Services

In 2014, it was announced that KPMG had entered into a deal with McLaren to 'apply the high-powered predictive analytics and technology normally used in Grand Prix races to improve its audit and advisory services.'[29]

At the time, Simon Collins, UK chairman of KPMG, had said, 'McLaren has honed sophisticated predictive analytics and technologies that can be applied to many business issues. We believe this specialist knowledge has the power to radically transform audit, improving quality and providing greater insight to management teams, audit committees and investors. The same is true of our joint advisory services.'[30]

At the end of that alliance, which a KPMG spokesman said had resulted in the development of 'predictive analytics tools unmatched anywhere else in the market, which allow KPMG to offer enhanced audit and advisory services to our clients', in 2017 it was reported that McLaren was entering into a similar collaboration with Deloitte, that would 'target the delivery of £1bn of annual benefits to the professional services firm's clients by 2022.'

The venture would 'seek to develop products based on the technical expertise of MAT's engineering and analytics functions drawn from the McLaren motorsport operations.'[31]

What is interesting about these examples of cross-industry application is that it is not just one, but a variety of aspects—sensor technology, aerodynamics, planning, project management, data analytics etc.—from Formula One that have led to exprovement in a variety of other industries.

FORMULA ONE TECHNOLOGY—FUTURE APPLICATIONS

Looking at the examples just listed, it is quite likely that innovatively inclined minds will continue to find parallel applications for Formula One technology in other industries. But, undoubtedly, there are some industries where Formula One technology will definitely play a vital role.

The industries mentioned below may have a closer relation to Formula One racing than those mentioned above, but they are, nevertheless, parallel industries.

Automotive Design

Formula One racing has, since its inception in 1950, pushed the boundaries and changed the perception of what a car can do. Always ahead of its time compared to what mass-produced cars can achieve, a lot of Formula One technology that has been experimented with and perfected for racing proves to be too expensive or impractical to integrate in mass production road cars. However, the 'trickle-down' effect, in reference to technology developed specifically for Formula One racing eventually finding its way into the cars we drive every day, has been felt in several instances.

Active suspension, for example, which gives a vehicle the ability to adjust itself continuously to changing road conditions via the use of sensors controlled by an onboard computer system was first used in Formula One racing in the Lotus Type 92 back in 1983. The technology eventually trickled down into passenger cars as well, with Land Rover, BMW, Citroen, Jaguar, Mercedes-Benz, Toyota and Volvo amongst manufacturers that use it in some of their cars today.[32, 33, 34]

Another example of the trickle-down effect is the use of carbon fibre in cars. 'A carbon-fibre vehicle chassis is lighter, stronger and has better aerodynamic properties.' McLaren was the first racing company to test a carbon fibre chassis, and when Formula One driver John Watson was involved in a horrific crash in the McLaren MP4/1 at the Monza racetrack in 1981, car manufacturers took notice, as Watson climbed unhurt from motor racing's first carbon fibre monocoque cabin. Had he been in an aluminium chassis, chances of him being severely injured were high. 'Lighter and safer' is a winning combination in car design, and today the carbon fibre chassis features in a number of production cars, including some of the cars manufactured by Aston Martin, Jaguar and Porsche.[35, 36]

Looking at the future, the trickle-down effect is going to have an even more important role to play as car manufacturers strive to make both, cars for the Formula One track and cars for on-road use, more sustainable.

The biggest impact will be in terms of enhanced engine efficiency and battery technology for hybrid cars, and in terms of the development of sustainable fuels.

'F1 hybrid cars are highly efficient, and the power units have significantly contributed to battery technology. The weight of the battery of the first energy store in 2007 was more than 100 kg, but today it stands at 20 kg. Lithium-ion batteries are rechargeable and are specifically designed for hybrid vehicles. This kind of technology is not only making Formula One cars more efficient but it also helps enhance the efficiency of road cars by improving their fuel consumption patterns.'[37]

In 2022, Formula One made the move to E10 fuel, a mixture of 90 per cent fossil fuel and 10 per cent ethanol. But with the launch of the new generation of Formula 1 engines, the aim is to develop a 100 per cent sustainable fuel to help achieve the goal of being net zero carbon by 2030.[38] The trickle-down effect of this move is poised to have a positive impact on the development of sustainable solutions for cars in general, public transportation and the reduction of carbon emissions.

'Formula 1 didn't invent the hybrid, but Formula 1 showed what a hybrid could be, and it moved people's perceptions of what a hybrid is capable of, and I think we can do the same with new fuel technology and hopefully demonstrate that another viable alternative energy source is possible,' says Pat Symonds, Chief Technical Officer, Formula One.[39]

It is not only the design of cars that could benefit from Formula One technology, but of other vehicles as well.

In 2011, McLaren collaborated with California-based Specialized Bicycle Components to completely reinvent the way a bike could be designed—they borrowed data-driven design from Formula One and applied it to bicycle design.

According to Duncan Bradley, head of high-performance design at MAT, 'Like any other bike-maker, Specialized would design by eye. Test riders would then ride the bike and give subjective feedback. That's exactly how we would design Formula One cars 50 years ago.'

After eight months of work that included attaching more than twenty sensors on the bike to measure various forces and vibrations that affect a moving bike, using a computer model that could be tweaked by changing parameters like shape, weight, stiffness of frame etc., they developed a formula based on the understanding of how people ride bikes. As Bradley put it, 'We completely flipped the way bikes were designed.'[40]

The result was the S-Works + McLaren Venge, which was 20 per cent lighter than Specialized's previous model without losing its structural integrity and was also the model used by Mark Cavendish to win the UCI Road World Championships—the first British rider to do so since 1965.

McLaren's Geoff McGrath said of the collaboration, 'Specialized later told me that they had learned more in six months about bike design than they had in the previous ten years.'[41]

In a similar collaboration that draws on the parallels between motor sport and cycling, such as materials technology and aerodynamics, Red Bull Advanced Technologies, the high-tech external solutions division of Red Bull Technology, announced that it 'would bring its track-bred technical capability to bear on bicycles being designed by BMC Switzerland . . . As such, Red Bull Advanced Technologies will harness the latest developments in race-refined technology, coupled with intelligent Human Performance Analytics, with specific focus on developing integrated electronic technologies to enhance the cycling experience for every bicycle rider.'[42]

Some of the other vehicles that have used Formula One design inspiration include air taxis and lightweight aircraft.

Scan the QR to learn about one such project:

Public Transport

Technology developed for Formula One racing will also find application in public transportation. For example, Formula One-derived technology to develop 5G infrastructure for connected road, rail and underground transportation[43], or Formula One sensor and data technology, as in the case of the McLaren and Singapore Mass Rapid Transit (SMRT) collaboration to track performance using race car condition-monitoring technology.[44]

As we move further towards autonomous driving, such technology will play a vital role in the management of public transport going forward.

Aerospace

And finally, it's not just here on earth that Formula One technology is poised to find parallel industry applications! In 2018, it was reported that Williams Advanced Engineering 'had begun work with Oxford Space Systems to help develop a new generation of lightweight, unfurlable boom arms and foldable antennae. These will be used on so-called nano-satellites that are lighter, less complex and cheaper than those currently in use. Their smaller scale presents a host of packaging and weight challenges—precisely the types of problem that are meat and drink to F1 engineers.'[45]

DEVELOPING AN EXPROVEMENT OUTLOOK

Here are some questions to ponder about applying Formula One technology to other industries:

- It is said that in most businesses, 'time is money'—Formula 1 is great at managing time. What parallels can businesses in various industries draw to optimize time?
- If Formula 1 is what paves the way for the future of the automotive industry, what is its equivalent for other industries?

- What parallels can be drawn with the ways in which Formula One cars manage heat, considering the cars regulate temperatures of over 2000°C?
- Formula One cars are built for safety even at very high speeds. What can the defence forces learn from Formula 1 about dealing with high-impact collisions?

6

Can a Popsicle Ease Global
Warming Problems?

What does eight-year-old Sam, who is about to enjoy an orange popsicle on a hot summer's day in May sitting at 105 metres above sea level in Florida, have in common with fifty-six-year-old Samstan Zangpo,[1] a 1.25-acre farmer who's about to begin sowing his crop in the village of Nang in Ladakh at 3700 metres above sea level?

They both stand to gain the benefit—though quite different in nature and scale—of a man-made, compressed, frozen body of water that has the ability to remain cool and melt slowly over an extended period of time.

While Sam's benefit is the pleasure of 'cooling off' on a hot day, Zangpo's benefit, though not immediately evident, has the potential to impact his life significantly.

What could a farmer, living in a cold desert and already surrounded by snow and ice-capped mountains, possibly stand to gain from an additional structure of ice?

The answer lies in being able to draw a parallel between a product from the food and beverage industry and using it as a solution to solve a crisis in the farming industry.

As far-fetched as that may seem on the surface, understanding the features of a popsicle enables a clearer picture to emerge.

A popsicle is, amongst other things, a solid block of ice that:

66

1. melts slowly at room temperature, and
2. releases a steady trickle of liquid (which would begin to drip down Sam's arm if he were not to eat it quickly).

It is these two features of a popsicle that present themselves as an exproved solution to the troubles faced by farmer Zangpo.

THE IMPACT OF GLOBAL WARMING ON FARMING IN LADAKH

To understand the benefit a 'popsicle' could bring to the farming community in Ladakh, it is important to first understand the problems faced by farmers in the region.

Winters in Ladakh, India's highest province, are severe to say the least, with temperatures dropping to -30°C. For centuries the agricultural community here has relied on the meltwater of glaciers high up in the mountains, using a system of canals that divert glacial water to farms for irrigation of crops.

In recent years, however, the effects of global warming and climate change (and this is true for most mountainous regions of the world) have put a spoke in this tried and tested method, leading to unreliable snowfall and receding glaciers.

The region is often no longer covered in heavy snow in the winter months of November and December like it used to be, but glacial water instead floods the area, cascading down mountains and either causing floods or going to waste; useless to farmers at this time of the year, as it is still too cold to plant anything.

According to estimates from the Yale School of Forestry and Environmental Sciences, a whopping 260 gigatons of water is wasted in this way, every year.

By the time the planting season of April and May comes around, the glacial streams have long dried up, leaving the farmers starved of water needed to irrigate their vulnerable saplings of barley and wheat—traditionally the main crops of the region—and reducing the farming season in the 80,000 sq km region of Ladakh to just four months, allowing for no winter crops, and locals having to import vegetables at a high cost.

In a nutshell, due to climate change, excess water is available when it is of no use to farmers; and during the time of the year when it is required and is crucial to the success of their crop, none is available.

THE QUEST FOR A HIGH-ALTITUDE, LOW-TECH SOLUTION

An innovation that has solved the problem to a certain extent over the past thirty to forty years has been artificial glaciers.

Many years ago on a winter morning, a young and curious boy born into a farming family in Ladakh noticed something that got him thinking—he saw that a puddle of water had frozen, while all around it water from streams flowed freely. On closer observation, the boy realized that the puddle had frozen because it was located under the shade of a tree that provided a colder temperature in that particular spot, and that water flowing slowly in a trickle could freeze quicker when compared to water flowing at a higher velocity.

Decades after his initial observation, in 1987, the-boy-who-had-a-theory was finally able to turn his idea into an innovation by creating the region's first artificial glacier in Phuktse village, the success of which would lead him—Chewang Norphel—to the building of more such glaciers, earning him, in the process, the nickname of Ice Man of India, and in 2015, the prestigious Padma Shri award.

As with many great innovations, the idea to create an artificial glacier began with a 'what if'.

In Norphel's own words, he thought, 'What if there were glaciers at lower altitudes which would melt sooner due to relatively higher temperature? Thus came the idea of artificial glaciers.

It's a technique to harvest winter wastewater in the form of ice. And by creating artificial glaciers at relatively lower altitudes, it was possible to get water when it was needed.'[2]

Norphel's idea had the potential to bring disruption to the region's agricultural community by figuring out a way to store water that is in abundance in winter—and that would otherwise go to waste—till it is required in spring.

He did this by using the simple physics principle he had seen play out in his youth to devise a system that involves diverting water in the form of slow-flowing streams from main glacial streams to a shaded, contained holding area in November, whereafter as winter intensifies, it freezes, creating an artificial glacier. This is done by creating stepped embankments that slow down the speed of flowing water, allowing it to collect and freeze easily recreating, on a magnified scale, what he observed with the puddle of water in his youth.

Come April the artificial glaciers begin to melt as temperatures rise, just in time to provide irrigation water required for crops in April and May.

Multiple glaciers are created at different levels, with the lower altitude ones melting first, thus ensuring a steady supply of water as each glacier at a different altitude begins to melt.

'In the winter of 1987, he created a unique water storage technique in Phuktse village. At an elevation of 4,000 metres, working with villagers, he moved large boulders to dam a shaded north-facing valley. The team then diverted a stream through channels that let the water trickle slowly. At sub-zero temperatures, it froze.

'Warm spring temperature thawed the ice and water trickled down to irrigate fields of barley in April, when glaciers high up in the mountains were still frozen solid. This technique offered one crucial advantage: it required no major masonry work. Villagers called it an "artificial glacier".'[3]

According to a report of 2015[4], using Norphel's artificial glacier method, farmers were able to gain an additional twenty to forty days of irrigation, allowing for the potential to grow even two crops a year and perhaps to raise cattle as well.

As of 2018, Norphel's innovation had led to the construction of seventeen such glaciers.[5]

But Norphel's design wasn't without flaws. Artificial glaciers have limitations:

- They have to be located at a high altitude, involving hard work and high cost.
- The concept doesn't work at lower altitudes where most of the people live.
- The concept only works in heavily shaded areas.
- They require regular maintenance—again a difficult and expensive proposition in the harsh winter.
- They require a large space.
- In some instances, the water evaporated before it could be used.

Sometimes an initial idea that causes disruption, while brilliant in concept, can have room for improvement or can lead to further innovation on the initial idea itself, if one is always seeking better ways to solve a problem.

ARTIFICIAL GLACIERS 2.0

If we were to look at drawing parallels, asking questions such as, how can one use all this ice that's around? (ice is water after all, just in a different form); or, what's something that is frozen but can be made to melt when required? (ice cubes, ice cream and ice popsicles!) could help find an answer.

About a quarter of a century after the first artificial glacier was constructed, Sonam Wangchuck—a mechanical engineer, co-founder of alternative school SEMCOL and a self-confessed problem solving addict—applied his mind to improving Norphel's idea when he realized, on observing an intact fragment of ice under a bridge, that it wasn't the warmth of the sun that melted ice, but rather, the fact that *direct* sunlight fell on it.

Wangchuck realized that if he could reduce the surface area of the artificial glacier he just might be able to solve its limitations. A smaller surface area would mean that the ice structure would have less area exposed to direct sunlight and so take longer to melt.

But how does one reduce the surface area of a large artificial glacier by about 600 to 700 per cent? For that was what his solution would entail.

High School Physics Comes to The Rescue

Applying basic mathematical logic, Wangchuk knew that a conical structure would be his best bet.

To test his theory, and in the process give his students at SEMCOL an interesting project to work on, he built a prototype at 'a spot that was fully exposed to sunlight and located at the lowest altitude—and hence warmest—possible in the whole of Leh valley.'[6]

He developed a system that would allow ice to form in the shape of a cone without the use of any machines or energy, but instead through the application of a basic physics principle he'd learned in school—if water at one end of a pipe is at a certain height, it will rise or fall to the same height at the other end as well.

Using a network of pipes laid below the frost line, cold stream water that hovers between a liquid and solid state was diverted to the designated spot, and at the point where the pipes turned vertical the water was sprayed into the cold air, causing it to freeze and form a conical ice structure. The result was the first prototype of a giant cone-shaped six-metre-high popsicle.

Water in the form of ice, when it begins to melt, flows at a slower velocity than water in its liquid form, at a normal temperature. So just like Sam's popsicle, which begins to melt on coming into contact with the hot Florida temperature and starts to trickle down his hand, the prototype conical ice structure began to melt when the warmer spring temperatures arrived, releasing a slow and steady flow of water at the time that farmers like Samstan Zangpo required it in their fields.

Constructed in October, the prototype was expected to last till May. It lasted eighteen days longer than expected.

The Project Garners Community Support

With the success of this prototype ice stupa, as it came to be called, Wangchuk was invited by His Holiness Che Tsang Rinpoche—'a passionate advocate of the environment and sustainable development'— to construct the next ice stupa at his monastery in Phyang Valley.[7]

This extract from TED explains the success of the project at Phyang Valley:

'Wangchuk's team planned to tap into the water of a stream flowing about one-and-a-half miles up the slope from the monastery. Into this stream they placed one end of a mile-and-a-half-long pipe, which ran downhill via a tunnel. When the pipeline reached the grounds of the monastery, it made a 90-degree turn, jutting out of the ground and rising—perpendicular to the ground—to roughly 35 feet, its mouth facing the sky. Since the mouth was at an elevation of about 65 meters above the monastery in the high mountains, the water should mirror that height at the other end of the pipe and rise 65 meters over the valley.

When construction began, several hundred locals volunteered to assist, lining up on the slope to dig the tunnel, lay the pipe, and then shovel earth over it. They also planted 5,000 saplings around the planned ice stupa, greening the valley. 'Generally, in Ladakh, there is a rich tradition of people coming out to help,' says Wangchuk. 'And that comes because it's a very harsh and difficult place, and you cannot survive if you only take care of yourself.'

By March 2015, the team was ready to open the pipe. When they did, the stream water entered and began to flow through it down the slope. As the water moved, it began speeding up thanks to gravity. By the time it reached the other end, its momentum helped it to rise and gush up before smashing against the fountainhead blocking the pipe.

The fountainhead was placed strategically, with the aim of splintering the water into a fine spray and sending it shooting in all directions like the florets on a dandelion head. As the miniscule drops broke out of the pipeline and met the -10 to -20-degree winter air, they froze. Bit by bit, these pieces of ice accumulated and began to grow upward like a stalagmite.

Gravity, speed, slope, acceleration, temperature—these physical forces all worked with the water and earth to build the ice stupa. It was a 'solution with no rocket science,' according to Wangchuk. Once the basic framework was put into place, everything took care of itself, 'using no machines or energy except gravity,' as he put it.

The tower rose to a height of 64 feet, containing nearly two million gallons of water.

With the stupa complete, the team waited. As April came, temperatures rose. The ice tower released a little rivulet of water that trickled into the serpentine channels circling the beds of saplings. The water continued to flow, but even when temperatures peaked in the upper 60s in mid-May 2015, the tower stood. It stayed through June, shrinking slowly until finally disappearing in early July.'[8]

A Low-tech, High-efficacy Solution

According to the latest available figures, with the government lending its support to the ice stupa project and the assistance of the Ministry of Tribal Affairs, there are, at the time of writing this book, twenty-six stupas in Ladakh, and Wangchuk is in the process of laying a pipeline that will help create fifty more stupas that bring 10 million litres of water a year to the water-starved region[9], bringing hope and reliability to small-scale farmers.

'A fifty-foot ice stupa, which can be created in less than a month, stores more than a quarter of a million gallons of water.'[10]

By controlling the state of water—converting it from a fast-flowing liquid into ice, and then later into a slow-flowing liquid state, while also ensuring that none of it is lost via evaporation—the ice stupa has inadvertently utilized freeze concentration in a new and unique way, adapting it to the farming industry.

While the melting of an ice popsicle might not be a source of joy to Sam, the same principle, coupled with the innovative application of some basic physics principles, has brought about an exprovement—a unique way to solve the irrigation crisis peculiar to the Himalayas.

Though the ice stupa in many ways improves on the concept of the artificial glacier, it is important to note that had Wangchuk's approach been one of improvement, i.e., asking questions like:

- How can one reduce shade requirements for artificial glaciers? or
- How can one minimize maintenance requirements for artificial glaciers?

it would have led merely to an improved version of the glacier, without coming up with an entirely new concept.

The fact that his approach seemed to be based on a question like 'How can one solve the summer water crisis without having to depend on economic resources or being at the mercy of changing weather patterns?' was what led to the development of an exprovement.

THE IMPACT OF THE ICE STUPA

What has been the impact of the ice stupas on farmers of the region?

'The ice stupas have transformed life for some farmers in the area, who talk about having a stable crop now, both to sell and to feed their families.

Tenzing Pitot says her family's financial situation has improved dramatically since an ice stupa was built. It became difficult to know when to plant vegetables, she says, but now there's a near-guarantee that water will be there when needed.'

'The ice stupas "help us with water at the right time," says Phunsuk Dolma. Dolma sells vegetables in Leh, a nearby town that shares is name with the local district. "We don't have to wait for the natural glaciers to melt," Dolma says. "The natural glaciers help us after the artificial glaciers melt."'[11]

While Sonam Wangchuk feels that more work needs to be done to improve the design of the stupas to make them more reliable, he says 'in the meantime, we can grow trees where trees would never grow because the land was too dry.'[12]

That rationale alone is reason enough to celebrate.

DOES A PARALLEL PATH TO EXPROVEMENT EXIST?

On analysis of the processes and methodology employed in the development of the ice stupa exprovement, we found that altering the state of a liquid to suit requirements is technology that already existed in the food and beverage industry.

Do you see the parallel between a popsicle and a glacier? They both use a process known as freeze concentration, which involves the crystallization of water to ice at first and then the separation of ice crystals from the concentrated liquid.

In the case of a frozen popsicle, the concentrated liquid begins to melt and trickle down once the popsicle has been removed from the freezer and remains at room temperature for a while. In the case of the ice stupa, the frozen conical shape forms and remains frozen in winter but begins to thaw once temperatures heat up as spring and summer arrive. Or looking at a different aspect of the popsicle—what drips is a concentrate, thereby leaving water behind.

Thus, by adapting the concept of freeze concentration, a process used in the food and beverage industry—not unlike the one used to make Sam's popsicle—to the conditions and requirements in Ladakh, Wangchuk devised a plan to capture and freeze the excess glacial water that was going to waste in winter, and store it till it was needed till summer.

Another noteworthy parallel is that freeze concentration in the food and beverage industry allows juice concentrates, coffee etc. to last longer, while in the exprovement just explained it also allows water to 'last longer'—till the ideal time and in the ideal form in which it is required. The ice stupa itself is a parallel to the popsicle.

WHAT THE ICE STUPA TEACHES US ABOUT EXPROVEMENT

Obstacles Can Provide an Opportunity for Exprovement

An approach of exprovement is often required when a problem presents itself in unusual or unique circumstances. In such situations, exploring the possibility of making the apparent 'obstacles' and 'disadvantages' a part of the solution could provide an answer.

In the case of the ice stupa, the main obstacle was plenty of water that was available at the wrong time of the year.

Generally, when one hears 'water shortage' the most common solution that comes to mind is to store water in some sort of a container or holding area, to be used later, or to transport water from a different source.

Adopting a change in perspective, Wangchuk decided to use the excess water when it was available, but by converting it into a different state (ice) and storing it in a different form (a cone-shaped structure that didn't require a container and used more vertical space than it did horizontal space, thereby using less land area than an artificial glacier) he turned the obstacle into an opportunity. The water that would have otherwise caused floods or gone to waste was retained for use when required. The second obstacle that Wangchuk integrated into his solution was the adverse condition of freezing temperatures, which played a key role in the working of his solution.

Improvements Help with Easy Adoption of Exprovements

The ice stupa strikes a deep connection with the farmers in this predominantly Buddhist province. It looks a lot like a Buddhist stupa—a shrine, which often contains relics and where people come to pray and meditate. Due to this similarity, it has quickly found acceptance amongst the locals. It is not uncommon to see people coming to pray at the ice stupas, structures that have given a new lease of life to many a farming family in the region.

'On seeing the stupa in Phyang Valley, many people in the community felt a spiritual connection to it. Not only was a part of their revered glaciers now standing in their own valley, but there was hope for water. They strung colorful prayer flags around it to break the wind and protect the ice, further highlighting its resemblance to Buddhist stupas.'[13]

Integrating culture and tradition into the solution played an important role in making the solution not just acceptable, but in this case, revered.

This shows that improvement based on behavioural economics theory or by employing design thinking can help make an exprovement a resounding success.

Here too, parallels can be drawn, for example, by asking questions like 'What already familiar experiences, beliefs or systems could be mimicked or integrated into the new solution being developed?'

BUILDING ON AN EXPROVEMENT: WHAT NEXT FOR THE ICE STUPA?

When it comes to the ice stupa, as Simant Verma, who has worked as a project manager on the ice stupas puts it, 'We don't look at ice stupas as just a solution to climate change...That's not how we're trying to put this out in the world. We are trying to foster innovation, so that other ideas can come out of it.'[14]

It is with this kind of a mindset that other ideas begin to pop up—where else can a new exprovement be useful? Which other industries can it find application in? How far can an idea be extended?

Wangchuk's work earned him the prestigious Rolex Award for Enterprise in 2016, and once word of his work got around, enquiries from other mountainous regions of the world, from Peru to Switzerland, started pouring in. Ice stupas have the potential to cause disruption because unlike other solutions, they work at low altitudes and in very warm temperatures—and more importantly, can find application in other parts of the world where farmers in similar circumstances are facing similar problems caused by climate change.

But besides agriculture, ice stupas have found application in other industries also being affected by climate change.

Disaster Management

In 2016, members of the ice stupa team travelled to Peru where they were able to successfully implement the concept, building two glacier bases in just two nights, confirming that the technique works in regions like the Andes as well, though temperatures get much hotter than those in Ladakh.

In Peru, the more pressing goal was to find a way to mitigate the effects of a natural disaster—in the form of flash floods—and to re-glaciate the area. In this way the ice stupa has also found a parallel use in fighting the effects of climate change.

Tourism

2016 also saw Switzerland's first ice stupa take shape, at Van Rosel. In this case the application had the dual goal of mitigating climate change and protecting the tourism industry. Here the team used twigs to help scatter the water, rather than the indigenous sea buckthorn plants that are generally used in the ice stupas of Ladakh.

Morteratsch Glacier, one of Switzerland's major tourist attractions, has been subject to a loss of 15 million tons of ice a year, due to global warming. The ice stupa project here 'creates an artificial snow cover for the glacier in summer to delay the retreat of the glacier.'[15] According to studies conducted by the ice stupa team, it is believed that in twenty years, they will be able to build back the glacier to what it currently is. Ice stupas are also being considered as a water solution for Alpine huts.

The stupas in their current form already serve as an attraction to visitors to Ladakh, which has a sizeable tourism industry, but Wangchuk foresees a future where the structures can house ice bars and ice hotels for a truly unique tourist experience, coupled with the double advantage that the income earned can be used to support struggling farmers in the region.

In fact, in the village of Gya in Ladakh, the youth group that built an ice stupa installed a cafe within its base, and then used the income generated from it to take village elders on a pilgrimage.

A concept that began as a unique solution to an irrigation crisis is now set to help in flood prevention, drought relief, rebuilding glaciers and boosting the tourism industry . . . who knows where its next application will be!

FREEZE CONCENTRATION—WHAT NEXT?

The technology of freeze concentration has till now mainly found use in the food and beverage industry, where it allows for foods like coffee, wine and fruit juice concentrates to retain their flavour, aroma and colour.

However, parallel applications are also in the offing.

Water Desalination

Using a desalination process invented by Alexander Zarchin, saltwater, when frozen in a vacuum, leaves behind crystals of pure water (since fresh water freezes faster than salt water). The salt that is left behind is drained off and the water crystals are then melted to produce desalinated water.

In some places that have extreme cold weather conditions this process can occur naturally as well, or by spraying sea water on to a pad during the coldest months, allowing the build-up of ice piles. The fresh water is then obtained during the warm months, when the ice begins to melt.

Wastewater Management

Studies on freeze concentration as a method to extract pure water from wastewater are being conducted around the world.

The principle remains the same—when waste water undergoes freeze concentration, the ice crystals so formed contain pure water, while the impurities remain in the liquid left behind, thus allowing pure water to be separated or extracted.

DEVELOPING AN EXPROVEMENT OUTLOOK

What are some of the types of questions that could have led Wangchuk to find exprovement in an unrelated industry?

- How can one save water when there is an excess of it, but use it only when there is a dearth of it?
- What parallels exist in unrelated industries that conserve water?
- What parallels can be drawn when examining the various forms in which water can be saved?
- What parallels exist where the shelf life of products containing water is extended?
- How can a glacier be made to behave like an ice cube?
- What parallels can be drawn with freeze concentration?

7

What Do a Pizza Box and Cancer Detection Have in Common?

'If I had waited, I might be dead.'

Few people know their bodies as well as high performance sportspeople do—they notice subtle changes in their output, are constantly on the watch for parts of their bodies not working like they usually do and can just tell when 'something's off.'

Yet it took Olympic high jumper Chaunté Lowe two years to convince doctors that the tiny lump she'd discovered during a self-breast examination needed further investigation, even though she had noticed a drop in her power and endurance during training sessions.[1]

On paper, it was unlikely that Lowe had breast cancer—she was only thirty-four, had no family history of the killer disease and was in remarkably good health otherwise. Her doctor was convinced it was an inflamed lymph node that had come to Lowe's notice because of how thin she was and advised that she return for a routine breast cancer screening after six years, once she had turned forty.

Lowe, however, couldn't shake the feeling that something wasn't right and so didn't wait for six years. Feeling that the lump had grown bigger, she approached another doctor two years later and insisted on getting an ultrasound and mammogram done, which revealed that the lump had actually tripled in size.

A biopsy confirmed the worst—Chaunté Lowe had triple-negative invasive ductal carcinoma, an aggressive form of breast cancer that disproportionately affects black women.[2]

At the time of writing this book, the American record-holding high jumper, thankfully, after undergoing treatment, is cancer-free and focused on making her fifth Olympic appearance, while also campaigning for early cancer detection.

The fact that she did not wait as long as she was initially advised is what probably saved her life. It is a well-known fact that early diagnosis is key to winning the battle against breast cancer.

Sadly, for women who aren't as proactive or as in tune with their bodies as Lowe, who do not have access to medical facilities, whose insurance packages do not cover breast cancer screening before a certain age, who follow the guideline that screening should begin only at the age of forty, who don't conduct self-examinations or who aren't 'at risk' for early breast cancer, the diagnosis can come too late, if it comes at all.

THE PROBLEMS OF DIAGNOSING BREAST CANCER

The statistics surrounding breast cancer[3] are grim:

- Breast cancer is the most common cause of cancer death among women worldwide.
- One in eight women will be diagnosed with breast cancer during their lifetime.
- One woman dies every minute in the world of breast cancer.

Coupled with these statistics are several problems that afflict the whole process of breast cancer screening.

Disparity and Gaps in Access to Medical Facilities

Depending on where one lives, there is a huge disparity in the probability of surviving breast cancer, ranging from 90 per cent in high-income countries, to 66 per cent in India and 40 per cent in South Africa. This is mainly due to a lack of early detection programmes and access to medical facilities, as well as delays in getting treatment.[4]

Never has the gap in breast cancer, and cancer screening in general, been more evident than during the Covid-19 pandemic. Whether due to the fear of catching the Covid-19 virus, successive lockdowns or the prioritization of directing resources towards seriously ill Covid-19 patients, many individuals around the world have missed or delayed getting their regular cancer screening tests done, and as has been shown in the case of Chaunté Lowe, an early diagnosis can make all the difference.

'Delays in screening . . . could mean that the 'missed' cancers might be larger and more advanced when they were ultimately detected. In general, cancers are easier to treat in their early stages.'

Because some cancers grow slowly, the impact of the pandemic on overall cancer deaths will not be clear for many years, according to Eric Feuer, PhD, chief of the Statistical Research and Applications Branch in NCI's Division of Cancer Control and Population Sciences.

'This is a complicated story that will reveal itself slowly over time,' says Dr Feuer. He notes, however, that recent studies have shown that 'screening rates dropped very sharply, very quickly' in the spring of 2020.[5]

Problems With Breast Screening Protocol

Generally, mammograms/breast scans are scheduled once in two years, beginning at the age of forty, and in some cases only at the age of fifty.

This, however, does not take into account some categories of high risk women[6] like Chaunté Lowe, who could develop breast cancer before they're forty, including women with BRAC1 and BRAC2 genetic mutations, women of certain ethnicities and women with rare types of breast cancer that aren't always easily detectable.

In addition, if it isn't considered an urgent case, women often have to wait an extended period of time to get their tests done. Lowe herself had to wait four weeks to get tested, in spite of the lump in her breast having tripled in size.

Problems With Current Testing Methods

• Sometimes mammogram results may be less accurate for women with dense breast tissue or breast implants. This is because dense breast tissue can appear white on the mammography image and mask the presence of tumours, which also appear white.[7]

• Mammograms sometimes produce inconclusive imaging results and require additional testing and/or follow ups.[8]

Problems With Self-Examination

• Not all women know how to properly conduct a breast self-examination.

• To cite just one example, in a study conducted in Turkey, where breast cancer accounts for 24 per cent of female cancers, it was found that 48.5 per cent of women were not able to distinguish the masses from normal breast tissue and 49.5 per cent of them did not feel confident in detecting the masses.[9]

• A study conducted in 2014, on women who were thirty-five years or older, revealed that less than 15 per cent carried out breast self-examinations and less than 10 per cent performed them on a regular basis.[10]

EARLY DETECTION—THE NEED OF THE HOUR

While one might rightly suggest that improving awareness, changing the screening system and revising guidelines is essential, given the worrying statistics, any tool that might help detect breast cancer early and give women more control over the whole process can only be a step in the right direction.

Welwaze, a US-based company, has developed an exprovement—heat-sensitive colour changing breast pads—that does exactly this, using thermography to detect abnormalities in the breast.

The product, called Celbrea, is a simple, non-invasive, pain-free, fifteen-minute thermal activity indicator test that can be done by individuals in the comfort and privacy of their homes. Some of the other benefits of using a thermal activity indicator like Celbrea are:

- It is a non-invasive, non-contact procedure that does not involve compressing the breast.
- It does not involve exposure to radiation.
- It can detect vascular changes in breast tissue that may indicate the presence of breast cancer many years before other methods of screening can.
- Hormonal and menstrual changes do not affect the procedure or the results.[11]
- When combined with an app, like Celbrea is, it offers a fully integrated breast health monitoring system that helps women 'predict, prevent and monitor their health, through different features targeting breast cancer, fertility and birth control'[12] and 'can alert one's physician to the possibility of breast pathology, including occult, thermally active cancer.'[13] The app also serves as an educational tool and a calendar to set reminders and track and record all important information related to one's breast health, giving women more control over their breast health.
- An improvement to the product, from a behavioural economics aspect, is being able to conduct this test at home, as it could encourage more women to do some form of testing, given that they can perform it in private. It also serves as an additional tool for women who are unsure of how to perform or interpret a breast self-examination properly.
- In cases where there are backlogs of pending screenings, a thermal activity indicator could, at the very least, help with testing prioritization.

While it is not intended to take the place of mammograms, a heat-sensitive colour changing breast pad like Celbrea can add to doctors' existing standard evaluation protocols with a quick, painless examination, and provide an additional way to screen for breast disease, including breast cancer.[14]

Given that one in eight women in the world will be diagnosed with breast cancer in their lifetime, this exprovement is poised to potentially help save a lot of lives.

DOES A PARALLEL PATH TO EXPROVEMENT EXIST?

The key technology that enables Celbrea to change colour when it detects an abnormal temperature is thermochromic material—material that changes colour when it comes into contact with heat.

On examination, we found that a direct parallel already exists in the labelling industry, which supplies thermochromic stickers to several other industries where they are used as warning indicators, building on the concept of using colour to indicate a change—look no further than traffic lights: red for stop, green for go.

Food and Beverage

Thermochromic pigments are used in the food and beverage industry as labels that indicate temperature change—on a beer bottle when it has been chilled to its 'perfect' drinking temperature, on pizza boxes to indicate that the contents are no longer at a desirable eating temperature or on a food carton to indicate that the contents are very hot and likely to burn your mouth.

This application imbibes the improvement of behavioural economics—just like our brains automatically know that red on a traffic light means 'stop', a particular colour on anything from a coffee cup to a cooking utensil could indicate that something is too hot or too cold or just the desired temperature without us actually having to touch it or take its temperature with a thermometer.

Medical Supplies

Heat-sensitive label manufacturers have also applied improvements through design thinking by developing reversible and irreversible heat-sensitive labelling options, which can be opted for depending on the particular application, making it more user-friendly depending on the need.

For example, a reusable heat-sensitive strip thermometer would make use of a reversible label, allowing for temperature to be interpreted via the colour the strip changes to, but then it would return to its original base colour, allowing for it to be used again.

On the other hand, an irreversible heat-sensitive label on a Covid vaccine vial being transported from a manufacturing facility in Baltimore, USA, to the village of Nqileni in South Africa could serve as an invaluable indicator, letting anyone who comes into contact with a particular vial see instantly whether the vaccine has ever been exposed to undesirable temperatures during transit.

While electronic sensors provide real-time data on consignments, the cost, time and effort involved makes putting a sensor on each individual vial an impractical solution. Irreversible temperature-sensitive labels solve this problem, adding value to cold chain tracking by providing vital visual information to the end user in situations where data transmission might not be possible, such as in remote regions of the world. The two technologies working in tandem could result in safer, more effective vaccination programmes across the world. According to a *Wall Street Journal* article of December 2020, 'temperature-monitoring labels will be used to track the integrity of Covid-19 vaccine vials in rollouts across nearly 190 low-and-middle-income countries.'[15]

The same goes for the food industry. You might pick up a tub of frozen ice cream from the freezer in your supermarket, but how do you really know that the tub has always been at its optimum temperature during all stages of its transportation and storage from its manufacturing facility up until you've picked it up?

In both the food and beverage and medical supplies industries, temperature-sensitive labels provide the opportunity to become more transparent with the end user, offering reassurance—something that goes a long way in building brand loyalty.

Learn more about another similar offering by scanning the QR code:

Besides being used on labels, thermochromic material has also been used to serve as a warning indicator by directly coating surfaces with thermochromic paint.

Piracy, Theft and Counterfeit Prevention

With the emergence of thermochromic printers, heat-sensitive pigments can now offer a covert ink-based security feature on things like concert tickets, medicines and high end cosmetics, helping to detect counterfeits, providing an additional level of security and serving as a deterrent to piracy.

In many cases, simply rubbing one's finger over the print generates enough heat to cause a colour change, thus making it an easy detection method that requires no additional equipment, and potentially replacing the need for holograms.

Products like Tamper Alert, an irreversible, heat-activated ink technology from Chromatic Technologies Inc., can help 'identify tamper evidence in labels and packaging for chemicals, pharmaceuticals, food, electronics and other products targeted for theft and counterfeiting.'[16]

THE COLOURFUL FUTURE OF THERMOCHROMIC MATERIAL

Besides serving as a temperature indicator, thermochromism, in conjunction with other technologies, could pave the way for more exprovements to come about, those that do something more besides just changing colour, such as:

In Conjunction with Machine Vision

When combined with a camera that monitors several items containing a thermochromic sticker, machine vision can trigger required actions.

For example, if components on an assembly line were coated with a thermochromic paint or labelled with a thermochromic sticker, machine vision would be able to detect and highlight those components that had been exposed to excessive heat because their colour would change. This in turn could be programmed to result in automatic removal of the item from the assembly line. Both processes could take place without human intervention.

In the Surface Coating Industry

Thermochromic material can already be applied as a coating on surfaces such as glass, polycarbonate or plastics to make use of the fact that, as the surface becomes darker, it would allow less light to pass through. Some examples where it serves this purpose is in photochromic glass lenses where the darkening of the lenses can shield one from the harmful UV rays of the sun or blue light emitted by computer screens.[17]

The darkening of car windows is another example, where when the temperature inside the vehicle gets too high, darkened windows can help bring down heat conductivity, and thus keep the inside temperature optimum.[18]

But going further, it could also help to cool larger surfaces and reduce cooling costs.

According to Mark Miodownik, a British materials scientist and engineer, 'A house that changes colour to white when it is hot will reflect more sunlight and require less air conditioning. It is such environmental considerations that are pushing forward thermochromic research, in particular as coatings for "switchable glass". In this case the transition is designed to be spectrally selective, affecting only the infra-red transparency of glass, letting heat through in the winter to take advantage of passive solar heating and blocking it in the summer. Given that forty per cent of the energy consumption of developed economies is consumed in heating and cooling of buildings, such coatings look like they could play an important role in the fight against global warming.'[19]

Heat-Sensing Robots

Soft robotics is poised to be able to do more than before with the emergence of robots that are capable of sensing heat, adding another dimension of humanlike capabilities—the withdrawal reflex on coming into contact with a hot surface—to what they can already do.

Researchers at Liverpool Hope University were able to develop such a system by adapting a sensor to react to extreme heat by using thermochromic paint.

'We demonstrated that we could easily sense temperature using the hue value by using different colours and layers of thermochromic pigments with varying thresholds of temperature on the reflective coating,' says Alexander Co Abad, lead author on the study.[20]

'The team measured a response time of just 643ms for cold-to-hot and hot-to-cold, which is comparable to the withdrawal reflex response of less than one second typical of the human autonomic system to extreme heat.'[21]

NEW DEVELOPMENTS IN THERMOCHROMIC TECHNOLOGY

An innovation by NASA in the form of a temperature-sensitive coating conjures up even more exciting possibilities, as this coating (which is probably the farthest the capability of thermochromic material has reached yet), developed at the Glenn Research Centre, offers some unique characteristics that could prove to be game changers:

- The coating can measure temperatures of up to 600°C
- Because it works in white light, 'colour changes can be detected and recorded using low-cost sensors instead of single-point or global-imaging-based detectors', making it an inexpensive option.
- It is capable of detecting a gradual temperature change, with corresponding colour change for a large range: between 25°C to 600°C.
- It can easily and uniformly be applied to large surface areas, even those with complex shapes.[22]

Due to its stability at extremely high temperatures, some obvious applications could be in the area of heat treatment of metals, but given the numerous other unique properties it possesses, perhaps thermochromic material is finally on the cusp of truly finding its moment in the sun.

DEVELOPING AN EXPROVEMENT OUTLOOK

What are some of the types of questions that could have led Welwaze to find an exprovement solution in an unrelated industry?

- Can breast cancer symptoms be diagnosed at home?
- How can one turn something as complex as breast cancer detection into something as easy as measuring blood sugar at home?
- Can the method of calibration by comparison that is used in the instrumentation industry be adapted for breast cancer detection?
- How does a 'stick on' thermometer measure temperature difference?
- Which industries need to know when the temperature of something has changed and what are the innovative ways they do this?
- How do pizza boxes indicate a hot pizza?
- In which other industry does one find visual cues that temperature or any other parameter has changed?

8

A '70s Fashion Fad That Saves Lives

If you lived through the 1970s, you might remember the fad that was the mood ring. Developed during the era referred to as the 'Me Decade' in America, the mood ring fit right into the burgeoning desire to express one's individuality and style.

Josh Reynolds was a burnt-out Wall Street broker who'd had enough of the high-stress environment and decided to focus on how biofeedback could direct one's attention to stress levels. He became known as a mindfulness teacher and even appeared on the Merv Griffin show as a biofeedback stress management guru. Based on studies that suggested that changes in people's emotions and stress levels resulted in corresponding changes in the temperature of their hands, after a year of research and development, Reynolds, together with Maris Ambats, developed what was at the time referred to as a 'thermal biosensor'—rings with clear quartz stones that had been treated with thermochromic crystals, so that a change in the wearer's body temperature would result in a change in the colour of the ring.

Accordingly, blue meant you were calm or relaxed, yellow indicated you were tense or excited, etc. Though based on studies related to changes in body temperature, it transpired that the accuracy of these rings was questionable, as it appeared that surrounding air temperature often played a role, and not just the wearer of the ring! Further, the material used in the mood ring only had a short life span of two years, after which it stopped displaying its colour-changing properties and turned permanently into a shade of black.

Nevertheless, at the time it was considered fashionable to own one of these fun rings and celebrities, such as Barbra Streisand, Sophia Loren and Cher, were amongst those who promoted the fad.

It has been reported that around the same time as Reynolds and Ambats were developing their mood rings, jewellery designer Marvin Wernick was separately also inspired to create colour-changing jewellery based on the same principle when he observed his doctor friend using thermochromic tape on a patient's forehead. However, since he didn't patent his idea, Reynolds and Ambats were the ones to cash in. Upon its release, and aided by a massive PR campaign, Reynolds was able to sell silver-plated mood rings for a whopping $45 each (remember this was the 70s) and is reported to have made $20 million in sales in just one year.

While the questionable accuracy and limited life span of the mood ring signalled the end of that fad, Reynolds was reported in 2020 to be looking at the return of a new and upgraded mood ring made out of a more accurate and sensitive material and accompanied by an app. His theory is that 'if we can measure stress, maybe we can control it', and he foresees an integrated wellness offering that could do things like prompt Alexa to play a happy song when you're feeling sad or text a mood emoji to a friend to let them know how you're feeling.[1]

Biofeedback measures 'information' from your body, such as breathing patterns, heart rate, brainwave activity, sweat gland activity, body temperature, muscle contractions etc. via electronic sensors, and using this feedback, 'helps you make subtle changes in your body, such as relaxing certain muscles, to achieve the results you want, such as reducing pain. In essence, biofeedback gives you the ability to practice new ways to control your body, often to improve a health condition or physical performance.'[2]

The mood ring, as a concept, can be considered one of the earliest attempts at developing a biofeedback wearable device.

Drawing inspiration from jewellery, what were once watches and rings are now the Fitbit tracker, the Apple watch, the Oura Ring and the Dhyana Meditation Ring, to cite a few examples of gadgets that comfortably straddle the domain of biofeedback, wellness and individual style devices.

DOES A PARALLEL PATH TO EXPROVEMENT EXIST?

Thermochromic material, which has also been discussed in the previous chapter, began to emerge from laboratories in the 1960s.[3] While in the earlier chapter, we were able to connect the dots to see how the use of thermochromic materials in the labelling industry as a warning indicator is a parallel to its application in the healthcare industry, in this chapter we connect the dots between how a development in the chemical industry—temperature sensitive, colour-changing pigments—found a parallel application in the fashion industry as colour-changing material, but more recently has formed the basis for exprovement in a variety of industries.

THE COLOURFUL HISTORY OF THERMOCHROMIC MATERIAL AS A STYLE STATEMENT

Reynolds may have intended for the ring to be a wellness tool, but it developed into a fashion/style statement. Besides several cheaper, knock-off mood ring manufacturers jumping on the bandwagon and generating sales worth $250 million in just four months, other mood jewellery in the form of necklaces, bracelets etc. also began to make an appearance.

'Over the years, Americans have slipped back and forth between selfless and selfish jewelry. While they became more kitsch than cool in the late '70s, mood rings came back moodier and cheaper than ever in the '90s, and again in later years thanks to '90s nostalgia.

In 2022, the liquid crystal technology of mood rings and LCD has come full circle. In partnership with mood ring creator Josh Reynolds, NFT Creative Enterprises has sold a smart wearable NFT of a gold mood ring (along with the real deal) for $65,000. A mood ring with liquid crystals inside of it is now displayable on an LCD screen.'[4]

With the advent of thermochromic inks and dyes, the colour-changing concept found its way into the fashion industry. In 1991, to celebrate the 150th anniversary of the Royal Society of Chemistry, a fashion show in honour of chemistry's contribution to fashion over the centuries featured tight-fitting thermochromic garments that resplendently showed off multiple colours as the clothes absorbed heat from the wearers' bodies.[5]

Since then, many brands have experimented with the material, beginning in 1991 with Generra Sportswear's heat sensitive T-shirts that showed a colour change when you placed your hand on one of them, as your body's temperature changed or even when you hugged someone. The fad made a more 'stylish' comeback in the 2000s when designer duo Anzevino and Florence featured heat-sensitive, colour-changing racerback dresses and scarves, and British designer Henry Holland came out with heat-sensitive T-shirts and a mini dress that retailed for $236, to cite a few names that experimented with the phenomenon.[6]

'Mood' nail polish and lipstick also work due to a thermochromic reaction.

Staying with its application in the fashion industry, thermochromic material has even found its way into in a certain niche segment of the footwear market.

When the husband of Kamala Harris's niece wore a pair of limited edition $2000 Dior X Air Jordan 1 sneakers to the 2021 Presidential inauguration, people took note; Twitter was abuzz with chatter about it.

Interestingly, Nikolas Ajagu wasn't the only person to wear sneakers to the inauguration that day. Joe Biden's twenty-year-old granddaughter also sported a pair of Air Jordan 1 Mid 'Sisterhood' sneakers, prompting *Vogue* magazine to state that 'Purple may have been the colour of the day, but it's safe to say Air Jordans will forever be remembered as the shoe of the 2021 inauguration.'[7]

Within twenty-four hours the value of both styles of shoes skyrocketed on sneaker trading sites like StockX and Flight Club.

Not the kind of shoes that instantly come to mind when you think 'formal occasion', Ajagu, (a self-confessed sneaker collector) and Maisy Biden's choice of shoes gives us an insight into the sneakerhead community—people who collect, trade and/or admire sneakers as a hobby.

Many sneakerheads are well-versed in the history of sneakers, study the market carefully and when presented with a pair, can even tell you their value, make and history.

For sneakerheads, wearing a particular pair of sneakers is indicative of a person's style, identity and 'swag'.[8] In fact, the global sneaker market was valued at approximately $79 billion in 2020 and is predicted to reach $120 billion by 2026.[9]

When it comes to the desire to own a limited edition or customized product, few segments can match the enthusiasm of the sneakerhead community. But while not all sneaker enthusiasts may be able to afford a $2000 high-end designer pair of shoes like Ajagu's (which incidentally went on to have a resale value of well over $10,000) they sure are always on the lookout for a unique pair of sneakers.

And shoe store Sir Castle Tees in Raleigh, North Carolina, caters to just this market. For anywhere between $150 to $300 you can buy a pair of sneakers (Vans, Nike etc.) custom painted by artist Mike Phillips Jr. He changes things up even further by using a temperature sensitive dye while creating his custom art on the shoes, allowing for the sneakers to change colour when exposed to fire or sunlight or in some cases when they get wet. Visit @sircastletees on Instagram and you can see videos that show a pair of Nikes that are white when in-store but change to rainbow colours once they're taken out into the sunlight, a fluorescent yellow patterned pair that turn to a dark green when water is sprinkled on them and a black speckled pair that turn hot pink as a lighter is passed alongside them. Many simple pairs reveal complex patterns when exposed to heat, thanks to the colour-sensitive paint.

These examples are just some of the ways in which thermochromic material has been making guest appearances in the fashion industry over the years.

Car Customization

Fashion is not the only area where being 'different' or expressing your individual style is what it's about. And interestingly, thermochromic pigments have found their way into another industry where being able to make a style statement is the name of the game—car styling.

While Plasti Dip (a temporary paint job for cars that just peels off when you want to remove it) is probably one of the most impactful products to ever hit the car 'pimping' market, DipYourCar featured a video showcasing its experiment with a colour-changing car! After applying a coat of Plasti Dip on an Audi A4, eight coats of a heat-sensitive paint were applied over it, and the now 'black' car was ready for some fun. As it was driven out of the cooler garage into the sun, the chameleon-car began to gradually change from black to green to blue and eventually to a deep purple! Besides the novelty factor, it was interesting to note that one could also see which parts of the car reached a higher temperature quicker than others on exposure to the sun.[10]

While this particular instance was just an experiment, the innovation of combining the two technologies could bring a quirky, customizable offering to the car styling market.

From sneaker enthusiasts to car enthusiasts, heat-sensitive liquid crystals, dye or paint have had several applications where personal style or novelty is key. A coffee mug that reveals an unexpected picture when a hot beverage is poured into it or a swimsuit that changes colour when it gets wet—from an entertainment point of view, the possibilities, though usually short-lived, are endless.

EXPROVEMENT AT THE INTERSECTION OF CHEMISTRY AND STYLE

Looking at applications of colour-changing material that go beyond just aesthetic appeal, here are two exprovements that are a parallel to colour-changing clothes from the fashion industry.

Professional Sports

Just like the principle behind the mood ring found a renewed application in heat-sensitive labels, the colour changing T-shirt has also found a renewed application in thermochromic sportswear that can detect and indicate physical exhaustion in endurance athletes, as this extract from an article published in the *Journal of Design, Creative Process and the Fashion Industry* highlights:

'Endurance athletes face a complex array of physiological changes as their skin temperature rises during vigorous exercise. Since endurance athletes do not typically have fiscally feasible and straightforward real-time physiological monitoring (outside of complex Bluetooth and wireless connectivity linking their heart rate, pulse oximetry, etc. to electronic databases), exercise reaching high levels of physical exhaustion is of great concern. To aid in easy and visual determination of physical exhaustion, thermochromic pigments were applied to Nylon/spandex fabric, using pigment activation temperature as an indication for exhaustion. Thermochromic pigments were chosen because these microcapsules contain leuco dyes capable of changing chemical structure to alter the dye molecule absorbance, leading to a visual tool for skin temperature indication. Each pigment was chosen to activate at a targeted physiological skin temperature range between 33 and 38°C. Nylon/spandex was chosen for high wearer comfort and excellent garment/skin contact. This technology was coupled with conventional textiles to create smart apparel with satisfactory abrasion and color fastness capabilities. Using targeted placement of thermochromic panels in garment construction, a garment capable of serving as a "warning light" for physical exhaustion in athletes was created.'[11]

Camouflage Material

The use of colour-changing fabric has been suggested for military use, where camouflage fabric—as uniforms or as material that hides ammunition—can be customized to change colour depending on the ambient temperature.

Research into 'adaptive camouflage', which 'refers to the adaptation of an object, such as a military vehicle or soldier, to its surroundings', in a study by Martina Vikova and Marcela Pechova, has focused on 'the development of an adaptive color changeable system based on selected thermochromic inks following the colors used in Czech woodland and desert combat uniforms. The printed color pattern mimics leaf design, which transforms into desert design based on thermal conditions (hot air and body temperature).'[12]

In another article from the *Journal of The Textile Institute*, the authors 'have developed color changeable (chameleon-type) printings on cotton fabrics using thermochromic colorants for defense applications. Different colored coatings, such as light green, dark green, black, brown, and sandal have been developed using blue and orange thermochromic colorants in combination with turmeric (a natural dye) and graphite. The printed color pattern mimics jungle motif design (classic green and brown camouflage) which transforms to desert color motif on application of heat from external sources (using hot air oven or electrical power). The response time and temperature for each color change and recovery were evaluated in case of direct heating. The printed fabrics' physical properties, such as tensile strength, elongation at break, flexural rigidity, and tear strength, were also tested before and after printing. The wash property of printed fabrics shows reasonably good fixation of colors to the fabric surface. The chameleon-type camouflage printing described in this work shows promise to use the same fabric for camouflaging at different terrains which essentially reduces the time for shifting troops to different locations.'[13]

Dynamic Tattoos

Another example of a parallel drawn from the fashion and style industry to develop an exprovement is tattooing.

This age-old form of creativity and self-expression has found application in the wellness and medical industries in the form of colour-changing tattoos that, in conjunction with other technology, could help detect a number of conditions, from elevated alcohol levels to skin cancer.

Here are a few examples:

- In 2016, the *Wall Street Journal* reported that 'Researchers at the Center for Wearable Sensors at the University of California, San Diego, have come up with a removable electronic tattoo that can sense your blood-alcohol level from the sweat on your skin and then send this information via Bluetooth to a smartphone or car computer.'[14]

Some of its potential applications include locking a car's ignition if worrisome alcohol levels have been detected in the driver, notifying a recovering alcoholic's sponsor if alcohol has been consumed, letting a bartender know if a customer has had too much to drink or simply providing a user who's concerned about their own drinking habits with a visual indicator if they've crossed the drinking threshold.

- Combining nanotechnology with invisible tattoos, Carson Bruns, Assistant Professor, Laboratory for Emergent Nanomaterials, ATLAS Institute, along with the team at ATLAS has developed a tattoo ink that contains a UV-activated dye inside a plastic nano capsule that is several sizes smaller than the width of a human hair. These UV-sensitive tattoos turn blue when the tattooed individual has been exposed to too much sunlight and serve as a signal to apply more sunscreen or to reduce time spent in the sun. The hope is that this exprovement can lead to a reduction in skin cancer cases.[15]

'When you think about what a tattoo is, it's just a bunch of particles that sit in your skin . . . Our thought is: What if we use nanotechnology to give these particles some function?' says Carson Bruns.

- In 2018, scientists at the Department of Biosystems Science and Engineering at the Swiss Federal Institute of Technology 'created a tattoo comprised of engineered skin cells and an implantable sensor, which could detect elevated blood calcium levels that are present in many types of cancers.'[16] This smart-tattoo uses biosensitive ink and changes colour to indicate the presence of breast, colon, lung and prostate cancers. It could help recognize cancer in patients before it develops to the tumour stage, thus improving chances of recovery and potentially saving lives.

- In 2019, it was reported that scientists at the Technical University of Munich had developed 'an intradermal tattoo that can change colour in response to changing levels of glucose, albumin, or pH',[17] biomarkers whose abnormal levels could indicate diseases related to the kidney, liver, heart (albumin), blood (pH) or help in the management of diabetes (glucose).

While most smart tattoo applications are still under laboratory trials, they hold the potential to serve as indicators of a medical condition much more quickly, rather than realizing it only when a symptom shows up.

Life-Saving Dot

Our last example is not related to colour-changing material, but it is an example of how a traditional Indian symbol, which has developed into a fashion and style element over the years, was transformed into a device that could supply women with a vital nutrient they're likely not getting enough of, especially in rural India.

The bindi, often seen on the foreheads of Indian women, dates back to the third or fourth century and is worn either for religious purposes or to indicate that one is married. In modern day India, however, it is commonly used as a mark of beauty and a fashion accessory, and is available in a plethora of colours, shapes and designs to match one's outfit.[18]

Thanks to the Jeevan Bindi or Life Saving Dot initiative by Neelvasant Medical Foundation and Research Centre, India, Grey For Good (the philanthropic arm of Grey Advertising) and Talwar (a prominent bindi distributor), the bindi could serve an additional purpose—provide women with iodine, a nutrient whose deficiency has been linked to depression, weight gain and brain development of foetuses during pregnancy.

'India is one country where iodine deficiency is a real threat. Many of its residents are vegetarian, and the soil is notoriously poor in the mineral. This combination of factors means that rural women in particular are at risk of suffering from iodine deficiency.'[19]

The group came up with the idea of coating the back of the bindi with iodine, which can be absorbed by the skin. As a result, a user can get up to 12 per cent of her daily iodine requirement, while staying stylish as well.

DEVELOPING AN EXPROVEMENT OUTLOOK

What are some of the types of questions that could have led to the exprovement of using heat sensitive labels in a variety of biomarker applications as highlighted in this chapter?

- What can changes in temperature tell us about the human body or a product?
- What parallels can be drawn from a wearable temperature sensor?
- How can fashion or style trends help in the adoption of new or unfamiliar technology?
- Is wearable tech a parallel from mood rings?
- Can the process of heat causing labels to change colour be reversed, or in other words, be made to change colour by getting rid of heat? What parallels can be drawn with this?
- What parallels can be drawn to ensure ease of use or acceptance? For example, fashion, jewellery etc.

9

What's a Bicycle Pump Doing in a Michelin-Star Restaurant?

Throughout the history of gastronomy, every now and then a new discovery or invention has changed the way the world prepares and consumes food.

Take the egg for example—a food that has been a staple of cuisines around the world since humans began to first eat eggs, reportedly from around 6000 BC. Eggs were used by ancient Egyptians and Romans in breads and cakes, purportedly on their discovering that eggs were a good binding agent. This property also led to the use of eggs as a thickening agent in various custards and sauces by the Greeks, around 25 BC.

Upon the discovery, supposedly in the sixteenth century, that beating egg whites produced a light, airy, foam-like texture, it led to their being used to make new and interesting dishes and desserts like meringues for example.

Till today, both these properties of eggs are still widely incorporated into cooking techniques around the world. As we know, eggs can be manipulated in a variety of other ways as well—heating at various temperatures, poaching, etc.—as eggs alone, or mixed with other ingredients. From ancient times till today, the numerous discoveries of what can be done with an egg have had an undeniably important impact on the history of gastronomy.[1, 2]

Another example is the process of fermentation. It is believed that as far back as 10,000 BCE, humans were inadvertently fermenting dairy to produce yoghurt out of camel, goat, sheep and cattle milk. 'It has been suggested that the first yogurts were produced in goat bags draped over the backs of camels in the heat of North Africa, where temperatures around 110°F during the day made ideal conditions for fermentation to occur.'[3]

But while the outcome of adding an egg to a sauce or fermenting milk may have been discovered centuries ago, the reason these outcomes occurred was in many cases discovered only much later, when scientific research into the 'why' was undertaken.

Staying with the fermentation example, 'it wasn't until the mid 1800s that people understood what was happening to make their food ferment. In 1856, a French chemist by the name of Louis Pasteur connected yeast to the process of fermentation, making him the first zymologist—or someone who studies the applied science of fermentation. Pasteur originally defined fermentation as "respiration without air", and he understood by his observations that fermentation never occurred in the absence of simultaneous cellular propagation and organization. At this time, fermentation was still being used solely to increase the holding and storing properties of food. It wasn't until 1910 that fermented foods were first considered as beneficial to health.'[4]

Today, we consume probiotic foods such as kimchi and kombucha, as well as a variety of other (good) bacteria-ridden foods to improve our health. Research into what happens when food is fermented and how it interacts with the human body has resulted in the process being used as not only a mode of preservation, but as a tool to healthy living too; not forgetting its various other uses of course, such as in the creation of alcoholic beverages.

In a similar manner, referring to our egg example, chemistry and physics can explain why fluid, transparent egg whites when beaten transform into stiff, white, foamy, cloud-like peaks.

These examples—and there are many more—of important, impactful food techniques came about by chance. But what if one were to work backwards and purposely put foods through various chemical, biological and physical changes to see what would happen?

The result, surprisingly, (but also in a way, logically) would be the alteration of edible items in terms of their look, structure and texture in ways that would entirely transform the concept of what food is, and the experience of eating it.

CREATING IS NOT COPYING—A MANTRA FOR EXPROVEMENT

One of the ways to judge the calibre of a chef is by how well they have perfected classical cooking techniques—methods of skilfully preparing reputed dishes that have been taught and handed down over the years from generation to generation.

Another way is by how creative a chef can get in terms of the taste and presentation of the food they serve.

In the early 1980s when a budding chef named Ferran Adrià joined an already well-established Michelin-star restaurant called El Bulli in Catalonia, Spain, the restaurant was serving food representative of both classical French cooking and nouvelle cuisine.

But Adrià, who quickly rose to become one of the head chefs after just one year on the job, had been inspired by a phrase he'd heard from Jacques Maximin, champion of nouvelle cuisine and chef at the Le Chantecler in Nice—'Creating is not copying'.

Adrià wanted to experiment.

So, together with the other head chef, Christian Lutaud, he first spent three years revisiting and reimagining classic dishes to create them in new ways. For example, reworking Partridge Escabeche (an ancient Spanish dish that uses techniques devised by hunters) in the form of a boneless pigeon.

But when Adrià became the sole head chef in 1987, he began to truly infuse life into the 'create, don't copy' maxim. 'Every afternoon, between the lunch and dinner services, he and his kitchen began to experiment freely with new techniques.'[5]

'This simple phrase (creating is not copying) was the catalyst for the change of attitude in our cooking, marking the transition from "recreating" to a firm decision to focus on originality. We were convinced that we needed to stop referencing the cookbooks of important chefs and carve out an identity of our own instead. It was the beginning of our creative journey at El Bulli.'[6]

In 1990, Juli Soler, who was the manager at El Bulli (and who had encouraged Adrià and Lutaud to travel around Spain and France to get inspiration for and experiment with dishes), and Ferran Adrià together bought El Bulli from its then ageing owners.

Once that happened, it cemented Adrià's commitment to getting creative with food. The premises were remodelled to include a new 3000-square-foot state of the art kitchen, and in 1998, after heeding the advice of Joel Robuchon to separate their creativity from the existing restaurant service, they purchased part of a small eighteenth century palace in Barcelona to set up the food workshop that came to be known as El Bulli Taller ('*taller*' means workshop in Spanish), where experimentations with food were to become the main focus.[7]

'By 1994, four years after becoming co-owner of the restaurant, he had moved away from classical cookery altogether. In its place was what he called "technique-concept cuisine", in which he subjected potential ingredients to rigorous experimentation and scientific analysis as a means of creating novel dishes that produced unexpected sensations.'[8]

A professional creative team—the 'development squad'—worked together to develop this new type of cuisine. The process would begin with the team analysing the way different ingredients behaved, noting down everything with the conscientiousness of a medical research lab. Over the years, the *taller* even developed its own system of symbols and classifications for products and procedures: what Adrià terms, the 'whys of things'.[9]

The team, consisting of Ferran Adrià, Juli Soler, Ferran's brother Albert Adrià (who had joined El Bulli in 1985 and was in charge of the restaurant's desserts) and chef Oriol Castro, 'tore down the culinary and gastronomic conventions. They took a critical and analytical look at all the essential, surrounding components before rebuilding. The idea was to forge new connections between elements that had never been linked before.'[10]

The result was that in the years that followed, El Bulli would go on to achieve three Michelin stars and have a waiting list a year long.

From 2002, the first year that 'The World's 50 Best Restaurants' list was compiled, till El Bulli's final year of operation in 2010-11, it found a spot amongst the top three rankings on the list every single year, claiming the number one spot a record five times.[11]

CREATIVITY INSPIRED BY UNRELATED INDUSTRIES

By the 1990s, El Bulli came to be known as a laboratory for daring innovation[12], with the team boldly experimenting with techniques based on ideas developed or discoveries made in other industries.

Some of the results of these experiments included:

- **Culinary foam:** Adrià supposedly developed culinary foam as a by-product of inflating tomatoes with a bicycle pump and then discovered he could achieve the same effect through a more refined process—by 'spraying out of a nitrous oxide canister the mixture of a main ingredient, such as raspberries or mushrooms, and a natural gelling agent.'[13] Food foam was born out of 'a quest to achieve a texture lighter than mousse with a more intense flavour.'[14]
- **Spherification:** A delicate encapsulation of liquids within spheres of gelatin, its best-known application was 'liquid olives,' which resembled solid green olives but burst in the mouth with olive juice.[15]
- **Frozen savoury cuisine:** When El Bulli served the Savoury Tomato Water Ice with Fresh Oregano and Almond Milk Pudding for the first time in 1992, it marked 'a new symbiosis between sweet and savoury, overcoming the boundaries previously found between mains and puddings.'[16]
- **Art-inspired cuisine:** An example is the Red Mullet Gaudi—a filet of red mullet covered with a mosaic of vegetables, this dish incorporated a creative technique inspired by the work of famous Spanish architect Antoni Gaudi, whose work predominantly features fragmented mosaic tiles.

- **Pluralist dishes:** In a nod to the philosophy of pluralism, El Bulli, in 1996, served the Mollusk Platter. Pluralist dishes are those made not of a single ingredient but various elements from the same product family—'each of them can be savored individually, but together they form a different, unique harmony.'[17]
- **Sixth-sense dishes:** This concept evolved from the notions of playfulness, provocation and irony, and the idea of challenging and interacting with the diner. An example is The Spice Dish, in which an apple jelly acts as a base for twelve aromatic herbs and spices whose names are revealed to the diner, but not the order in which they are presented.[18] Taking the parameter of provocation to the next level, 'in 1997, when the debate about foams was at its height, El Bulli served a snack that was specially created to provoke a reaction in the diner. The *espuma de humo* is a small glass filled with smoked water foam and served with oil, salt and croutons. The idea was for the diner to "eat smoke".'[19]

The list of six examples above is by no means exhaustive, and considering El Bulli produced 1846 different dishes during the course of its existence, neither is it representative of all the techniques used by Adrià.

But it does serve as a list of examples of borrowing inspiration and techniques from a variety of unrelated industries, disciplines and artistic forms, philosophy, and even psychology, to develop an exprovement—the creation of food in forms that the world had never seen before. We are also able to draw a parallel between how a scientist conducts experiments in a laboratory to make new discoveries, and how Adrià experimented with food in the El Bulli Taller to discover new expressions of food.

As Adrià himself says in the short film *elBulli*, by Alison Chernick, 'Cooking involves everything; whatever discipline you like. For example, it's health, economics, psychology, science, design, artistic expression . . .'[20]

He also draws a parallel between the restaurant and Picasso, saying that in the same way that Cubism is a rupture in modern painting, El Bulli could to some extent be considered the place where there's a break from the past and a new world is created.[21]

Going even further, he views the art of cooking as a parallel to
language: '. . . the alphabet is the ingredients, the words are created
with techniques. Ingredients and technique turn into words. With these
words you can make sentences. And with sentences you can make verses.'[22]

A NEW ERA OF GASTRONOMIC INNOVATION

Though Adrià has been proclaimed by many to be one of the greatest
chefs of all time, with *The New York Times* describing how 'he rocketed
beyond the standard-fare celebrity chefs into the rarefied air of the
gastronomic geniuses', according to Adrià, 'There is no such thing
as the world's best chef. What matters is who is the most influential;
because this can be measured.'[23]

The impact of Adrià's experiments at El Bulli was that the culinary
world was exposed to forms and combinations of food it had never
experienced before. It was great-tasting food that was accompanied by
an unmatched dining experience that hit all the senses at a different
level, influencing gastronomy in a variety of different ways.

When the restaurant was closed for the six months before it was
to open for its last season in 2011, there were reportedly 3000 people
on the waiting list, vying for one of the approximately four dozen
available seats.[24]

Beyond what one could experience at the restaurant, Adrià's
philosophy of 'question everything' helped bring a number of exciting
and far-reaching consequences to the culinary world as we know it
today, some of which include:

Culinary Trends and Techniques

It was thanks in large part to Adrià and the work at El Bulli that
deconstruction or de-structured cooking became popular in the 1990s,
when El Bulli began to create dishes that physically looked nothing like
the original dishes but retained the essence and flavours of the originals.

'One of the examples that best illustrates this is Adrià's potato
omelet, which is a radical breakaway from its usual presentation as each
ingredient is dealt with separately and served in a cocktail glass.

The first layer is a golden onion jam, the second is the hot liquid egg and the third is a potato foam, made using a siphon. The serving and the consistency have been changed, but when you spoon out the three layers and mix them in your mouth, your taste buds immediately recognize that what you are eating is potato omelet.

The dish is "reconstructed" through the tasting memory of the person who eats it, although its appearance and even the way it is eaten may be completely different.'[25]

According to Sarah Todd, consulting chef and former Masterchef Australia contestant, "'In the culinary world "deconstruction" is the art of separating the components of a dish and then restructuring them in a unique and innovative way to tantalise the senses, while staying true to the original dish. To do this successfully, it's vital to understand what makes the original dish memorable." She goes on to explain that the flavour is nostalgic but in terms of texture and method, it might be a basic dish. She emphasises that the difference is in the preparation of the ingredients, and this is where you can make a version of a classic dish your own.'[26]

This style of cuisine gave chefs the freedom to really get creative with their own interpretations of what a dish could be.

Besides deconstruction as a broader concept, El Bulli played a key role in several of the techniques used at the restaurant becoming popular as food trends—food foam, spherification and molecular gastronomy to name a few, as well as other modernist techniques.

Inspiring a New Generation of Chefs

El Bulli's influence also had a positive impact on subsequent generations of chefs. Anne Willan, culinary historian and founder of Ecole de Cuisine La Varenne, credits Adrià, along with other chefs like Juan Mari Arzak and Heston Blumenthal, with being the luminaries that drove the experimental cooking movement, but calls Adrià 'the ringleader'.[27]

Further, several chefs who used to work at El Bulli went on to open their own successful restaurants or work at some of the best in the world, including Noma chef Rene Redzepi and Mugaritz chef Andoni Luis Aduriz, while three El Bulli sous chefs joined forces to open Disfrutar, a two-star Michelin restaurant also reputed amongst the world's best restaurants.[28]

Kitchen R&D

'From 1995 onwards, El Bulli pioneered the concept of "kitchen R&D" and is still the restaurant most people associate with using science and experimentation to create its menu.'[29]

Chefs across the world were inspired by Adrià's practice of closing El Bulli for six months of the year in order to allow his chefs ample time to experiment at the *taller*, and created test kitchens of their own, 'applying scientific rigor to and dedicating space in their organizations for creative culinary explorations.'[30]

'Nowadays, from The Fat Duck to Noma, research chefs are almost a necessity at the highest level of restaurant. Vaughn Tan, an assistant professor of strategy and entrepreneurship at University College London, in 2020 published *The Uncertainty Mindset*, a ten-year study of how R&D has become integral to the success of modern, forward-thinking cooking. "Places with that intensity, to keep their standards, can't just test as they go," said Tan. "They need people dedicated to coming in, trying things, failing, studying, reworking and innovating."'[31]

ELBULLI—A CREATIVE LEGACY WITH MORE TO COME

With the closing of the El Bulli restaurant in 2011, Ferran Adrià was able to shift his focus from developing never before seen food creations to compiling everything he had discovered about food and sharing what he had learnt over the years with those that were fascinated by the process that had led to exprovement in culinary art. It wouldn't be correct to term this a 'shift' however, but rather a reinforcement of his commitment to discovery and creativity, one of the outcomes of which were his food creations.

Adrià believes that his methodology can be applied not just to getting creative with food, but that the process can be applied to developing creativity in any field.

Exprovement stems from a change in perception, a shifted perspective and creativity, as many of the case studies highlighted in this book confirm.

While the world may know him best for his dishes or as the chef that experimented or as the person whose restaurant was known for several years as the best in the world, Adrià has always kept his focus on the process more than the outcome and is now attempting to keep creativity alive long after his time.

The setting up of the El Bulli Foundation in 2013, which aims to take on the entire notion of creativity, is a testimony to this dedication.

The foundation operates as a non-profit and is intended to appeal to 'chefs, as well as anyone who is interested in the creative process.'[32] Adrià says it is neither a charity nor a traditional commercial business, but instead refers to it as a 'think tank for creativity.'[33]

Amongst the undertakings at the foundation is the development of the ambitious Bullipedia project—a type of Wikipedia for haute cuisine—currently available in the form of over thirty 500-page books in encyclopaedia format.[34]

'Mr. Adrià has nominally divided the foundation into two main strands: knowledge, which is the group focused on creating BulliPedia; and creativity, which is focused on, in his words, "deconstructing the entire process of creativity". He calls this group El Bulli DNA.

Other projects include 'a search engine known as SeaUrching (named in part for the delicacy) as well as a language to describe gastronomy known as Huevo, Spanish for egg. Huevo, it was noted by one of Mr Adrià's colleagues, could ultimately be a digital language coded for use by refrigerators or other kitchen appliances.'[35]

Visit the El Bulli Foundation website to learn more about the interesting projects currently underway:

The creation of the term Bullinianos which refers to 'all those people that have participated in projects undertaken by Ferran Adrià, Albert Adrià and Juli Soler, along with those participating at the present time or in future projects'[36] is another validation of the concept of exprovement.

Take a look at the multidisciplinary team listed on the El Bulli Foundation website and you will see the coming together of minds from completely unrelated industries and disciplines (museography, philology, geopolitics and social management, amongst the more unexpected ones) to keep the foundation's tagline of 'feeding creativity' alive.

DEVELOPING AN EXPROVEMENT OUTLOOK

What are some of the types of questions that could have prompted the development of exprovement in the food industry by drawing parallels from a variety of other industries? How could this thought process be taken even further?

- What happens when a parallel is drawn between a vegetable and the bicycle industry?
- What are the parallels that could be drawn between the food industry and the English language?
- Can one draw a parallel between the food industry and the glass-blowing industry? The concept of spherification is one example.
- What applications from the world of physics can be applied to food?
- The entire software industry has been leaning towards incorporating Human-Computer Interaction. The parallel to this in the food industry would be Human-Food Interaction. What exprovements could this give rise to?

10

How Is a Voltmeter Similar to a Mind Reader?

At forty-three, editor-in-chief of *Elle* magazine, Jean-Dominique Bauby, was in the prime of his life, at the pinnacle of his career and a man about town living the good life in Paris.

One day in 1995, when he was out for a drive with his son, he suddenly started seeing double. He was rushed to the hospital but slipped into a coma—he had suffered a debilitating stroke.

Sometime after waking from a twenty-day coma, Bauby began working on his book *The Diving Bell and The Butterfly*.

From a literary point of view, at less than 150 pages, it is a beautifully composed book in terms of structure, story and language. But what makes the book truly remarkable is the method by which it was put together.

When Bauby woke from his coma, he was completely paralysed— he couldn't speak or move.

In Bauby's words, 'Up until then I had never even heard of the brain stem. I've since learned that it is an essential component of our internal computer, the inseparable link between the brain and the spinal cord. I was brutally introduced to this vital piece of anatomy when a cerebrovascular accident put my brain stem out of action. In the past it was known as a "massive stroke", and you simply died. But improved resuscitation techniques have now prolonged and refined the agony. You survive, but you survive with what is so aptly known as "locked-in syndrome". Paralysed from head to toe, the patient, his mind intact, is imprisoned inside his own body, but unable to speak or move. In my case, blinking my left eyelid is my only means of communication.'[1]

So how was Bauby able to 'write' a book when he was completely speechless and the only thing he could move was his left eyelid?

It happened that Bernard Chapui, a friend and former editor of *Men's Vogue*, who was visiting him in hospital one day, noticed that Bauby's left eye was twitching. He promptly asked Bauby to blink if he could understand him, and when Bauby did, it was discovered that though his body couldn't function properly, his brain was actually still active—his left eyelid being the only way he was able to let anyone know.

Upon this fortuitous discovery, 'Bauby started work with a speech therapist who specialised in the "alphabet of silence". The therapist would call out and point at letters (arranged by how frequently they are used in the French language), and Jean would make words and sentences by blinking his eye when she got to the letter he needed.'[2]

'"When he learned that the Paris rumour-mill was describing him as "a total vegetable", Bauby resolved to prove "that my IQ was still higher than a turnip's".'[3]

The entire book was written by Bauby blinking his left eyelid.

It took ten months (four hours a day) to complete. Using partner-assisted scanning, a transcriber repeatedly recited a French language frequency-ordered alphabet (E, S, A, R, I, N, T, U, L, etc.) until Bauby blinked to choose the next letter.[4]

'It took more than 200,000 blinks to write the book.'[5]

Over twenty years after Bauby's book was published, Rodrigo Hübner Mendes became the first person on the planet to drive a Formula One car—one that had no steering wheel, gear stick or pedals—using just his mind.[6]

No, Mendes is not a magician. And though on the surface it would seem like someone with the ability to drive an Formula One car wouldn't have much in common with a person with locked-in syndrome, there are many similarities in the conditions and the methods used by both men to achieve their goals.

Mendes is a quadriplegic.

He was able to drive the Formula One car using the technology of brain-computer interfacing (BCI), which is a direct communication pathway between a brain and a computer that is programmed to perform a desired activity.

To put it simply, a wearable EEG device was able to interpret his brain signals/intentions and accurately convert them into commands that a computer (with the help of steering algorithms and track mapping) was able to carry out to steer the vehicle.

In comparison, Bauby's brain activity, when combined with a rudimentary algorithm and accurate interpretation by another person, resulted in him being able to produce letters, words and ultimately write his book.

The common element was that both men, though physically incapacitated, used only their minds to achieve their goals—though each used a very different method to translate or interpret their thoughts.

But while it took Bauby ten months for the activity in his brain to be correctly interpreted into a book of less than 150 pages, Hubner's brain activity was understood and translated into action in real time—in no less of a dynamic environment than driving an Formula One car on a racetrack!

The technology that allowed Hubner to achieve this amazing feat, as is the case with many examples of exprovement, has its roots in an unrelated industry and stems from something invented for an entirely different purpose.

ELECTRICITY MEASUREMENT: THE FOUNTAINHEAD OF BCI

One of the major quests of the late 1800s was to find an accurate way to measure the flow of electricity and its consumption in order to make electric measurement more precise while conducting experiments and to be able to charge the newly acquired customers of the burgeoning electric industry in a fair and accurate manner.

The inventions of the ammeter, the voltmeter, the galvanometer and the watt-hour metre were all steps in this direction, and years later, volt and ammeters formed the basic building blocks of many sophisticated marvels of technology, including CTs, MRIs and photo sensors—highlighting the parallel between the seemingly unrelated electrical and healthcare industries.[7, 8]

The billions of nerve cells of the human brain produce tiny electrical signals that form patterns called brainwaves. It was the study of this phenomenon that led Hans Berger to play a critical role in the development of the electroencephalograph—an instrument that measures and records the electrical activity in the brain. The recording thus produced either via a computer screen or on a graph paper is called an electroencephalogram, commonly known as the EEG.

Berger employed the basic principle of the voltmeter to measure electrical activity—except in this case, it was of the human brain.

He was also able to notice and characterize brainwave patterns, classify and explain many EEG phenomena as 'normal' and 'abnormal', and recognize EEG changes associated with mental effort, increased attention or those associated with brain injury.[9, 10]

FROM DIAGNOSTIC TOOL TO TREATMENT TOOL TO INTERPRETATION TOOL

Traditionally EEGs have been used as a diagnostic tool in the medical industry to study unwell brains.

But beyond serving as merely a diagnostic tool, EEGs can also be used as a therapeutic tool to bring about positive enhancements to unwell brains.

Neurofeedback therapy uses the information made available through an EEG to assist in the reconditioning or retraining of the brain, helping it to function optimally. It can be useful in managing depression, anxiety, ADHD and other conditions that can benefit from improved cognitive functioning. It does this through 'auditory and/or visual positive reinforcement in the form of watching a video, listening to ambient music, or playing a video game.'[11]

However, conventional EEGs require one to go to a lab, hospital or clinic. The electrodes, wires and bulkiness of the gadget mean that one typically has to be sitting in a fixed spot while the machine is working.

Until, that is, the innovation of portable, wireless EEG devices.

BRAIN MONITORING ON THE GO

Improvements to the design of traditional EEGs have led to solving their immobility problem, while also enhancing the comfort and aesthetics of these devices.

For example, dry sensor technology, rather than the use of electrodes that need to be attached with sticky gel, and Bluetooth technology, have helped develop designs that allow the user to wear an EEG during day-to-day activities, entirely changing what is possible with EEG technology today and in the future.

With as much ease as you'd wear a fitness tracker on your wrist, a Muse headband can help you stay focused and become better at meditation, to cite one example. When your mind begins to drift, the signals detected through the headband activate 'stormy weather' music through your headphones, letting you know you've gone off track. When your mind is calm, you will hear the sounds of peaceful weather.

Further, by gamifying the process—being able to track your progress via the Muse app, set goals, take on challenges, earn points and bonuses—improvements in the form of behavioural economics play a role in keeping you motivated.[12]

Another device is Emotiv, a wireless neuroheadset that can measure and track cognitive, behavioural and mental well-being, and send signals to various devices, providing information that makes it easier to take advantage of neuroplasticity—'the brain's ability to modify, change, and adapt both structure and function throughout life and in response to experience.'[13]

A Performance-Enhancing Tool

No longer is the EEG merely a tool to understand and improve unwell brains from the confines of a lab. Due to its portability, low cost and visualization via connectivity to a computer, mobile phone or tablet, advanced portable EEG units like Emotiv allow for well brains, in everyday situations to also be studied in order to enable superior performance.

For example, a student using an Emotiv device can begin to understand whether they learn better early in the morning or late at night, to classical music or to no music at all; or which lighting and what temperature best suit their personal learning ability, simply by observing their brain patterns under different conditions, and then implementing more of what works best for them.

Each person learns in a different way, and Emotiv can allow you to create a customized learning environment for enhanced performance. An example of this is the innovative workplace learning system developed by SAP and Emotiv, which combines SAP's learning platform with Emotiv's neurotechnology.[14] It can detect when a worker has lost focus, where in the workflow a user is struggling and suggest a break or appropriate learning material in a format best suited to the particular individual. In this way BCI could be a useful tool in human resource development at companies as well.

Everyone, including those with learning disabilities, could have the opportunity to improve their performance on a daily basis, without having to go to a lab or clinic or have cumbersome gadgets strapped to their head. Using a combination of improvements that incorporate design thinking and behavioural economics, wearable EEG devices make it easier to monitor and provide valuable feedback for both, well and unwell brains, as one goes about their day.

Mind Over Matter

What Mendes was able to achieve was through a combination of BCI, steering algorithms and track mapping. An on-board computer in the car translated Mendes's thoughts (which were captured via his brain activity using Emotiv) into commands that were able to act on all the mechanical elements of the car.

Combining wireless EEG technology and BCI allows for exprovement—being able to move an object with your mind is no longer the stuff of dreams!

'I grew up loving *Star Wars*, so the idea of moving an object with my mind is already the stuff of science fiction and the stuff of fantasy— that alone is cool. But driving a Formula One car—that takes it up to another level . . . The ability to translate thought directly into action is one of the most exciting new frontiers opened up by neurotechnology,' says Tan Le, founder of Emotiv.[15]

This application of Emotiv also opens up the possibility of making not just sports, but many types of jobs more inclusive as well, which previously would not have been an option for people like Mendes.

Hearing about how Mendes was able to drive an Formula One car using just his mind, one can't help but wonder how much this technology could have helped Bauby, who died just two days after his book was published and had written of his condition, 'Something like a giant invisible diving-bell holds my whole body prisoner.' But, he also observed, 'My mind takes flight like a butterfly. There is so much to do.'[16]

A BCI system could potentially have enabled his mind to do many of the things he longed to achieve.

On another note, it also raises the question of whether we may be able to see Michael Schumacher race again one day.

TURNING THOUGHTS INTO ACTION ACROSS VARIOUS INDUSTRIES

Some of the industries where BCI has found and can find further application have already been covered earlier in the chapter, such as brain-controlled driving in the automotive and racing industries and real-time adaptive learning experiences for human resource development.

Here are a few more parallel industries that are making use of the possibilities offered by technology that is able to link our brains directly with computers.

Wellness

Through neurofeedback therapy, BCI can assist people with conditions such as ADHD, addiction, anxiety, depression, sleep disorders, PTSD and learning disabilities.

In addition, devices like Muse, Emotiv's Insight and Neurable's Enten can help users perform better in everyday life. While Muse can help users sleep and meditate better, Insight and Enten help users understand under what conditions they learn best, what helps them focus best (including what type of music), when their brains need a break from work or studying, what activities cause distractions, and make productivity recommendations based on the same, all by tracking the user's brain waves.

Devices like Enten and Muse, which are intended for mainstream everyday use, have much sleeker designs than many of the other portable/wearable EEG devices. Enten, for example, looks exactly like a normal set of headphones—an improvement on traditional EEGs that makes use of behavioural economics, as people are more likely to try out something that looks and feels akin to something they already know well and use often.

Gaming

Adding another dimension to virtual reality (VR), Neurable launched a brain-controlled interface in 2017 with a completely hands-free VR gaming experience that allows players to do things like pick up objects and fight robots using just their thoughts.[17]

Home Automation

With products from companies like Paris-based NextMind, any internet of things (IoT)-enabled device in your home, including lights, microwaves, music systems, air conditioners etc., could potentially be controlled with your thoughts, taking home automation to the next level.[18]

Disability Sector

The ability to control devices with one's brain could allow people with physical disabilities to perform a range of activities, for example opening and closing a prosthetic hand or moving a wheelchair simply with their thoughts. In one recorded instance, a paralysed man was able to translate his thoughts into text on a screen, with 94 per cent accuracy, simply by imagining the motion of his hand physically writing the text.[19]

Thanks to brain mapping and machine learning, the more the user engages with such devices, the better they become at interpreting the user's thoughts/brainwaves.[20]

Neurolutions, a US-based company, has developed a product called IpsiHand, a 'lightweight, adjustable, battery-powered, robotic device worn over a stroke patient's impaired hand, wrist and forearm. The IpsiHand exoskeleton physically opens and closes the patient's hand in response to the patient's thoughts.'[21]

This product is based on the fact that though many paralysed people cannot move their arm, they can still imagine moving it, and BCI provides the opportunity to turn that intention into an action. In fact, continued usage can lead to a rewiring of the brain (thanks to neuroplasticity) up to a point where the uninjured part of a stroke patient's brain slowly begins to take control of the paralysed limb and improve movement in that limb.

Marketing

One of the insights most important to a marketer is consumer behaviour—understanding things like what consumers' preferences are, what motivates them to buy a product or service or at what point they actually make the decision to buy something.

One way to do this is to measure consumers' neural activity when they interact with a product—the raw physiological data that is untarnished by poor communication and psychological factors like embarrassment, forgetfulness or poor framing or understanding of a question. This information, when used in marketing tools like ad campaigns, colour choices etc. is what is referred to as neuromarketing.

With the advances in wearable EEG already described, marketers would be able to gain potentially more accurate data, even as consumers go about their normal lives, without having such studies confined to labs or testing rooms.

Industry 4.0

Mind control technology can also enable mind-controlled robots to perform tasks in a factory, with the benefits of increased productivity, improved safety and remote monitoring. In fact, Altran has developed 'Factory Avatar'—an immersive and adaptive remote factory control system that supports the use of cognitive-control technology in the context of the emerging Industry 4.0 revolution.[22]

WHERE DO WE GO FROM HERE?

With BCI being able to translate our thoughts into actions, what are some future scenarios that are likely to play out?

Smart Adaptive Environments

Merging the feedback that EEGs can provide us with on the one hand, and the ability to execute commands that control devices with just our thoughts on the other, we could be looking at a future that allows us to live in a smart, adaptive environment.

For example, when your wearable BCI detects that you are fatigued, no longer would it just send you a notification, but instead would automatically, taking full advantage of IoT, send a signal to your coffee maker to start brewing a cup to revive you; or perhaps it would adjust the light setting in the room you're working in.

If your device detects that you're struggling to understand a particular document at work, it could automatically play a video that explains the concept clearly, or start a podcast instead, depending on what artificial intelligence and machine learning has taught it is your best learning methodology.

In this way, feedback and control would combine into a single seamless loop.

Next-Gen Neural Hardware

Technology can sometimes seem to come full circle. Mobile phones, when they first came out, were large and bulky, and one of the next phases of improvement was to make them as small as possible so they would be more convenient to carry around. But later, as the use of a mobile phone changed, we saw a gravitation towards bigger devices once again.

Drawing a similar parallel to EEGs/BCIs, scientists worked on developing devices that didn't need to be inserted into a person's brain, so their use could be more widespread and one wouldn't require medical expertise to use them.

But as what is possible with an EEG has evolved—mainly due to improvements in supporting technology—companies like Neuralink and Synchron are developing tiny, battery-operated brain implants that work on Bluetooth, making a return to the use of devices that need to be inserted into the human brain.

Primarily these companies are looking at helping people in whom the signal pathway from the brain to the spinal cord to the muscle is damaged (such as those with paralysis), as the brain implants are able to pick up neural signals.

Today, the recording power of devices like N1 from Neuralink can transmit 2048 electrodes worth of information wirelessly and of a quality far improved to what has been possible in a lab till now.[23]

In fact, neurotech start-up Synchron, in March 2022 announced long-term safety results from their fully implanted endovascular BCI Stentrode for severe paralysis—after one year of usage, four patients with amyotrophic lateral sclerosis (ALS) reported no side effects and were able to perform daily online tasks. Their device doesn't require open-brain surgery, but is fed through a patient's jugular vein to their brain.[24]

At Kernel, founded by Bryan Johnson, the focus has been on improving the measurement capability of BCIs with the development of more accurate hardware like Flow, which uses spectroscopy to offer a more detailed look inside the human brain. This device has effectively taken what an fMRI does in a room-sized setting and shrunk it down to a device you can wear on your head like a helmet.[25]

With the ability to easily and with greater accuracy scan a person's brain multiple times a day, such technology opens up the possibility of conducting all kinds of brain research in an easy manner, from studying the effects of caffeine on the brain to studying sleep disorders, with data being collected from much larger study groups than before.

Sensory Substitution

As mentioned earlier in the section on disability, EEG combined with BCI can not only help someone with paralysis move a prosthetic limb or exoskeleton, but also restore motor skills to some extent, thus improving brain-to-body (motor) signals.

More difficult, however, is the ability to restore somatosensory or body-to-brain signals—the ones that let us experience the sensation of touch.

When the human brain is not able to receive this feedback (usually due to spinal damage) it becomes difficult to modulate motor skills, for example to adjust one's grip based on whether one is holding an egg or a heavy dumb-bell.

Researchers have found that in some cases where spinal damage has occurred, some residual fibres with a degree of neural activity do remain—a residual body-to-brain connection that can be picked up by advanced EEG devices.

In one instance, researchers at Battelle Memorial Institute and the Wexner Medical Centre at Ohio State University were able to simulate the sensation of touch in a paralysed man by developing a system that converted the data recorded when the patient touched something into a haptic motor, which they placed on his biceps where he was still able to experience the sensation of touch. When the haptic device buzzed on the patient's arm, it provided haptic feedback that nudged him to adjust his grip accordingly. While he didn't actually 'feel' the object, he was able to judge how much to adjust his grip.[26]

At Neosensory, the company founded by renowned neuroscientist David Eagleman, a lot of work is being done on engineering sensory substitution devices. By developing a system that is capable of capturing sound waves and translating them into a pattern of vibration on a vest called versatile extra-sensory transducer (VEST), Eagleman and team have been able to help deaf people interpret sound through their ability to feel things, using a non-invasive method that is forty times cheaper than a cochlear implant.[27]

Using neural activity in this way puts human beings in a position to broaden and improve their perceptual experience, moving from accessing data that has to be monitored and interpreted through numerous screens to simply 'feeling' them on a wearable device.

Scan the QR code to read about how Neosensory Buzz is changing the lives of deaf children in China:

To give an idea of the varied potential applications, which it is not possible to entirely expand upon in this chapter, Eagleman, at a TED Talk in 2015, spoke about an experiment being conducted at his laboratory where an individual (who was unaware of the type of data being relayed to him), was fed real-time data relating to the stock market via the Neosensory VEST to determine whether his ability to trade on the stock market improved over time.[28]

'With just a few weeks of training, Eagleman says users can learn to associate the patterns with specific inputs—the sound of a letter, say, or news of a particular stock appreciating.

Eagleman predicts that over time, perceiving data through the VEST will become second nature. "It's an unconscious thing, just the same way that you hear,' he says. 'We don't know for sure what it will actually feel like, but what we can say is it's not an effortful, cognitive translation."[29]

ACCESIBILITY

Looking at how far technology has progressed since the time Jean-Dominique Bauby wrote his book, attention must also be brought to how much more accessible the technology is becoming to the common man today.

The price list below shows that neurotech devices aren't as inaccessible as one might imagine:

Device	Starting price in USD (March 2022)
Muse	200
Neurable Enten	200
Emotiv	500
NextMind	400
Kernel	5000

DEVELOPING AN EXPROVEMENT OUTLOOK

What are some of the types of questions that could have led to the interpretation industry finding exprovement solutions in the medical industry?

- Can telepathy be made real? Could technology from a parallel industry (medical) make it happen?
- Can a computer help mediate between the brain and the world?
- If a computer can help, can it help communicate with machines as well?
- Can wearing an EEG probe be made easy and perhaps even into a fashion statement?

11

Broken Bones Fix Disaster Zones

How do you fit a building into a bag?

And no, we're not talking about the temporary canvas or polyester tent type. We're referring to a permanent structure made out of concrete.

Two industrial design students who entered a design competition to try and win some money could tell you how:

1. Open an approximately 3 m x 2 ¼ m x 1 ⅕ m polyethylene, airtight, waterproof, rot-proof sack.
2. Activate an electric fan to inflate the package (the way you would a kid's blow-up pool) until it forms a self-supporting structure. When fully blown up you will see it has achieved a dome like shape and contains entrance doors as well.
3. Spray water on to the structure (non-potable or sea water will do).
4. Wait for twenty-four hours.
5. Your permanent, 50-square-metre concrete structure is now ready for use![1]

But we have still not told you how they got the building into the bag in the first place.

For that, let's go back to where it all began.

In 2004, when Peter Brewin and William Crawford from the Royal College of Art, London, entered a competition sponsored by the British Cement Association, in part to earn some money for their studies and in part to showcase their design ideas, they probably didn't realize they were on the cusp of developing an exprovement that could change the way concrete is used in the construction industry. Their focus was on brainstorming new uses for concrete.

Intrigued by the compressive strength of cement on the one hand and the possibility of rapidly installing a structure using inflation on the other, they combined the two concepts to develop an inflatable structure made of a type of pliable fabric containing a specially formulated dry concrete mix, which when hydrated and inflated could form a hard structure in less than twenty-four hours.

AN EXPROVEMENT BORN OUT OF HUMANITARIAN CONCERNS

After the competition, the duo spent a month in Uganda conducting research to determine the applicability of their invention. They spent time with non-governmental organizations and aid agencies and visited refugee camps, observing first-hand how vulnerable the hut-like shelters at the camps were to weather, thieves and rebel forces.

During their time there they witnessed a tropical storm at a refugee camp in the northern part of the country and found that in less than twenty minutes, the tents housing the refugees had flooded, and rain had leaked in through the fly sheets, soaking the mud floor, while panicked children were forced to desperately scatter in search of shelter.

In another part of Uganda, they saw housing made of wooden frames covered with flimsy plastic sheeting and heard from residents how easily and frequently members of the rebel-led Lord's Resistance Army set fire to these fragile homes, breaking in and abducting their children to induct them into their ranks.

Elsewhere in the country, at a World Food Program initiative, they were told about thieves slashing through the storage centre's soft-skinned walls to steal precious food supplies.[2, 3]

Their experience in Uganda led to the realization that their invention had found a truly meaningful application—one that could offer protection from the elements of nature acts and of human violence, and one that could potentially save lives—in the form of 'rapidly deployable hardened shelters that require only water and air for construction.'[4, 5]

Effective Emergency Shelters—A Global Requirement

War-stricken Uganda is just one of the examples of the situation faced by refugees and the victims of war-torn regions around the world.

According to the latest statistics from UNHCR, the UN Refugee Agency, the world has 89.3 million people who have been forcibly displaced due to persecution, conflict, violence, human rights violations or events seriously disturbing public order. Out of these, 27.1 million are refugees, and 4.6 are asylum-seekers.[6]

Oftentimes refugees and other displaced individuals are crowded into flimsy shelters with no protection from either natural calamities or violence such as arson in turbulent regions or war zones.[7] In extreme environments, a refugee is more likely to perish from exposure than from hunger. The existing infrastructure for refugees also takes a long time to construct and is usually made of traditional soft-skinned fabric tents that are not sturdy and are vulnerable to external forces. Natural elements like rain, snow and wind can easily damage them.

In war zones, violence inflicted by opposing armies can cause harm and destruction to such structures and their residents.

In areas of difficult terrain, like Afghanistan and Kashmir, transportation and assembly of permanent structures is not easy, further exacerbating the problem, creating a severe threat and leaving millions homeless, injured or dead.

Besides displaced individuals, there is also a requirement for easy-to-install, sturdy infrastructure when a natural disaster like an earthquake or flooding occurs.

Emergency housing and structures in which medical facilities can effectively function in turbulent environments such as the ones just mentioned are an absolute necessity. Building traditional concrete or even wooden houses in such emergency scenarios is not feasible and even if it were, would take a considerable amount of time. But Concrete Canvas Shelters (CCS), which is the name by which the duo's invention later began to be sold, allows for all the benefits of a concrete structure, with the additional one that they can be installed in twenty-four hours.

'CCS have two major advantages over conventional tented shelters:

Operational – CCS enable a hardened structure from day one of an operation. They provide much better environmental protection, increased security and vastly improved medical capability.

Financial – CCS have a design life of over ten years, whereas tents wear out rapidly and must then be replaced. CCS are a one-stop solution, saving effort and cost over the lifetime of medium- to long-term operations.'[8]

In addition, the waterproof structure can also be converted into a sterile environment and used as an emergency medical facility at a disaster zone.

Watch how a Concrete Canvas Shelter deploys by scanning this QR code:

FROM EXPROVEMENT TO SUCCESSFUL BUSINESS VENTURE

While working on developing the CCS for commercial production, however, the inventors realized that the concrete-filled geotextile material used for shelters had much greater potential as an erosion protection product within the civil sector.[9]

The unique material, sold under the name Concrete Canvas (CC) by Concrete Canvas Ltd, the company founded by Brewin and Crawford in 2005, is a three-dimensional fibre matrix containing a specially formulated dry concrete mix.

Hydrophilic fibres on one surface aid hydration by drawing water into the cement, while a PVC backing on the other surface ensures that the material is waterproof[10,] so although it hardens on contact with water, it does not get damaged if it comes into further contact with water, making it suitable for several underwater applications as well.

Some of the most notable properties of CC are[11]:

- **Flexibility:** It has drape characteristics, allowing it to closely follow the ground profile and fit around existing infrastructure. It can also be cut or tailored using basic tools like scissors and held together with a variety of fixtures including nails, screws, staples and bonding sealant.[12]

- **Rapid installation:** CC can be laid at a rate of 200 m² an hour—up to ten times faster than conventional concrete solutions.
- **Strength:** The material's fibre-reinforcement prevents cracking, absorbs energy from impact and provides a stable failure mode.
- **Durability:** CC is five times more abrasion-resistant than ordinary Portland cement concrete, has exceptional chemical resistance, good weathering performance, and will not degrade when exposed to ultraviolet radiation. It has a durability of 120 years when used in erosion-control applications.
- **Fireproof and waterproof:** Thanks to its PVC backing, CC is completely waterproof and resistant to fire damage.
- **Easy to use:** CC eliminates the need for a concrete plant to be set up, requires less personnel, and no on-site mixing or measuring, except for the addition of water directly on to the product. It is also available in bulk or batched rolls.
- **Lower project costs:** The speed and ease of installation of CC—it can be laid up to ten times faster than most concrete solutions—makes it more cost-effective than conventional concrete, with less logistical burden. For instance, a single lorry of the 7mm thick CCT2 material can substitute the requirement for thirty 17T mixer trucks.
- **Eco-friendly:** CC is a low-mass, lower-carbon technology, and uses up to 95 per cent less material than conventional solutions. A single pallet of CC can cover the same area as two 17T mixer trucks for many types of applications.

As a result, CC has found applications in several industries where easy-to-install structures that provide protection are required on a regular, and often unexpected, basis:

Defence

By drawing a parallel between the use of CC in disaster relief and its applicability in military defence, it was found that the material could also be useful in the construction of protective walls for army personnel and equipment during times of war.

Since CC is fireproof, it provides protection against gunfire and explosion impact, while its lightweight property allows for ease of transportation along borders. This permits its use even in the most remote areas where equipment can only be transported using helicopters. With the introduction of CC, building concrete walls for defence is far less cumbersome due to the simplicity and time taken to install.

The British Army has used CC as a substitute for sandbags in Afghanistan.

"'The problem is the sandbag walls are getting a lot of incoming and outgoing fire that's degrading the sandbags, and once they've been shot up . . . the sand leaks out and they no longer provide the protection from incoming shrapnel," Brewin says. The Concrete Cloth holds the sand in and is also fireproof, which prevents sandbag degradation.'[13]

CCS found use in military applications in other countries as well, with their rapid deployment and security features making them ideal in remote areas. The American, Swedish, Dutch and UAE militaries have tested out the shelters, with the Swedes even testing them against mortars![14,]

In war-striken zones, infrastructure is prone to damage and destruction, and roads become the only viable way to transport equipment. When these are damaged, getting emergency and defence supplies from one place to another become next to impossible—in such cases CC can be used to reinforce vehicle tracks.[15] Further, CC can be used as a quick, effective and cheap method for on-site treatment of surfaces, such as the flattenning, compaction and curing of radar or ground-to-ground missile sites.

Construction

Concrete Canvas has found several applications in the construction industry, especially in circumstances where a concrete surface or structure is required to be put up quickly, but without the involvement of a lot of material, equipment and labour.

Shotcrete has traditionally been used for slope protection. Using CC in place of shotcrete has made it convenient to install landslide protection on slopes simply by unrolling the sheets of CC on to the slope. On hydration, the sheets turn into hardened concrete that provides durability and protection.

This has also greatly reduced the demand for heavy machinery and labour, as well as alleviated potential health hazards, such as the deafening noise caused by some of the other slope protection methods.

For example, in Maraval in Trinidad and Tobago[16], Concrete Canvas was successfully employed as an erosion control measure at a roadside slope that was eroded, overgrown with vegetation and a threat to the stability of adjacent roads and buildings. Bulk rolls of Concrete Canvas were delivered to the site, unrolled from the top of the slope using spreader beam equipment and secured to the undulating surface using steel ground pegs and rock anchors, before being hydrated with water from a local source.

The entire 475-square-metre installation took a team of four men just eight days to complete, highlighting the material, equipment, labour and time saving potential of CC.

Concrete Canvas also works well when an add-on or additional concrete structure is required after the initial work has been completed.

For example, when a small public access boat ramp originally built in the 1970s in East Fork Lake in Illinois needed to be extended in order to accommodate longer boat trailers, Concrete Canvas was found to be the most effective solution, costing half of what traditional concrete would have and saving nearly two weeks of installation time.[17]

Another application has been channel lining. For example, when in Northumberland, UK it was decided to formalise a channel to prevent river water from coming into contact with metal-contaminated waste heaps—the result of the nineteenth and early twentieth century mining activities of the now abandoned Coalcleugh mine—Concrete Canvas was chosen as the ideal material for lining the channel, due to its rapid installation rate, ease of application in a remote area and its ability to provide erosion control, especially during high flow events.

At the time of installation in 2019, it was estimated that the project would 'help prevent about half a tonne of lead, cadmium and zinc polluting the river each year.'[18]

Mining

Concrete Canvas can be used as an alternative to poured or sprayed concrete or as a quick way of erecting strong permanent or temporary blast and vent structures and spall lining, and has been successfully tried in Mpumalanga, South Africa.[19]

Underwater Applications

Due to its property of water resilience, CC has begun to be commercially used for the construction and protection of underwater pipelines. Using CC for underwater tunnels and piping reduces wear and tear due to its ability to toughen with water. Additionally, it is time and cost-effective.

Furniture

As one begins to creatively explore the applications of Concrete Canvas, we start to see its use in unlikely areas such as furniture creation. Because of its multifaceted characteristics of being safe, eco-friendly, time-efficient, highly durable, strong and easy to use, various furniture designers have begun to incorporate CC into their designs. Integrating metal frameworks with concrete cloth enables the creation of unique and sturdy furniture designs with finer detailing—at notably lower costs and within a shorter period of time.

An example is the RUG'N ROLL collection of concrete stools by Johannes Budde, which was exhibited at Milan Design Week 2022. Made from Concrete Canvas, these waterproof and fireproof stools can be used as either outdoor or indoor furniture and were showcased as having an 'extraordinary life span'. The installation process was reportedly ten times faster thanks to the use of CC.

The Concrete Canvas stools are a unique design, since they look very much like folded rugs, yet possess the strength of concrete, described by *Designboom* as a 'fascinating symbiosis'.[20]

Emergency Landing Sites

Concrete Canvas can reduce the time, effort and equipment required to build emergency helipads, such as those needed at disaster evacuation zones where every minute is precious. Used around the periphery of existing helipad sites, CC can also help with the suspension of dust generated by helicopter rotors.[21]

A HYGROSCOPIC PARALLEL

But where did the inspiration for Concrete Canvas come from?

This is where broken bones played a part.

In the early nineteenth century, a technique known as *plâtre coulé* became popular in Europe. When a person fractured or injured a bone, it would be encased in a wooden construct over which plaster of Paris was poured. The idea was to immobilize the limb to avoid movement so the fractured bone could heal. However, due to its weight, the patient was largely confined to a bed during the healing process.

In the 1850s, a Dutch military surgeon, Antonius Mathijsen, while working in Haarlem, discovered that by soaking bandages in a mixture of water and plaster of Paris, he could create a cast that hardened in minutes. His bandages consisted of strips of coarse cotton cloth with finely powdered plaster rubbed in. To this day, the concept of plaster bandages remains an advanced version of Mathijsen's starched bandages.[22]

It was by drawing this parallel with the plaster cast that is used to fix broken bones that Brewin and Crawford, while completing their post-graduate degree at the Royal School of Art in 2004, were inspired to create Concrete Canvas.[23]

In the medical industry, plaster casts for injuries are made of gauze and plaster strips soaked in water. These are wrapped around the injured body part over a stockinette and cotton padding. As they dry, the strips begin to harden, and take twenty-four to forty-eight hours to harden fully before forming a solid structure immune to cracking and damage.

As a parallel to this, Concrete Canvas is made of dry cement-impregnated fabric that solidifies on hydration. It is laid using rolls of concrete sheets that are flexible before hydration, but solidify within twenty-four hours of installation, on exposure to water. The two students emulated the plaster concept by creating a canvas that solidified in water.

TOWARDS GREENER CONSTRUCTION

There are plenty of other countries that are now adapting Concrete Canvas into their conservation and infrastructure efforts such as Saudi Arabia, Canada, the USA, the UK, India, Russia and several more. It is fascinating to see the range of applications, which only keep expanding over time. From the launch of the CC shelter in 2004, the company has expanded into several nations and has won many awards for its work.

A significant point to note is that in this day and age, it is important for solutions to be green and sustainable. In addition to saving about 95 per cent of the previously required construction materials, any untreated material will naturally 'green' over time as it allows moss growth, while the fibre-reinforced concrete will later prevent root-growing vegetation. Thanks to these properties, Concrete Canvas directly reduces the CO_2 footprint of construction work.

In terms of what is to come, the future lies in further experimentation with Concrete Canvas. Given its unique and efficient properties, there is a world of applications for which Concrete Canvas or a variation of it could be utilized. As of now, it does have certain limitations with regard to its width and height. For Concrete Canvas to completely disrupt the traditional concrete industry, it requires innovation and modification to suit the needs that may arise from further exploration of its uses.

Already, as of June 2022, the company announced the upgrade of its product to one that has higher performance and a lower carbon content than before.

The new T-series has 33 per cent less embodied carbon than standard CC, providing more than 60 per cent savings when used to replace conventional poured concrete for erosion control applications and has 25 per cent higher abrasion resistance, providing longer-lasting protection in erosion control applications.[24]

DEVELOPING AN EXPROVEMENT OUTLOOK

Questions such as the following, which seek parallel applications in a variety of other industries, could help spark further ideas for Concrete Canvas inspired exprovements:

- What are the different industries into which Concrete Canvas can branch out?
- Fibre-reinforced plastic uses a mesh of fibres to make the support structure of the material. Was that the parallel for the plaster cast?
- Since concrete is now available in the form of a textile, what parallels can be drawn with the garment industry?
- Wearable tech is now capable of embedding conductive material into the fabric itself. What parallels can be drawn by introducing conductive materials into CC?
- The BMW Gina is a concept car made of fabric. What parallels can that spark keeping CC in mind?

12

Can Human Beings Become Electronic Circuits?

A music video made in 2009 shows globally renowned DJ, producer, singer and songwriter Calvin Harris's track 'Ready For The Weekend' come to life in an unusual way.

Every time Harris and a member of the group of dancers who are part of the video high-five each other or tap their feet, the sound of a different instrument—guitar, drums, piano, bass guitar, electronic sounds etc.—seems to magically emanate from them. When 'played' together in harmony, the group effectively becomes a human synthesizer, successfully recreating a version of the hit track.

In the video (which you can view by scanning the QR code), Harris explains what makes the magic happen, to create what he refers to as the Humanthesizer, a collaboration between Harris, Sony Music UK and four masters students at the Royal College of Art Industrial Design programme. The Humanthesizer is enabled via the use of conductive paint—the brainchild of students Bibi Nelson, Becky Pilditch, Isabel Lizardi and Matt Johnson—which is capable of 'wiring' human beings to a computer when their hands and feet are covered in the substance, essentially making the dancers extensions of a circuit.[1]

As Sony's Steve Milbourne explains:

'We read about the conductive ink "Bare" that the students at the RCA (Royal College of Art) had invented, and we thought it was pretty cool. We wondered if we could make some kind of musical instrument from it, so we spoke to Calvin and asked him if he'd be up for collaborating.

After quite a bit of mulling over various methods of doing it, we decided to try and create a choreographed routine where people touching hands would close the circuits and trigger sounds somehow.

With the help of the guys from the RCA we began to draw a schematic for the synth, and conceptualize how it would operate; we eventually decided on a layout and that we'd control it using MIDI, by connecting the paint "electrodes" to an Arduino, which connects to Max/MSP. This then controls individual tracks in Ableton, and in the live mode automatically quantized them on the fly as the performance took place.

Behind the scenes it was two days of setting up, testing and working out the routines before the day we filmed it. On the day we spent the morning letting the dancers rehearse and get the timing more or less right (so the notes were quantized into the right places at the BPM running in Ableton, a bit slower than the original track, but dancing at 140 bpm was a little difficult for them!) and then we filmed several takes before we got one we were happy with.'[2]

THE JOURNEY TO EXPROVEMENT

As we've seen in the two case studies on thermochromic material, an exprovement isn't always born as an exprovement—it becomes an exprovement once it finds the right application.

Conductive paint was born out of the idea the students had, as part of their final year project at RCA, to print an electrical circuit on to the human body. After extensive research and a lot of experimentation, the idea morphed into conductible paint.

Beginning with the basic idea taught in high school science that distilled water, which is a non-conductive medium of electricity, turns into a great conductor when mixed with salt, they began to explore the idea of adding something to the paint to make it conductive, such as copper (one of the best and most economical conductors of electricity) mixed with glue. After much trial and error, they developed a successful formula that would make the paint conductive and non-toxic—by adding carbon to the mix of ingredients. Initially the team did not have a clear idea of what the new product's applications could be and how the lab-borne idea could be implemented across any, let alone multiple industries. While the Calvin Harris video generated a lot of interest online, the four students still weren't sure about the commercial viability of the product.

One of the things they considered was its use as a body paint, but the complex manufacturing regulations of the cosmetic industry put a spoke in that idea. Eventually, in 2010, they decided that their product would find a broader market in the electronics industry as 'paintable wire'.

This idea began to catch the attention of investors and government agencies. The students went on to form a company, Bare Conductive, which received the prestigious Innovate UK Award with a funding prize of £1,00,000 in 2010[3], which not only helped the Bare Conductive team expand their business but also gave them the confidence to pursue new ideas.

Driven by its product innovation, Bare Conductive amassed £4,50,000 from seven private investors by 2014.[4] Furthermore, in 2017, Bare Conductive participated in the Arrow Certification Program, and as one of the Arrow flash funding winners, received $1,00,000.

A creative idea propelled by funding and confidence in the product's viability bolstered Bare Conductive's product roadmap and helped the idea that had originated from a final-year college project expand into numerous product portfolios spread across multiple industries.

ELECTRONICS FOR EVERYONE

In general, when putting together an electronic product of any kind—simple or complex, small or large—one requires a plethora of conductive wires to be connected to components such as resistors, capacitors and inductors.

What the exprovement of conductive paint does is eliminate the need for these wires, making it possible to create the function the wires serve by simply drawing a line of paint wherever a wire needs to be used.

This exprovement also makes it much easier (and way more fun!) for anyone, from a student to an engineer, to effortlessly create something that comes to life with the use of an electronic circuit.

For example, an elementary school student can easily paint a picture of a house with a doorbell, a dog in the garden and birds in the sky, using the conductive paint. By connecting the painting to an audio circuit, the doorbell could be made to ring when pressed, the dog could be made to bark when petted and the birds could be made to chirp when touched.

Today, Bare Conductive manufactures and sells Electric Paint and Touch Board—products that allow one 'to create interactive installations or build sophisticated prototypes'[5]—and a variety of other kits that enable putting together a range of projects.

From musicians and artists to advertisers and educators, Bare Conductive's products have been used to create interactive projects at museums, art installations, promotional events, conferences, retail experiences, gaming events and more, mainly in the form of interactive wall murals.

Bare Conductive paint can also be used on a wide variety of other materials including paper, wood, cement and even textiles.

THE CREATIVE PARALLEL

A parallel for conductive paint, the starting point of Bare Conductive's journey, can be drawn with the art supplies industry.

The art supplies industry sells products that enable artists and creators to create art or develop projects that put together a variety of materials to deliver something engaging.

Conductive paint adds another element to this industry by enabling the addition of electronic circuits to any installation. In the same way that one can draw or paint a brush stroke to add an element to a painting or wall mural, one can now paint a stroke of conductive paint to integrate surprising and exciting interactive elements into the piece.

Further, it allows one to turn an installation into a piece that can be educative, informative or just enjoyable in new and imaginative ways.

ELIMINATING WIRES IN A NUMBER OF INDUSTRIES

Here are some of the current applications of conductible paint.

Electronics

Bare Conductive's paint is a non-toxic, water-based, water-soluble, electrically conductive paint.[6] As per the technical information printed on the product, it can be utilized in electronic circuit boards or printed circuit boards (PCBs) in a variety of forms such as:

- A painted resistor element
- A capacitive electrode
- A conductor in designs that can tolerate high resistivity

In short, the use of conductive paint in PCBs is intended for applications that can run on low direct current (DC) voltages and at low currents. It can also come in handy when repairing broken electronics such as remote controls.

To test these intended applications, Bare Conductive started running Kickstarter programmes for its products. In one instance, with the launch of a programmable circuit board, the product was oversubscribed eightfold! Amazed by the response to their products and modular kits, the company started making Arduino starter kits and by late 2011, they began to promote accessories, such as pens that can draw electric circuits.

This alone has a gigantic potential to cater to a multi-billion-dollar industry globally.[7]

In addition, the pandemic-induced pressure on the supply chain of the electronics industry and the challenge of resolving the shortage of PCBs[8] could be addressed with creative solutions, such as Bare Conductive's conductive paint.

Music and Entertainment

Given that musical instruments, such as pianos, guitars and drum sets, can cost hundreds, if not thousands of dollars[9], the idea of creating your own piano or drum set for just a few dollars is an appealing proposition.

Similar to what Calvin Harris did, Bare Conductive's paint can be used to 'build' your own piano simply by painting piano keys onto a paper or cloth.

While the piano built at a cost of a few dollars might not have the musical range or look half as luxurious as a high-end Steinway & Sons or Fazioli piano, it does have one major advantage over its original counterpart—it can be rolled up and carried around with ease.

To further demonstrate the possibility of foldable and printable musical instruments, EJTech (an art and technology lab from Budapest) has built a working model of a flexible musical instrument digital interface (MIDI) controller on textiles.[10]

The team at EJTech successfully leveraged the capabilities of an Arduino Mega ADK kit to build a textile-printed keyboard that plays MIDI notes when touched.

With the possibility of textile-based MIDI players, hobbyists and music professionals could explore untapped opportunities to rethink the design of musical instruments.

Gifts and Greeting Cards

Hampered by the popularity of social media-based greetings and digital e-cards, paper-based cards, in an attempt to sustain and grow with the changing demands of the consumer, could take the form of do-it-yourself (DIY) personalized greeting cards, such as the conductive paint-based greeting card kits offered by Bare Conductive, which also serve as educational toys—playing around with the electronic kits helps kids learn amazing things about science while sending greeting cards to friends.[11, 12]

Advertising

Advertising plays a significant role in catching people's attention and promoting products. It is a dynamic field that requires a lot of creativity—creative commercials that are different from conventional advertisements stand a better chance of becoming deeply engraved in the minds of consumers, as unconventional things catch our attention quicker than conventional and mundane ones.

Companies vying for attention amidst competitors and attempting to make a positive and long-lasting impression in their customers' minds have the opportunity to do 'something different' using Bare Conductive's products.

The company's products have been used in interactive advertising in a wide variety of industries ranging from retail to banking.

For example, Rabobank has experimented with Bare Conductive's paint on a wall, to create an interactive smart surface. Icons of the products offered by Rabobank were painted on the smart surface. When touched, the icon revealed information about the respective products being offered. Unlike conventional signboards and large banners displaying product information, this interactive wall helped the bank attract visitors to its exhibition stand and hold their interest for a longer period of time.[13]

In a similar vein, companies such as Alibaba[14] and Siemens[15] have also used Bare Conductive's paint to create interactive walls that effectively showcase their products and encourage customer interaction. The growing trend of companies adopting creative ways of advertising through interactive walls gives us an idea of the considerable opportunities for products like conductive paint to flourish in the future.

The Bare Conductive blog has more examples of their products being used in creative ways in several industries. You can read about these by scanning this QR code:

SMART SOLUTIONS FOR A SMART FUTURE

In the twenty-first century, everything seems to be getting 'smart'— smart TVs, smartphones, smartwatches, smart glasses (for augmented and virtual reality), smart speakers and more.

It would appear that 'smartness' has become the need of the hour; some might even say—if a device is not 'smart', it doesn't belong in the twenty-first century!

So why should buildings be left behind in this race for 'smartness'?

The concept of 'smart buildings' has also started gaining traction as digitization penetrates every nook and corner of the world. Technologies such as artificial intelligence, machine learning, data analytics, internet of things, robotic process automation, etc. are becoming household terms as they make devices 'smart'. With the help of such advanced technologies, more and more buildings are being equipped with intelligent detection systems and smart appliances.

You might wonder what this has to do with Bare Conductive and its painting solutions.

Sensing the need of the hour in the smart building field, Bare Conductive entered the arena by launching its spin-out brand LAIIER in 2021. With this, they are venturing into smart building management systems and industrial smart surface applications.[16]

Advanced digital tools and technologies coupled with Bare Conductive's unique paint solutions could open the door to countless opportunities. Some of them are:

- **Switchless walls:** 'Art is the elimination of the unnecessary', said Pablo Picasso, one of the most influential artists of the twentieth century.

    Bare Conductive's unique and multipurpose paint is an example of art that can eliminate conventional things, in this case—switches. The walls of a house could be painted with conductive paint to do away with switches. A wall would then act as a switchless switch! Could this potentially eliminate the need for switches across the globe?

- **Intelligent floors:** LAIIER's conductive paint could be applied on floors to detect any change in the surroundings such as leakages in walls or pipes carrying water or any other liquid in industrial buildings, thereby transforming surfaces into connected sensors.[17]

    LAIIER's smart building suite also offers cloud-based predictive maintenance solutions. It collects data sensed by smart surfaces and sends it to the cloud for analysis that can predict costly accidents. In short, all vital information regarding the functioning of a building can be made available at the tap of a mobile phone or tablet.

- **Smart appliances:** LAIIER has already started offering non-contact liquid-level sensors that can be applied like a sticker to the surface of an appliance to sense a variety of parameters, such as the level of water and detergent inside washing machines and dishwashers.[18]

These sticker-like sensors could also be applied to the outer surface of detergent bottles to estimate the level of detergent remaining inside the bottle and accordingly send a reminder to effectively replenish the stock.

The market opportunity for the global liquid detergent segment alone is in the multibillion-dollar range as it was valued at over $27 billion in 2017 and is expected to go over $40 billion by 2025.[19]

DEVELOPING AN EXPROVEMENT OUTLOOK

Who would have thought that paint could be more than a decorative (and protective) element that can be applied to the walls of buildings?

With Bare Conductive's unique and multipurpose paint, it can now be a switch, an instrument, a sensor and much more.

The big insight from Bare Conductive is that we are increasingly moving towards using DC power and away from the use of alternating current (AC) power. DC generally operates at very low voltages so does not give an electric shock or electrocute a person.

- With the above in mind, why do we still need to conceal our electrical wires?
- Since wires do not need to be concealed and can be placed (or painted) on exposed surfaces, can they be made to look beautiful?
- Wearable tech has gained a lot of popularity; could this tech be painted on to our skin? What exprovements can that bring about?
- Could the paint being used on our walls communicate with us to tell us more about the structure itself?
- Every product we use, uses paint/colour/dyes in some form or the other. By making them out of conductive ink, can all these products be made 'smart'?

13

A Gamer's Take on Physiotherapy

A man waves his hand from right to left. Mirroring his movements, an animated fish on the screen in front of him moves from right to left as well, chasing a little green dot as its target.

You would be excused for thinking this is a description of a video gamer using his Xbox 360 with Kinect motion sensing technology to play a game, but it's not.

The person playing the game is actually a seventy-four-year-old man who recently had a fall, broke his arm, had surgery and is now doing physiotherapy remotely, from the comfort of his home.

If you have ever had to undergo or observe someone undergoing physical therapy, you know how long the process takes, the kind of discipline it requires and how frustrating it can get. This is especially true of the elderly, for whom just getting to the physiotherapy centre can be a huge barrier, let alone the actual process of recovery and rehabilitation.

When Canadian doctor Seang Lin Tan suffered a stroke in 1993 and required physiotherapy as part of his rehabilitation programme, he was at risk of becoming one of the 65 per cent of patients who, when released from hospital, either 'don't do the prescribed exercises or are only partially adherent because they get fatigued easily and the exercises themselves are tedious.'[1]

BARRIERS TO EFFECTIVE PHYSIOTHERAPY

There are several reasons that contribute to this high percentage:

- When patients are asked to engage in self-directed physiotherapy at home, often the only guidance is in the form of a sheet of paper they have been given with figures showing them what to do—there is no real-time feedback, motivation or progress monitoring, not to mention that the monotony of it can be demotivating.
- Having a physical therapist visit your home can be expensive, especially if recovery is a particularly long process.
- Many doctors have come to rely on years of data collection that suggest patients reach a 'recovery plateau' after a certain amount of therapeutic success, though they aren't sure why this happens. Unsatisfactory outcomes are thus often readily accepted without much questioning.
- Patients are not able to see the results of their efforts, especially when exercising by themselves at home. As recovery is generally a slow process, it's hard to measure just how much progress you've made week-on-week, other than your therapist telling you that you have, when you go in for a session. This can be demotivating and often leads to many patients dropping out of therapy and accepting their condition instead.

CHALLENGING THE WAY THINGS ARE DONE

Dr Tan's son, Justin Tan, was a first-hand witness to his father's tedious journey to recovery, which revealed many of the hurdles mentioned above.

Justin, who holds a bachelor's degree in biological engineering from MIT, realized that he could combine his technical knowledge with his other big passion—gaming—'to create something that was more interesting. Something that patients could use and engage in, in a more interesting fashion.'[2]

He also challenged the 'recovery plateau' theory when he found that 'it's not actually true . . . studies since the 1990s have shown that this concept of recovery plateau doesn't actually exist for the majority of patients and in fact intense continuous and varied rehabilitation even several years after a specific incident can yield functional improvement.[3]'

AN EXPROVEMENT IS BORN

While in his final year of university, he developed Jintronix—a virtual rehabilitation software for stroke victims that makes use of Kinect technology to gamify it.

To understand how Tan used the technology, it might help to first understand how the Kinect works:

Photographic cameras have come a long way and been through many iterations over the past 185 years, starting from the initial daguerreotype to the use of dry gelatin plates, and further on to using 35 mm film, single reflex cameras, the instant Polaroid camera, analogue electronic cameras and finally, digital cameras, which led to the most widely used form of cameras today—those on our smartphones, smart TVs and webcams. Each innovation improved on previous capabilities: dry gelatin plates allowed for smaller-sized cameras; Polaroid cameras allowed for ready prints in less than a minute; and digital photography allows for the shooting of compressed pictures and their storage in a digital form besides other advantages.

Microsoft Kinect, however, takes the use of cameras to another level, combining it with technologies like advanced motion and depth sensors, which enable full body mapping, and that working in tandem allow users to control characters on the screen via their own body movements that are mirrored in the movements of their onscreen avatars. The addition of a microphone enables control via voice command, while internet connectivity enables real-time feedback.

The key to making all this work together to deliver the required outcome lies in the Kinect's software, which uses large amounts of collected data on things as they would move/work in real life. Using artificial intelligence and a machine learning algorithm, the Kinect is able to 'learn' how to analyse what it 'sees', and to deliver an output in the form of making the onscreen avatar do exactly what you're doing in front of the screen.

THE PARALLEL BETWEEN GAMING AND PHYSIOTHERAPY

Tan wanted to develop similar software, but one that was tailored to work for the requirements of physical therapy.

By bringing together various areas of expertise—physiotherapy, software programming, hardware engineering, video game designing—Tan created the exprovement of Jintronix, which allows patients to do their physiotherapy in the form of an interactive game that provides real-time feedback.

'Using Microsoft's Kinect motion sensing technology and any kind of home computer, the system is calibrated to the patient's range of motion.

The infrared camera captures the person's movements and shows them in a small box at the bottom of the screen. So while the patient is sitting in a chair and playing various games on-screen, they're doing their rehab exercises at the same time.

For instance, one game (described at the beginning of the chapter) has the player virtually moving a fish in the water, gulping down food. The patient must move their arm in various figurations, such as a box or a figure eight, typical in rehab exercises.'[4]

Another game has a lady kicking a football to score a goal, while inadvertently carrying out physiotherapy to improve her leg movement. Yet another has a user 'pushing' an object forward to increase their range of motion, while they get real-time feedback in the form of numbers on a metre on the screen in front of them.

By adapting Kinect technology to physiotherapy requirements, Jintronix applies behavioural economics (improvement) to make the process of physiotherapy much more enjoyable. What was once a tedious, repetitive task is now a gratifying game where you can see your score, have a more tangible goal to work towards and have a bit of fun in the process—all of which work as motivators.

Each person's game can be tailored according to their needs, they don't have to leave the comfort of their home to do physiotherapy, the need for devices that must be attached to the body is eliminated, a person can be monitored remotely by professionals, and thanks to the technology used, progress analysis is now more precise.

Examined from an improvement point of view, the Jintronix system works in a way that improves the entire experience for the user and makes it a more effective one, bettering the chances of people sticking with a physical therapy programme.

To test his innovative idea of applying technology from the gaming industry to the rehabilitation therapy industry, Tan's prototype consisted of reimagining technology like laptops and TVs to figure out how to make software that would allow people to use technology they already owned, how to make the system 'on demand' and how to enable online interaction among patients, doctors, family and friends. Occupational therapists assisted in the development of the innovation by helping build clinically validated games that were safe and in alignment with required physical therapy outcomes.

BORROWING TECHNOLOGY FROM AN UNRELATED INDUSTRY

It is a well-known fact that the Kinect peripheral for the Xbox, which was intended to revolutionize the gaming industry and which at one point was the fastest selling game peripheral, was eventually not considered a success . . . in the gaming industry. However, Tan's unique application of it to the physical rehabilitation industry goes to show that with a little imagination, thinking out of the box, seeing the correlations between systems and drawing parallels, an innovation that doesn't meet expectations in one industry can find application in another—in this case an application that could potentially give new meaning to someone's life.

Not only does it borrow technology from the gaming industry, it also taps into another aspect of human nature that the gaming industry relies on—the compelling nature of competition.

A FUN SOLUTION TO A SERIOUS PROBLEM

According to the World Health Organization (WHO), 'globally, one in three people are living with a health condition that benefits from rehabilitation. Many countries are not equipped to respond to existing rehabilitation needs, let alone the forecasted increase that is arising from health and demographic trends. Rehabilitation is often not prioritized in countries and continues to be under-resourced. As a result, countless individuals do not have access to rehabilitation services, leading to an exacerbation of their condition, further complications and lifelong consequences. In some low- and middle-income countries, more than 50 per cent of people do not receive the rehabilitation services they require.'[5]

It is with this in mind that the WHO began the Rehabilitation 2030 initiative, which at its second meeting in 2019 estimated that 2.4 billion people are in need of rehabilitation services worldwide.[6] A system like Jintronix can make a difference in bridging this gap in the following ways:

Effectiveness

An exprovement like Jintronix or Evolv (a system developed by Microsoft on similar lines) has the potential to convert the 65 per cent of unmotivated patients to recovered success stories.

It addresses the problems described earlier in the following ways:

1. A tedious, boring, solo and often frustrating activity is now made interactive and engaging. Being able to visualize and monitor your progress and successes via your on-screen avatar in real time is far more exciting and inspiring than hoping that you're correctly remembering what you were told to do and accurately following it.
2. When the activity gets tiring, the 'game' motivates you to keep going.

    'The first time my patient stood in front of Jintronix, she went for twenty minutes, wanting to win the ski activity. She changed my mind about the role of games in rehabilitation,' says Dr Aaron Bunnel, Stroke Programme, University of Washington School of Medicine.[7]
3. Since the technology allows for real-time feedback, positive results are likely to be seen quicker. If it is brought to your attention immediately, you will do the exercises correctly much sooner than if you had to wait till you saw a physical therapist at a clinic. Jintronix or Evolv can give a patient real-time feedback vis-a-vis their progress from a previous session and let them know whether their

posture is correct in the first instance, saving time and potentially leading to reduced injury and quicker results.

Besides home use, Jintronix has found application at in-patient rehabilitation hospitals, skilled nursing facilities and assisted living facilities, where it not only keeps patients more engaged and motivated, but also helps clinicians and physical therapists do their job better, as they can obtain real-time feedback as well as detailed reports from the system. Patients were also found to be far more enthusiastic about doing their exercises than before.

'Jintronix is an amazing tool to use . . . I can individualize it to the patient so it's really patient-centred and it's fun to use, and I get objective information for my documentation,' says Suma, a therapist at Vertis Therapy, Indiana, USA.[8]

But does it work in practice? There are several studies to prove that it does. Here is an extract from one of them:

> 'In this study of 48 previously independent older adults who had suffered a minor injury, researchers compared 12 weeks of in-home Jintronix use to 12 weeks of supervised community-based exercise program and a control group that was not given an intervention. Jintronix participants showed improvement in gait speed, chair-stand test performance and balance compared to the control group, who showed no improvement. The in-home Jintronix technology provided similar results to the participants of the community-based group exercise program.'[9]

Ultimately, one of the biggest testaments to how life-changing such a system can be can be found in what patients who have used Jintronix have to say about how it has helped them improve:

'I couldn't even stand on my feet for five seconds and within six weeks I'm walking. Jintronix really helped,' says James, a patient.[10]

Wider Market Penetration

Being able to do physiotherapy from home—also known as telerehabilitation (TR)—improves accessibility, both logistically and financially, becoming available to people who otherwise do not have access to physiotherapy clinics or who cannot afford the expensive in-person sessions.

Research shows that: 'TR is less costly and equally as effective as clinic-based rehabilitation at improving functional outcomes in stroke patients. TR produces similar patient satisfaction. TR can be combined with other therapies, including VR, speech, and robotic assistance, or used as an adjuvant to direct in-person care.'[11]

Though telerehabilitation has been around for a while, Jintronix makes the offering more viable and effective. It can be used for rehabilitation in a wide variety of scenarios, including sports and accident injuries, stroke and multiple sclerosis rehabilitation programmes and for people with congenital and intellectual impairments, especially as there is a high demand for at-home physiotherapy services across all age groups.[12, 13]

Borrowing advanced 3D motion sensing technology from the gaming industry enhances the sub-industry of telerehabilitation (virtual care), whose importance came to the forefront during the Covid-19 pandemic.

One article interestingly notes that even when in-person services resumed, 64 per cent of people preferred to continue with telerehabilitation, showing that the scope for wider market penetration does exist.[14]

Here's the conclusion from another pilot study:

> 'Telerehabilitation, which combines Kinect-based exergaming, remote patient monitoring, and CVT follow-up, is acceptable and shows promise as a potential alternative to in-person outpatient therapies to improve ambulation and mobility outcomes in veterans with MS. The potential physical benefits are further complemented by reduced barriers to access and reduced travel burden to maintain appointments.'[15]

Reduced Burden on Resources

Given the sheer number of people needing to undergo physiotherapy—in the US alone, the average physical therapy clinic sees between

101 and 200 patients each week, which equals 300 million therapy sessions a year![16]—an exprovement like Evolv or Jintronix can help to drastically lower the strain on hospital services and other resources while simultaneously creating a huge positive impact on the lives on those suffering from immobility.

Scalability

Physical therapy, in its traditional form, is not scalable, but an 'at home' version changes that, bringing potential disruption to the industry. By removing the need for one-on-one interaction, not only are costs dramatically brought down, but looking at figures cited from 2013, 'it's estimated in North America alone that there are 50 million patients who currently suffer from physically chronic disabling conditions, whether it be from a stroke or a traumatic brain injury after a sports accident or after a car accident a spinal cord injury,'[17] suddenly what seems like a mathematical impossibility now looks like a requirement that can be met.

Another factor that makes Tan's model scalable and disruptive is that he uses technology that already exists in most homes—a laptop or a smart TV already contain the technology required. The fact that people don't have to go out and buy additional (and potentially expensive) equipment could encourage a lot more people to try out the software.

Measurability and Standardizaton

From the business owner's point of view, the software helps in other ways as well. According to Paul Riccio, vice president of finance and development at Vertis Therapy,

> 'In our industry our customers need measurable outcomes. It's where payment reform is going, it's where regulatory change, reimbursement is going. It's a necessity that our industry is becoming standardized and Jintronix has been by far the best technology we found, after a very long time of searching . . . The ability to measure the outcomes so quickly, easily in a standardised manner [is] . . . second to none.'[18]

This could play an important role when it comes to developing an unbiased standard for insurance claims as well.

THE PARALLEL BETWEEN GAMING AND SKILLS TRAINING

But could there be even more potential? If the use of technology from the gaming industry can help unwell people improve their skills, why can't it help well people improve or learn new skills as well?

Skills Evaluation and Training

An October 2020 article headline from the Canadian Broadcasting Corporation's website reads: 'Physiotherapy graduates say their careers have been stalled by industry's failure to offer COVID-safe exam.'

It goes on to relate the plight of students waiting to take the clinical, in-person portion of their exams: 'Almost one year after completing his master's degree in physiotherapy, Jeremy Lynn was prepared to finally take his clinical exam in November to become a fully licensed physiotherapist.

And then the exam was cancelled—again.'[19]

Besides its current application, couldn't Jintronix also be used as a skills testing and skills training tool for students of physiotherapy or any discipline that requires a person to achieve and maintain postures and movements in a particular manner?

Take dance for example. Professional dance course instructors, like most teachers during the pandemic, had to make the sudden shift to teaching online via Zoom. Dance instruction was probably one of the areas where the transition to online teaching was even more difficult, as Suzanne Ostersmith, assistant professor and director of dance at Gonzaga University, explains: 'Students are used to following instructors' backs as they demonstrate in the mirror and watch students to assess their learning. With Zoom, it is more normal to face the students; but then, students ask the teachers to turn away. But if the teachers turn away, they can't see the students to assess learning. It's challenging to know which is the "right" or "left".'[20]

3D motion sensing technology could be useful in teaching skills such as these, in a similar manner that Jintronix is using it for physiotherapy.

Back in 2017, a professor from the Indian Institute of Technology, Bengaluru, developed algorithms that, when combined with 3D motion sensing technology, would recognize the poses and expressions of Bharatanatyam dancers and then, using machine learning, predict the expertise level of dancers. This recognition and evaluation could be applied to the identification and classification of Bharatanatyam videos found on the internet, making a more refined and accurate search possible.[21]

Studies that same year at a Taiwanese dance school class that used a motion capture (MoCap) system concluded that:

'Using a MoCap system and high-speed camera to document dancers' movements can provide reference materials for students to improve their skills through self-practice. Second, using a MoCap system and high-speed camera as teaching aids at a dance studio can enhance the effectiveness of dancing teaching. Third, incorporating MoCap and high-speed camera technologies into dance art is becoming necessary for achieving peak performance.'[22]

This technology can be used at the very least as a supporting tool to help judge skill level and aid in the process of skills training for diverse fields, ranging from surgery to grape harvesting.

Scan the code to read about how advanced motion sensing technology can teach or improve grape harvesting skills:

Borrowing Other Technology From the Gaming Industry

With the emergence of new technology from the gaming industry, skills training could take on an entirely new dimension.

Besides motion capture technology, other technology from the gaming industry opens up new possibilities for enhanced and more effective training.

Scan the QR code to read about how augmented reality can pave the way to safer, cheaper and more engaging industrial skills training programmes, thereby improving worker retention and gaining the interest of a younger generation in a rapidly ageing industrial engineering industry, 'with at least a quarter of all workers estimated to be over 50 years old and starting to think about the end of their careers.'[23]

This concept of using augmented reality for industrial skills training could easily be gamified as well, to make it more challenging and competitive to keep things interesting.

THE EMERGENCE OF NEW SUB-INDUSTRIES

Borrowing from the gaming industry has created the sub-industry of exergaming, something that took flight during the pandemic.

Whether it's Just Dance, an app that helps you get in some exercise while your smartphone or game console tracks and scores your movements as you dance solo or with others, or the Wii Fit, which tracks and monitors your progress in yoga, strength training or aerobics, 3D motion sensing has brought a new dimension to exercising at home, making it fun, interactive and more accessible.[24]

Exergames have even proven to be effective in improving mobility and balance in older adults,[25] supporting another emerging field—that of gerontechnology, which focuses on assistive tech that enables safe, sustainable and independent living for the ageing population.[26]

Gamification and the use of gaming technology can be both a fun and motivational way to overcome problems that come with age. For example, a study conducted by geriatric and physiotherapy researchers in Montreal showed how combining virtual reality and a dance class helped incontinence in a group of ageing women, the element of fun encouraging them to participate in the class.

'Our challenge was to motivate women to show up each week. We quickly learned that the dance component was the part that the women found most fun and didn't want to miss. The socialization aspect shouldn't be ignored either: they laughed a lot as they danced!'[27]

From the creators of Pac-Man to the creators of the Wii, game developers are creating experiences specifically targeted at keeping the elderly fit.[28]

Using Kinect technology or a Wii controller means that the elderly can get their bodies moving, via games designed to target particular muscle groups and fitness levels, without even realizing it, as they're swept away by the fun and competition of a game.

Scan the QR code to read about how the Nintendo Wii is helping the elderly stay fit at a senior home.

THE FUTURE OF MOTION SENSING TECHNOLOGY

Going beyond the aspects of 3D motion sensing that relate to 'exercise' at its core, the technology is poised to play a role in a number of other parallel industries as well, where its application will herald a new way of living.

Automotive Industry

Motion sensing is the primary technology that makes the concept of autonomous vehicles possible, by allowing for scanning, mapping and recognition of objects around a vehicle. 'Failure to identify those objects correctly in a timely manner can cause irreparable damage, impacting our safety and society.'[29]

Even in driver-driven vehicles, the technology can be used to monitor driver alertness and activate autonomous driving or a warning alarm, or alert emergency services if it senses that the driver has become incapacitated.[30]

Inclusive Design

Since technology like Kinect or Leap Motion can be used to develop a system that recognizes gestures, it opens up the possibility of enabling new avenues of communication between deaf and mute people and those who do not understand sign language or understand a different dialect of it, especially when integrated with voice recognition and interpretation.[31, 32]

Digital Twin

A digital twin is a virtual representation of a physical object. 3D motion sensing technology captures and represents what is happening to the physical object on to the virtual representation. This allows for real-time testing, adjustment, simulation and improvement of the object, say for example, an assembly line machine or a wind turbine.[33]

DEVELOPING AN EXPROVEMENT OUTLOOK

What are some of the types of questions that could have led to the physiotherapy industry finding exprovement solutions in the gaming industry?

- How can one make 'therapist equivalent' physiotherapy happen from home at a fraction of the cost?
- What parallel can one draw where movement or motion of any kind is monitored?
- What parallel can one draw where instructions can be seamlessly and instantly communicated from a remote location?
- How can one ensure great training quality irrespective of the trainer?
- Which industry brings the physical and virtual worlds together?

14

Spiderman, Goats and Haute Couture: What's the Link?

One of the most memorable moments from the movie *Spiderman 2* is the scene where Spiderman brings a runaway train to a standstill using just the strength of his webs.

As with many science fiction and superhero movies, we're often left wondering if the unimaginable feats pulled off on-screen would be possible in real life.

As it turns out, this particular one—using spiderwebs to stop a train—theoretically IS a possibility!

Spiderwebs, which look extremely delicate and can be destroyed with one sweep of a broom on cleaning day, are made of spider silk, a protein fibre spun by spiders that has remarkable properties:

- It has a high tensile strength, which means it can withstand a high load or stress before breaking.
- It is extremely elastic, which means it can be stretched to several times its own length before breaking.
- It has very low density, which means it is lightweight.
- It is water resistant.
- It has adhesive abilities.

While a single strand of this fibre might be easy to break, when scaled up, the story changes entirely.

According to *Science ABC*, the high tensile strength of spider silk makes it capable of absorbing a lot of kinetic energy—the momentum of a fully loaded subway train going at full speed was measured to be well within the limits of the elastic limit of the silk of the golden silk orb-weaver spider,[1] confirming that the scene from *Spiderman 2* is not as far-fetched as one might think.

A combination of some or all the properties of spider silk in a material thus opens up the possibility of several potential applications where lightweight but strong and/or elastic material capable of absorbing impact easily is required, such as ropes, cables, bulletproof vests, boat sails, parachutes etc.

According to *Science ABC*, 'independently conducted calculations point to a pencil-thick strand of spider silk being capable of catching a Boeing 747 and bringing it to complete rest.'[2]

The *New Yorker*, which describes spider silk as a 'wonder material' says of it, 'Famously tough, it can be stronger than steel and more tear-resistant than Kevlar. Although a human can walk through a spider web with relative ease, that is because each strand is only three-thousandths of a millimetre in diameter. Scaled up to a full millimetre, it's estimated that a spider web could catch a helicopter as effectively as it currently entraps flies. Spider silk is also extremely elastic and lightweight; some silks can stretch up to five times their length before breaking, and a strand long enough to encircle Earth would weigh just over a pound.'[3]

SPINNING A TANGLED WEB

So why aren't we harvesting spider silk the way we do silkworms?

For one, it requires a lot of spider silk to achieve any of the applications mentioned. The Boeing 747 example would require about 30 km of silk line, with the pencil-thick strand requiring silk from more than 1,00,000 spiders![4]

In another example, in 2012, a spider silk cape on display at the Victoria and Albert Museum took three years, eighty people and the silk from 1.2 million golden orb spiders from Madagascar to make.[5, 6, 7]

For another, spider silk is not easy to harvest. These tiny creatures aren't efficient at producing silk at the level or pace required for spinning into fabric, and neither are they cooperative. Compared to silkworms, spiders require a large space to spin their webs.

And finally, another major consideration is that spiders tend to be cannibalistic.

The problem therefore lies in the inability to scale up the production of natural spider silk to make it a viable operation.

This isn't for lack of trying though.

After numerous amateur attempts dating back several centuries, in the 1800s, France made a serious endeavour to turn spider silk into a proper industry, spurred on mainly by the efforts of Jesuit missionary Paul Camboué, who, whilst in Madagascar, along with M. Nogué invented 'a device to reel the spider's butter-yellow silk right out of its abdomen. The contraption, grimly termed "the guillotine", looked like a bite-sized version of the medieval stocks: the spider is placed in a wooden yoke, with its abdomen protruding out one side, and its legs and head the other. With a light touch to the arachnid's spinnerets, the dragline adheres to your finger, ready to be reeled out . . . this odd device represents the first real attempt to industrialise the process, to graft the living creature into a machine.'[8]

According to a piece in *The Literary Digest* magazine's December 1900 issue:

'It is to the ingenuity of M. Nogue, one of the sub directors, that we owe the apparatus which permits the thread to be wound mechanically and to be twisted and doubled in the quickest and most practical manner. This is done by means of a curious little machine, not easy to describe, in which the spiders are imprisoned by the throat while undergoing the operation. Young Malagasy girls go daily to a park near the school to gather three or four hundred spiders which they carry in osier baskets with wooden covers to be divested of their webs . . . Generally after having submitted to the reeling operation the spiders are put back in the park for a couple of weeks . . . [The silk's] color when first spun is a beautiful gold and it requires no carding or preparation of any sort before being woven. Will this be the silk of the future?'[9]

Sadly, it wasn't, as the cannibalistic nature of spiders eventually ended up making this attempt at commercialization impracticable. 'Forced into close proximity, they "spun their webs over the walls of their prison until it was so completely covered that no mosquitos or other insects could get in. Thus deprived of food, on the principle of the survival of the fittest, the stronger went on devouring the weaker until only a few were taken out alive, but these had attained an enormous size".'[10]

'Perhaps this is why spiders have failed to supplant silkworms: they are too factious to be farmed.'[11]

AT THE INTERSECTION OF MILK AND SILK

Scientists and researchers, though, were not yet ready to give up on industrial-scale spider silk production, and fast forwarding to modern times, one of the breakthroughs came in 2000, using a process—genetic modification—that had previously been associated with improving certain functionalities of organisms, and which began with the work of biochemists Herbert Boyer and Stanley Cohen, who in 1973 developed genetic engineering by inserting DNA from one bacteria into another.[12]

Since the first consumer genetically modified organism (GMO) product—human insulin to treat diabetes—was developed through genetic engineering in 1982,[13] the process has mainly been used to solve problems such as poor plant yield in agricultural crops and insufficient insulin production in the bodies of those with diabetes.

As a direct parallel to this type of bioengineering, why couldn't genetic modification be used to solve the problem of uncooperative, low yielding spiders?

This is where the curious case of the spider goat came in.

While the term spider goat may conjure up images of eight-legged goats shooting Spiderman-type webs from their hooves, the goats in question possess no such fascinating abilities. The only thing that makes them different from other goats is their milk, which contains an extra protein that can be extracted and spun into spider silk.[14]

The breakthrough came when Jeffrey D. Turner, drawing a parallel with the process of genetically modified organisms and combining it with the knowledge and experience he had gained while working on lactation at McGill University's animal sciences department in the mid-to-late 80s, arrived at the conclusion that the mammary gland is a perfect natural factory for the synthesizing and production of proteins.

He realized that 'theoretically, one could introduce foreign genes into an animal's mammary gland and get any given protein out of the animal without killing it, much as one milks a cow.

Given the enormous expense of manufacturing drugs artificially, transgenic animals offered a brilliant way to make dirt-cheap drugs; $50,000 worth of proteins could be extracted from a few buckets of milk at a cost of about $12 of hay! The logic seemed irresistible: the udder as factory outlet.'[15]

'In 1993, Turner was approached by the two venture-capitalist godfathers of Canada's budding biotech industry, Bernard Coupal and Ed Rygiel',[16] who had heard of Turner's work and were interested in the transgenic goat idea.

Together, they realized that instead of focusing on manufacturing drugs via the process—which was a risky proposition and involved complicated processes like obtaining FDA approvals—focusing on manufacturing a material instead might be a better business idea. Once they began to explore the potential uses of spider silk they were convinced.

In 1998, Turner learnt that Randy Lewis, a leading expert on spider genes at the University of Wyoming in Laramie, along with others had isolated the genes for spider silk and called him to help with the golden orb-weaver genes.[17]

Turner's subsequent company, Nexia Technologies, revealed in 2000 that it could transplant a spider's dragline silk gene into goats' DNA so that the goats could produce the silk protein in their milk. This silk-milk could then be used to manufacture a material called Biosteel that contained the properties of spider silk.[18]

Though Nexia Technologies went bankrupt in 2009[19], and Biosteel did not end up getting used on a mass scale, it nevertheless goes down in history as the first transgenic material ever made and showed the potential that genetic engineering could serve in developing biomaterials on a large scale.

THE LURE OF SPIDER SILK ENDURES

The focus over the past ten years or so has shifted to developing artificial spider silk rather than attempting to harvest it naturally.

To cite some examples, in 2017 Cambridge University revealed it had developed lab-made spider silk composed of 98 per cent water[20]; in 2020 Future BRH and University of Manchester scientists announced that they had successfully produced synthetic spider silk to create a new biodegradable glue alternative[21]; in 2021, Washington University announced that the synthetic spider silk it had been working on was actually stronger than its natural counterpart.[22]

While in 2002 Nexia Technologies foresaw 'tapping into the $500 million market for fishing materials as well as the $1.6 billion market for industrial fibers'[23], today's forecast is that the global sports fishing equipment market is expected to reach $16 billion by 2027[24] and the global synthetic fibres market is expected to reach $85.07 billion in 2025.[25]

SPIDER SILK: SPREADING ITS WEB ACROSS INDUSTRIES

A number of entrepreneurs, seeing the vast potential for spider silk in markets like these and others, have started up companies that manufacture artificial spider silk for applications in a variety of industries:

Polymers

Polymers find applications in many industries as they essentially combine the characteristics of different molecules to create a stronger chained network. Stronger products and economical large-scale production remain the two main goals of the manufacturing process of polymers. Biotechnology companies like US-based Kraig Biocraft Laboratories synthesise spider silk and its polymers to enable the next generation of biomaterials. The company develops multiple types of polymers that incorporate its patented spider silk protein sequences.

The solution reduces the overall cost of production to a level that allows for the mass adoption of the technology.[26]

Textiles

The display of the spider silk shawl and cape (mentioned earlier) at the Victoria and Albert Museum in 2012, which was a result of the collaboration between textile expert Simon Peers and fashion designer Nicholas Godley, generated a lot of interest in the fashion industry.

'I've been fascinated by spider silk since I saw the gold spider-silk cape of the V&A museum,' says Dutch fashion designer Iris van Herpen, known for fusing technology with traditional haute couture craftsmanship.[27] He sees tremendous potential in artificial spider silk and is in talks with biotechnology company Spiber to explore how the material can be made to work in his designs and couture processes.

'Founded by two Keio University graduates in bioinformatics, Kazuhide Sekiyama and Junichi Sugahara, Spiber spearheads innovation in the protein-based materials space. The company uses a library of thousands of genetic samples from a variety of arachnids and insects as a base for devising an inventory of materials, from textiles to "leather", "fur" and even "plastic".'[28]

British fashion designer Stella McCartney, renowned for her conscious fashion philosophy, collaborated with another company, Bolt Threads, in 2017 to create a unique spider silk custom dress, which was displayed at the Museum of Modern Art in New York.

'US-based company Bolt Threads manufactures spider silk fibers without spiders. The production process replicates the technique used by spiders to produce the webbing while the artificial spider silk mimics the high strength, flexibility and durability of the naturally produced version.'[29]

Beyond haute couture and conscious fashion, spider silk is also finding applications on account of its strength and durability.

'High-performance textile firms are starting to exploit the substance. The North Face teamed up with Tokyo-based Spiber to create a biotech concept jacket called the Moon Parka. Priced at $1000, the parka is created from genetically engineered silk-protein DNA sequences which researchers insert into bacteria that are then fed sugar. The extraordinary item has a luminous "moon gold" sheen ascribed to the hue of the orb-weaver's silk on which the material is based.'[30]

With further genetic modification, such as Washington University's announcement that its version is stronger than the natural spider silk, the material, which is touted to be stronger than steel, tougher than Kevlar and more flexible than nylon, could find a host of applications in industries where the strength of such a textile could play a life-saving role, such as defence, sports and even aerospace. Artificial spider silk with the combination of less expensive and easily available materials could take the applicability of spider silk to the next level.

Furthermore, digital technologies, such as artificial intelligence and machine learning, coupled with advanced data analytics, could play a vital role in identifying combinations of materials to make the spider silk lighter, stronger and more flexible—in short, to improve the specific strength or strength-to-weight ratio of the material, and, at the same time, make it affordable.

Thus, in equal parts for its aesthetic appeal, feel, strength and environmental friendliness, biodegradable synthetic spider silk is poised to be one of the next big things in the textile industry, which today faces the external pressure of coming up with more ethical alternatives on the one hand, and severe competition within the industry to produce innovative products that attract buyers and consumers, on the other.

Environment-Friendly Plastic Alternative

The emission of hazardous gases, such as carbon dioxide, its impact on global warming and resulting attempts to establish a more sustainable ecosystem, are topics being discussed now more than ever.

Eco-friendly material is one of the topics in particular garnering tremendous traction globally.

To promote eco-friendly practices, countries across the globe are taking numerous measures to control the use of materials hazardous to Mother Nature. As per a report published by the United Nations, more than seventy-five countries across the world have institutionalized laws and policies to limit the use of plastic bags by partial or complete bans.[31]

What does this have to do with spider silk? Well, genetically modified spider silk could hold the answer to the problem of single-use plastic.

'A vegan spider silk, created by researchers at the University of Cambridge, is a plastic-like, freestanding film that can be used to replace plastic in common household products.'[32]

Xampla, a spin-off of the University of Cambridge, is working on commercializing the biodegradable alternative to single-use plastics that is made out of plant products but where the molecular structure is manipulated to resemble spider silk.[33]

Military

Another area of large potential is military applications, where several spider silk properties come into play. Here are some examples:

Michigan-based Kraig Biocraft Laboratories, which is in contract with the US Army, has developed an elastic yet durable material called Dragon Silk, born out of genetically engineered silkworms that contain spider DNA. The material can be converted for use in military helmets, uniforms, body armour and tents. It is said to be stronger and far more elastic than Kevlar, which is what is generally used in army combat helmets—while Kevlar's flexibility is 3 per cent, Dragon Silk's flexibility is 30 per cent to 40 per cent.[34, 35]

In 2018 the company also announced that it had delivered ballistic panels made of Dragon Silk to the US Army where they were to be evaluated for their ability to stop bullets and other ballistic threats like shrapnel.[36]

Being lightweight, material made out of spider silk stands to benefit military personnel in particular, who often have to carry heavy loads (around 15 kgs or more) over long distances in the form of protective clothing, tactical vests, parachutes etc.

Scientists at the Air Force Research Lab (AFRL) and Purdue University have also been working on introducing natural silk's temperature-regulating properties to synthetics like artificial spider silk.

Enhancing body armour and adding comfort for troops is one of many improvements hoped for by a team led by Dr Augustine Urbas

at the AFRL Functional Materials Division of the Materials and
Manufacturing Directorate.

'Understanding natural silk will enable us to engineer multifunctional
fibers with exponential possibilities. The ultra-strong fibers outperform
the mechanical characteristics of many synthetic materials as well as
steel . . . These materials could be the future in comfort and strength in
body armor and parachute material for the war fighter.'[37]

Medicine

It is said that in the times of the ancient Greeks and Romans, wads of
spider webs were used as wound dressings to stop bleeding and to speed
up the process of healing in those injured in battle.

While it might seem odd, spider silk is an incredible material when
it comes to first aid. It is biocompatible, biodegradable, protein-based,
and it isn't known to cause any immune, inflammatory or allergic
reactions.[38]

Building on this idea, in 2017, scientists from the University
of Nottingham announced that they had, after five years of work,
succeeded in developing an antibiotic synthetic spider silk that could
be used as a dressing to close open wounds and in drug delivery as well.

This genetically modified substance uses E.coli bacteria-synthesized
silk and adheres molecules to its structure, infusing it with different
substances that make for a better bandage.[39]

Seevix, a company based in Israel, manufactures artificial spider
silk that possesses such self-healing capabilities. Its 'composite bio-
medical materials can be used in 3D tissue engineering technologies
as well as in medical devices, which require higher strength, durability
and impact absorbance, better wear and tear resistance, lighter weight,
miniaturization and antimicrobial properties.'[40]

Some of its products include bio-ink, 3D scaffolds, bio-dressing
and surface coatings for implants, to modify the biocompatibility of
materials, such as those used in reconstructive implants, catheters,
leads, valves and stents.

In a recent development, scientists from the Karolinska Institute in
Sweden and the Swedish University of Agricultural Sciences announced

that spider silk proteins can be fused to biologically active proteins and be converted into a gel at body temperature.

This means that it is likely to be possible to develop an injectable protein solution that forms a gel inside the body. 'The ability to design hydrogels with specific functions opens up for a range of possible applications. Such a gel could, for example, be used to achieve a controlled release of drugs into the body.'[41]

Cosmetics

Eco-friendly biopolymer spider silk can enhance cosmetic products in several ways and boost 'the performance and capabilities of cosmetic products by enhancing elasticity, strength and durability to achieve significant visible improvement in skin and hair care.'

It can thus find applications as an antioxidant and in pollution protection, moisture retention, anti-ageing and sun protection products. Companies like Seevix and AMSilk manufacture high-quality synthetic silk biopolymers for such applications.

Aerospace

A material that is lightweight yet strong and flexible is of immense interest to the aerospace industry.

It was announced in 2018 that Airbus has signed a partnership with German biotech firm AMSilk to develop a new biomaterial to be used in the construction of future high-performance planes.[42]

At the time a spokesperson for AMSilk said, 'In recent years, the aerospace industry has shifted from metal or steel fuselage and wings to carbon fiber composite materials, mainly to decrease the weight of planes and as a consequence save fuel . . . The new composite material AMSilk and Airbus are developing could be used to develop complex and more flexible structures on the one hand, and to reduce repair costs and plane downtime on the other hand.'[43]

Further, since the manufacturing process is a biotechnological one, this is also a sustainable option.

THE FUTURE OF GENETICALLY ENGINEERED MATERIAL

While genetic modification has generally been used to create or enhance products meant for human consumption or ingestion in some form, the case of genetically engineered spider silk draws a parallel, showing how the technology could be applied to create materials with desirable properties that can add tremendous value across industries. Further, with the elimination of approvals and time taken to bring a product for human beings to market, one can start to commercialize the idea immediately.

Beyond spider silk, nature has a whole world of biomimetic inspiration waiting to be tapped in such a manner.

Read about another nature-inspired genetically engineered product by scanning the QR code:

The spider silk case also brings into focus that while we may turn to nature to find a parallel, and often better solution to problems in a variety of industries, it is not always possible to directly apply what nature has to offer. In such circumstances science could help us turn our understanding of  the parallel into an exproved solution in terms of not only performance, but environment-friendliness as well.

DEVELOPING AN EXPROVEMENT OUTLOOK

Here are some examples of the type of thinking that could lead to further biomimetic exprovements:

- Nature is made up of a lot of materials with a diverse range of properties. Which of these properties can the world benefit from?
- What parallels can be drawn with statements like 'I wish my car could leap like a kangaroo'? By drawing this parallel, can

a kangaroo's gene help develop the next generation of car tyres or shock absorbers?

- What other fictional material can come to life? Could it be Superman's bullet-proof suit, for example?
- Can nature become our factory for making more materials?

15

A Fifth-Century Invention Helps Solve a Twenty-First-Century Problem

That the world needs more sustainable forms of energy, and quickly, is not new news.

However, it does merit bringing into focus events of the last few years that have highlighted the urgency to move away from fossil fuels. Without getting into the environmental aspects—an entire emergency of its own—looking at it purely from an economic and political point of view, the world is facing an energy crisis that is only deepening with each passing year.

As the global economy began to recover from the Covid-19 pandemic, 2021 saw demand-driven record high energy prices.[1] Another more recent driver has been the war in Ukraine, prompting the International Energy Agency (IEA) to urge countries to reduce their dependence on oil and gas.[2]

One of the countries most affected by the crisis is China.[3]

According to a *Bloomberg* article of October 2021, 'The hit from China's energy crunch is starting to ripple throughout the globe, hurting everyone from Toyota Motor Corp. to Australian sheep farmers and makers of cardboard boxes. The extreme electricity shortage caused by soaring prices of coal in the world's largest exporter is set to hurt China's own growth, and the knock-on impact to supply chains could crimp a global economy struggling to emerge from the pandemic.'[4]

It is perhaps fitting then, that one of the newer solutions to tackling the energy crisis draws its inspiration from a simple invention that is said to have originated in China in the fifth century.[5]

A HIGH-FLYING IDEA

The invention in question is the kite, which flies because of the energy it draws from the wind.

But what if this energy could be captured and utilized to power other things?

It is with an idea similar to this, which draws a parallel between how a kite is powered and asking what else that power could be used for, that Stephan Wrage, founder of SkySails, while flying a kite as a teenager on the beach, began to envisage a system that could make use of the clean, abundant and free natural resource of wind.[6]

Over 2000 years after the first kite was purportedly invented in China, a giant computer-controlled SkySails power kite, similar in look to a paraglider's sail, could be seen floating high above the beautiful beaches of Mauritius.

The kite flies in a figure-of-eight pattern in order to get the strongest pull possible to produce energy and is autonomously flown via the aid of software. There are no turbines up in the air; the energy is generated on-ground via the tug on a tether line from the sail, which is wound around a winch. As the kite flies across the wind, it pulls against the tether and unwinds the winch, driving a generator on the ground that produces electricity. The kite is then allowed to float while it is reeled back in, and the cycle begins again.[7]

This pilot project between SkySails and Mauritius-based IBL Energy Holdings Ltd, which is supported by a national scheme that aims to make renewables 40 per cent of the country's energy mix by 2030, has the gigantic, three-bedroom-apartment-sized kite harnessing enough energy to power fifty homes. It became the world's first fully autonomous commercial 'airborne wind energy' system in 2021.[8]

At present, in this fairly new sector of the wind energy industry, most kite-powered systems are capable of generating enough electricity to power only around fifty to sixty homes, which in comparison to a

2.75 MW wind turbine doesn't seem like much. However, many of the companies in the business have plans in the pipeline to develop systems that would be capable of generating 3.5 MW or enough energy to power around 2800 homes.

HOW A FIFTH-CENTURY INVENTION COULD FACILITATE TWENTY-FIRST-CENTURY EXPROVEMENT

While the International Energy Agency has predicted that wind energy will increase elevenfold in the next thirty years (and the cost of wind power reducing by 40 per cent over the past decade has supported this prediction), wind energy harvesting in its current form—via windmills—faces a number of drawbacks that the kite-flying exprovement has the potential to overcome.

While most advancements in the field of wind energy have focused on improving the design of the windmill (a design and system that was developed in 644 AD[9]) the exprovement of power-generating kites incorporates an entirely new design and new way of harvesting wind power—one that is cheaper, has improved accessibility and larger potential application.

Exponential improvement in the renewable energy sector could be achieved in the following ways:

By Reducing Burden on Precious Resources

Land: Traditional wind farms or solar power plants generally require a sizable amount of land. A system like Skysails' SKS PN-14 requires just a 30-foot container as its ground station to deliver up to 200 kW average cycle power.

Time: Typically, a single 500 kW wind turbine project would take no less than two years from the wind feasibility study phase to the installation and commissioning phase, while a 1 MW solar plant would take about sixteen to twenty weeks to install. Kite-powered energy systems take considerably less time to set up, with some taking less than twenty-four hours to install and begin generating electricity, thanks to their plug-and-play operation.[10]

Material: 'A study by Airborne Wind Europe, a trade association, found that a 50 MW kite farm would use 913 metric tons of material over a twenty-year lifespan, compared with 2868 metric tons for a typical wind tower farm. Using less material could make kite-based systems both greener and cheaper to build.'[11]

Capital: Given that they require less material (up to 90 per cent less than wind turbines[12]) land and time, power kites, manufactured by companies like Germany-based SkySails, Netherlands-based Kitepower and Norway-based Kitemill, require less investment to begin a project that can gradually be scaled up.

By Improving Accessibility to Wind Energy

Geographically: In some remote locations and in deep waters, traditional windmills can be impossible to install, whereas airborne wind energy (AWE) systems can be 'tethered to an anchored barge in deep waters, where a traditional wind turbine cannot stand firm.'[13] This could also help make territories like isolated islands self-reliant or less dependent on external energy sources.

'Airborne wind energy systems work extremely well on islands due to high coastal winds ensuring strong steady power generation. Islands offer fundamental challenges for any energy supply, as the cost of running a power line or even supplying fuel to local generators is often several times what the same would cost on the mainland.'[14]

Kites could also make it possible to build wind farms on land that isn't windy enough for conventional wind turbine towers.[15]

While AWEs may not always be a viable option in crowded cities, for some remote and inaccessible regions of the world, they may be the only possible electricity generation solution.

Logistically: While each individual unit of a traditional windmill is bulky, heavy and involves huge transportation costs, the more compact kite power units can be transported in a single twenty- to thirty-foot container.[16]

'These systems come in a container and can be dropped off wherever there's a road or dock.'[17]

By Offering a More Adaptable Wind Energy Design

There is a limit to the maximum height a windmill can reach—it simply becomes impractical to construct one beyond a certain height. The height of AWE systems, however, can be adjusted as and when required, depending on where the wind is blowing hardest at a particular time—something that often changes with the seasons.

Most importantly, these systems can reach 'up to 800m high (half a mile), far above the 200 to 300m (660 to 980ft) tip of the tallest wind turbines. The theoretical global limit of wind power at high altitude has been estimated to be about 4.5 times greater than what could be harvested at ground level.'[18]

AWE systems are also quieter than traditional wind turbines.

By Making Sustainable Energy a Short-Term Power Requirement Alternative

The easy-to-install kites have the added advantage of making sustainable, off-grid energy a possibility for short-term energy requirements, such as for military installations, mining operations in remote areas, disaster relief and at festivals and other events.

By Enabling Another Form of Energy Hybridization

While solar power has been the main electricity hybridization alternative—from large installations to individual homes—kite-powered energy now opens up the possibility for wind power to supplement traditional electricity sources.

Like solar power, AWE systems have the huge advantage of putting control in the hands of the end user, enabling them to make a more sustainable choice, without having to depend on government policies.

KITE POWER: TAKING WING IN VARIOUS INDUSTRIES

While kite power is in no way poised to replace traditional windmills just yet, airborne wind energy has a lot of potential going forward, reflected in studies and reports such as the US Department of Energy's 2021 report submitted to Congress, which concluded that such systems are 'likely to be capable of harvesting the same order of magnitude of energy as ground-based wind systems in the US.'[19]

Some of the barriers that are yet to be properly understood and are being studied include the potential threat these kites pose to birds or to the flight path of drones; or what could happen if a tether line of the system breaks.

But the evidence to support their envisioned success is strong— here are some examples of industries that are already using AWE systems.

Defence

Interestingly, kites have been used in military operations going as far back as the times of the Chinese Song Dynasty, when a kite called a Fire Crow, carrying incendiary powder, a fuse and a burning stick of incense, was developed as an aerial weapon.[20]

There have been recorded instances of kites being innovatively used in different parts of the world for signalling, communication and reconnaissance missions from way back in 647 right up to the Second World War, when the British Army used kites in various ways, including as anti-aircraft target practice, for lofting communications antennae and even to 'haul human lookouts into the air for observation purposes.'[21]

A reflection of the times we live in, 2021 saw the launch of a project between Kitepower and the Dutch Ministry of Defence as part of the latter's aim to 'reduce dependence on fossil fuels across its worldwide campaigns' and to test the potential of an 'environmentally friendly solution for deployments in remote locations, where logistical supply lines cannot be guaranteed, by reducing diesel consumption and increasing energy independence.'[22]

The project, which is being carried out in Aruba, serves to validate some of the advantages of AWE systems mentioned earlier, which are also particularly relevant to the defence industry as it often requires electricity in remote areas that have challenging terrain:

Easy Transportability: The consignment of Kitepower's Falcon 100 kW AWE systems was shipped from the Netherlands to Aruba and then transported via narrow roads in two trucks to the remote location of the project site—something that would have posed a huge problem and likely been impossible with a windmill.

*Potential for Use in Remote Areas:*The island of Aruba serves as a good testing ground to prove the efficacy of AWE systems in remote areas, especially islands, which in general pose a challenge for traditional energy supply systems, yet have the ideal geographical and climate conditions, such as strong winds, to make wind energy a successful solution.

As of March 2022, 'test results from the Aruba project have shown that the Falcon 100kW kite is capable of generating about 100kW worth of electricity, which is enough to power around 150 average households. For the moment, the system is still too expensive for averagely populated areas where other sources of energy are available as well. For more remote and isolated places though, such as Aruba and other small islands for example, but also locations like mines, offshore oil rigs and infrastructure projects, the Falcon 100kW could make a real difference as alternatives tend to be much more expensive in such locations.'[23]

Agriculture and Farming

Some farmers are beginning to look at installing these systems as an additional source of income or to power their own requirements, making maximum use of their lands in a sustainable way, like at the dairy farm

Kaasboerderij Mulder in the Netherlands. Scan the QR code to learn more:

'In agriculture, an energy supply disruption of even a short duration could mean a substantial reduction or the complete loss of an entire growing season.'[24] At the same time, farmlands, with their huge open spaces in rural areas, are a great place for taking advantage of wind energy. While wind turbines are already well established in this area, AWE systems present an additional, cost-effective, even 'cash crop' alternative as shown at the Mulder farm, while also reducing farmers' dependency on the grid.

Shipping

Though the Mauritius project is SkySails' first fully commercial system of its kind, it is not the first time the company has demonstrated the ability of its AWE systems. In fact, the business began with the purpose of using kite energy to tow ships at sea, something that has generally been reliant on a crude polluting fossil fuel called 'bunker fuel'.[25]

Back in 2008, the world's first commercial ship powered by a giant kite invented by Stephan Wrage set sail from Germany to Venezuela.[26] This test voyage achieved a saving of between $1000 to $1500 per day in fuel costs.[27, 28]

According to the company, by generating up to 2000 kW of propulsion power in good wind conditions, the SkySails system can save up to ten tonnes of oil per day.[29]

The success of this auxiliary fuel-saving energy source in the shipping industry can in many ways be seen to have served as a prototype to test its efficacy and viability, and to show how its effectiveness in the shipping industry paved the way for it being applied in the broader renewable energy industry.

Offshore Energy

Offshore AWE systems present a lightweight, flexible and cheaper alternative to traditional offshore wind energy solutions, which generally require concrete foundations and steel structures.

The AWE alternative requires only a floating platform out at sea, and the entire system can be shut down quickly during bad weather, making wind power generation possible in previously unfavourable waters and in regions prone to hurricanes and typhoons.[30]

Solar Energy

Besides the hybridization of conventional sources of power, such as that from diesel generators (where the conventional source can be turned into a backup source, reducing the need to be at the mercy of fluctuating oil prices and minimizing carbon footprints in the process), kite power could even hybridize renewable sources of energy, especially at solar energy parks, where the installation of windmills isn't effective as they can cause a shadow effect on solar panels and involve considerable set up costs and time.

In addition, wind power can comfortably cater to a solar plant's energy consumption requirements at night, when there is no sun, improving the economic viability of such projects.[31]

SOARING TO NEW HEIGHTS

The next era of kite power is poised to feature alternate kite designs as well as the integration of new technology from other parallel industries.

Onboard Electricity Generation

Some companies, such as Kitekraft, have AWE systems that generate the electricity onboard the kite, not on the ground as in the SkySails system. 'Onboard generation uses a rigid kite, similar to an aeroplane wing, which supports small wind turbines. When the kite flies, the wind runs the turbines and electricity generated by the craft is sent down the tether to the ground station.'[32]

Technology Integration 2.0

In early 2022, a company called Airseas, which was founded by former Airbus engineers, installed its 10,000-sqare-foot kite system called

Seawing on a cargo ship called Ville de Bordeaux, which, in its six-month trial period will sail back and forth between Europe and North America, with the company hoping to show that 'Seawing can decrease the carbon footprint of the shipping industry while making business sense too', while also noting that 'fuel bills account for over 50 per cent of a ship's operational costs.'[33, 34]

What makes this event notable is that it is the first-ever cargo ship to be installed with a fully automatic kite-power system—one that drew its inspiration from automated flight control systems developed for the aerospace industry. The company guarantees 100 per cent automation due to the use of digital twin technology in the following way:

'Leveraging our aeronautical expertise, Airseas has developed an advanced automation system that manages all aspects of the wing's operation and optimises the vessel's routing. The kite and ship are entirely recreated in a simulation model, which acts as a "digital twin" for the physical system. Equipped with various sensors (inertial unit, GPS, anemometer, etc.) the physical system is in constant dialogue with the digital model, with updates every 300 milliseconds to guarantee the most efficient use of the system.

Our digital twin technology places the kite in its ideal flight window to maximise traction power and fuel savings. Based on digitally calculated scenarios, the wing adjusts its position depending on the wind direction and speed, as well as the ship speed and route. This optimises performance, thereby reducing engine effort and generating maximum savings.'[35]

Seawing uses a nylon parafoil kite, which is a type of kite that has no rigid spars, is easy to fold and store, and maintains its shape by wind filling the space between its upper and lower layers.[36, 37] This improves aerodynamics and is the kind used by NASA and SpaceX during landings.[38]

Tidal Kites

Besides being used to harvest energy from the skies, companies are also developing underwater kites that can harvest energy from another abundant natural resource—flowing water.

Some of them include SRI International's manta ray-inspired underwater kites and Minesto's 'sea dragons', which are similar looking to aircraft and whose 'movement is generated by the lift exerted by the water flow—just as a plane flies by the force of air flowing over its wings. The moving "flight path" allows the kite to sweep a larger area at a speed several times greater than that of the underwater current. This, in turn, enables the machines to amplify the amount of energy generated by the water alone.'[39]

The latter have been used to harvest power from a fjord in the Faroe Islands and supply the same to the islands' electric company SEV—the first time a tidal kite has successfully produced electricity for a grid. Going forward, this project is expected to play a key role in the ambitious goal of the Faroe Islands relying 100 per cent on renewable energy by 2030.[40]

Another project of Minesto's in Northern Wales was the company's first utility-scale project and the world's first low-velocity tidal energy project—proof of tidal kites' ability to make a significant contribution to renewable energy in the future. After the successful test of a 0.5 MW demonstrator in 2018, the project is set to become a commercial tidal energy array with a total installed capacity of up to 80 MW.[41]

FULL CIRCLE EXPROVEMENT

An interesting and perhaps slightly ironic point is the observation that the shipping industry in its earliest days relied on wind to power its sails, and has now seemingly come full circle, after using steam, coal and then other sources of power over the years.

This also brings the realization that sometimes an exprovement can be born from returning to an original way of doing things, but with a new perspective and more often than not, advances in technology.

According to Kitepower CTO Joep Breuer, the idea to generate electricity via a kite existed back in 1980, when 'Miles L. Loyd published a paper with several formulas which illustrated how a kite can generate energy . . . It later gained traction in our country thanks to the Dutch astronaut Wubbe Ockels. He personally noticed by the way his hand got burned when flying a kite on the beach just how big a force it was capable of. "We should do something with that", he thought.'[42]

But it was only many years later that these ideas were able to come to fruition because the materials that could make it happen and the computational software that runs these systems didn't yet exist. As an example, Breuer highlights the Dyneema lines used to tether the kites, which are seven times lighter than steel, but just as strong.

DEVELOPING AN EXPROVEMENT OUTLOOK

What are some of the types of questions that could have led to considering a kite as a tool to generate wind energy?

- How can one capture wind energy at higher altitudes where the wind is stronger?
- How can one reach a higher altitude without having to build massive structures to get to the altitude?
- Can the energy used to fly a kite be captured?
- Can the energy used to fly a paragliding unit be captured?
- Instead of propelling a ship, can the sail of a ship capture wind energy?
- Can a kite be flown and controlled automatically?
- Can the process of unfurling the string of a kite in order to make it go higher be converted into a system that produces energy?

16

Can Banks Borrow and Lend Time?

'Hello, I'm Nora. Until recently I was living on my own and was managing well, despite a few health problems. I'd been living there my whole married life, had friends in the neighbourhood and my daughter lived near enough.

I'm eighty-five, and my husband died a few years ago. After that I did start to have a bit of trouble managing around the house. If I'm honest, I felt I was getting a bit forgetful at times. About a year ago I had a fall at home and my daughter called the ambulance, and I had to go to hospital.

I was checked over and returned home quickly enough but while I was still getting over that I became sick again with an infection. My daughter started to stay with me more as I wasn't sleeping well. She also helped to make sure I took the right tablets. I was supposed to get home help and see a specialist doctor for older people—a geriatrician doctor I think. This was taking a long time, and while I was waiting I had another fall at home, and this time I broke a bone in my pelvis . . . it took a long time to see all the people I needed to see—therapists, social workers and every 'ologist' under the sun. To cut a long story short, I ended up in hospital for weeks.

I tried my best; the nurses and the staff took good care of me, but it was tough. It was noisy, which kept me awake at night, and I was in a busy ward with people of all ages and stages of life coming and going with all sorts of problems. I had to keep repeating my story to the nurses and the doctors. I was in pain; too sore to move around by myself. I got lonely and was upset at times. I hated that I couldn't do normal things or take care of myself.

I just wanted to go home and get back to myself, but eventually the doctor decided I needed a nursing home and that's where I am now.[1]

This is an extract from a video made by the Health Service Executive (HSE), the publicly funded healthcare system in Ireland that is responsible for providing health and personal social services.

Though the video was made to highlight how the agency's 'Integrated Care Programme for Older Persons could provide person-centred, coordinated care across health and social care services for the elderly', it also highlights the plight of ageing people across the world.

Besides advancements in geriatric medicine and the emergence of fields like social gerontology and biogerontology, improved eldercare management can help reduce long-term hospital stays, make the experience more pleasant and allow the elderly to live in their own homes, where they are the happiest, for a longer period of time, rather than at a nursing home.

A proactive, rather than a reactive strategy is the need of the hour, which includes things like early identification of at-risk elderly people and better coordination among doctors, nurses, rehabilitation staff, insurance companies, pharmacies and at-home help, as well as having a single point of contact.

THE ELEPHANT IN THE ROOM

But while all these improvements help to ensure longer, better lives, there is no skirting around the fact that they all require money—and a lot of it—as anyone who has had to care for an elderly person will attest to.

There is, however, one more parallel requirement, other than money, that is needed to enable successful eldercare, and that is time. Of the two, time is also the element that brings comfort and meaning, something that all the money in the world cannot buy.

So what if there was a way to 'buy' people's time . . . with time?

As confusing as that may sound, a time bank does exactly that.

When it comes to eldercare, time banking involves someone giving their time to look after, provide a service (such as doing grocery shopping or providing physical rehabilitation coaching) or simply spend time with an elderly person. The time they've 'spent' gets 'credited' to their 'account', which they in turn can 'withdraw' in terms of services or time they can 'buy' when they reach senior citizen status.

Several countries, including Switzerland and China, are using the time banking concept as an old-age assistance programme.

'While time used to be donated on a voluntary basis or as part of a mutual support agreement among neighbours or friends, technology has made time banking a reality. A huge number of individuals can track their time accurately and quickly, turning it into money that can be banked and exchanged for desired goods and services.'[2]

In China, 'the services for the elderly range from physical assistance to emotional comfort, and include recreation, education, travel companionship, health knowledge, legal aid, financial advice and computers.'[3]

AN OLD CONCEPT GETS A NEW APPLICATION

The exprovement of using time banking for eldercare, which conceptually is a parallel from the unrelated industry of banking and financial services, is a new way of paying it forward.

Usually, providing for the future is done in terms of saving money, which is subject to the negative effects of inflation, resulting in people having to scale down their lifestyle when they become old.

With a shift in perception and by drawing a parallel to how money is banked, one can see the value of banking time with regard to caring for the elderly in a more beneficial way, while the creation of this parallel form of currency brings about an entirely new way to be able to afford eldercare.

With time banking, one hour today will still hold the value of one hour forty years in the future. Some might even argue that forty years from today one hour will be much more valuable than it is today!

A TOOL FOR EXPONENTIAL IMPROVEMENT IN ELDERCARE

According to the World Health Organization, by the end of 2030, the number of people sixty years and older will grow by 56 per cent, from

962 million (2017) to 1.4 billion (2030). By 2050, the global population of older people will more than double, to 2.1 billion.[4]

These staggering numbers leave no doubt that healthcare systems around the world are going to be overloaded in the years to come, especially in developing countries.

Here are the ways in which the exprovement of time banking can make a difference when it comes to eldercare:

Increased At-Home Care

According to a 2018 article in *Wharton Magazine*, 'with the senior population increasing dramatically, caring for them at home isn't just the cheapest method—it might be the most effective, too.'[5]

The time bank concept for eldercare could be the catalyst that helps this come to fruition. At-home services today can be quite expensive, but if elderly people are able to access at-home care that doesn't cost anything, more people would opt for it, also freeing up capacity at hospitals and nursing homes for those who absolutely require it. In turn, service providers could dedicate a certain number of their working hours to offering such services, as an investment for when they are older.

Opting for at-home care could improve the quality of life for senior citizens in the following ways:

- One-on-one assistance at home tends to be more personalized, which could lead to speedier recovery, as opposed to an individual's particular needs potentially being overlooked in a larger group living facility.
- Being able to continue living in one's own home has been known to help maintain or increase confidence levels—a key element in mental health and well-being.
- 'Research indicates seniors who remain in their own homes enjoy active and productive lives. Older adults are happier and feel more secure while living in familiar surroundings, and they have the freedom to come and go as they please. Seniors with cognitive impairment are also less likely to feel agitated or confused in their own homes.'[6]

- It also allows the elderly to potentially live close to their family. Sometimes opting for a good eldercare facility might require having to move far away.

Alternative Earning Ability

There is sometimes a gap between when one retires and one begins to start needing assistance as one ages. With time banking, this period can be used to earn time credits for the future. 'According to Wei Na, a professor of the School of Public Administration and Policy at the Renmin University of China, time banks can also tap the potential of relatively younger elderly who have enough time and energy after retirement to volunteer for the senile elderly who need help. "It is a low-cost strategy to deal with an aging society," she said.'[7]

Psychological Benefits

Volunteering one's time, whether in a professional capacity or just as someone who wants to help out, often leads to building connections between the two people involved and can go a long way towards improving the mental well-being of both parties. For example, as an article about time banking in China describes, a ninety-seven-year-old lady who recently lost her son and the younger lady who volunteers to help her and who recently lost her parents, are able to derive strength and comfort from each other, grieve together and in some ways fill the void in their lives.[8]

Time banking is in many ways similar to volunteering, which at its core is deeply rooted in altruism. Because of how it operates, it thus allows for more opportunities of deep and meaningful connections, when compared to what happens when one exchanges money for a service.

PARALLEL APPLICATIONS OF TIME BANKING

Time banking has been operating in various countries around the world for many years, but as a concept, is said to have originated in Japan with the work of Teruko Mizushima, who first proposed it following World War II, with the first-time bank being founded in 1973.

At the time, given the traditional role of women in caring for the elderly, which often involved women giving up all other roles and activities (including education, paid work or hobbies), Mizushima's time banking concept was developed as a way to benefit women caregivers and was designed to operate within the framework of traditional Japanese society.

'The direct target group as beneficiaries was women carers. They benefited directly by the opportunity to connect and organise mutual help within their group and by the possibility that by sustaining their groups over time through continuous recruitment they could also secure help for themselves in their old age by banking time credits and redeeming these in later life. This "purist" model of time banking can be considered as a person-to-person exchange, using only time as currency.

Mizushima's model had a mix of horizontal time exchange (giving and receiving services in the current period) and vertical time exchange (banking of time credits for future use).'[9]

The spread of time banking internationally, though, had a lot to do with the work of the creator of Time Dollars and founder of TimeBanks.org, Edgar Cahn, who was keen on experimenting with a new way to link untapped social capacity to unmet social needs.

A 2015 article[10] by Cahn and Christine Gray gives examples of time banking applications in other industries besides eldercare:

Business Development

In Los Angeles, a network of time banks came up with a dual-currency loan that reduced the burden of loan repayment for those wishing to start a small business. Under the system, borrowers could use time credits to pay associated loan processing fees. Borrowers could also participate in a programme that matched entrepreneurs with mentors providing expertise in areas such as strategy, business plan development, branding and communications.

Social Services

The Parent Support Network of Rhode Island uses time banking to offer services to parents who have children with bipolar disorder, schizophrenia or autism. 'Through the network, parents receive time credits for providing child care, coaching, transportation, and personal support to each other. The children, meanwhile, earn time credits by participating in their own mutual support group. This use of time banking has enabled parents to prevent the institutionalization of their children, and it has saved the state government millions of dollars that would otherwise be spent on support services.'[11]

Repairs and Maintenance

An example is the Westside Repair Café programme run by Our Time Bank in Los Angeles. At a four-hour event that is held every two or three months, one can bring their faulty appliances, broken furniture etc. and have it fixed by volunteer repair experts. 'One goal of the event is to give people an incentive to keep old items that would otherwise end up in a landfill.'[12]

Such a programme is easily replicable and can be designed so that people can earn and spend time credits while encouraging a 'Don't Refuse To Reuse' attitude.

Disaster Relief

An example of time banking resulting in exprovement (in the form of quicker response time) during a disaster (a circumstance where response time is crucial to saving lives) is when TimeBank members responded in the wake of Hurricane Andrew (Florida, 1992) before the National Guard or the Red Cross were able to arrive, and provided guidance to relief teams that were unfamiliar with the terrain.[13]

In 2019, another report spoke about the effectiveness of the Lyttelton TimeBank during the disaster management of the New Zealand earthquakes.

'During the earthquakes, the Lyttelton TimeBank had the best local communication system through which vital information flowed to members and local residents. Using a range of communication modes, timely information was provided to residents on practical and safety precautions, as well as the availability of clean water, food, services, and other resources. As a partner working with emergency workers and first responders, the Lyttelton TimeBank had a better knowledge of the community. It acted as a hub organisation activating its extensive social network through which valuable resources could flow. For example, when at-risk families and groups were identified, TB members offered home visits, emotional support, food, accommodations, repairs, and so forth. Problems were solved in the immediate aftermath of the earthquakes, such as dismantling chimneys that could be safely removed, thereby freeing emergency workers to assist on projects that needed greater skill. Or, TB members visited elderly residents providing emotional labour, which freed medical personnel to deal with more acute medical problems.'[14]

THE NOTION OF A PARALLEL TIME-ECONOMY

Is it possible that in the future, just like cryptocurrency, we could have a parallel currency of time credits? A scenario where, instead of swapping skill for money, people swap skill for time, via a transparent, decentralized platform?

Many of the proponents of time banking certainly think so.

Eldercare could be one of the big areas of growth for this parallel currency, but as has been shown via the other industry examples, it could be applied to exchanging a variety of skills and services.

While the policies, regulations and how-tos of enabling this don't fall within the purview of this book, understanding how drawing a parallel from another industry could bring accelerated improvement and additional benefits, does.

Here are some of them when it comes to banking time, not money.

Social Change

> 'Long before Occupy Wall Street, time banking represented a commitment to pursuing a more equitable and inclusive economic order.'
>
> —Edgar Cahn, Christine Gray

Time banking could enable social change in ways that money cannot, by making it possible to assign a currency value (in terms of time credits) to a number of unpaid but vital jobs such as raising children, caring for a sick person that no one else is willing to make the time to care for, home schooling a child, taking the initiative to clean up your neighbourhood, setting up a neighbourhood watch etc. People like Edgar Cahn refused to give money a monopoly on the definition of value, and by developing and promoting time banking, have created a medium of exchange that has the potential to bring about social change, such as women's empowerment or valuing one person's time as much as the next, no matter their skill or the opportunities life has handed them. One of Cahn's principles for time banking as laid out in his book, *No More Throw-Away People,* is that everyone is an asset and has something to contribute.[15]

Some economists believe that time banking is a crucial tool to help empower women in those developing countries where unpaid labour is not considered 'real work' and is often devalued by the men and society in general.[16]

Along with this, our definition of work could also change to include otherwise unpaid and care work—allowing, for example, a stay-at-home parent to finally be 'paid' for all the work they do.

Community Building

With time banking, the exchange of time for skills tends to happen within a closer geographical setting, and when it takes on the nature of 'volunteering' as highlighted in the eldercare example, it can lead to building a stronger community, which in turn leads to people living in a more sustainable way by sourcing what they need locally, rather than from far away.

It also helps time bank members get to know their neighbours/ local community better, fosters a feeling of belonging and promotes intercultural learning.

In relation to the previous point on social change as well, time banking, by valuing everyone and celebrating and honouring equity, can stimulate 'a community-wide cycle of action, learning, gathering, projects, initiatives, and rewards that enlists people's untapped capacity to extend trust, build mutual support, reduce social isolation, and advance shared purpose'.[17]

New Job Opportunities

In 2015, *The Guardian* shared a story about Cheryl Hughes, a Welsh stay-at-home mum who lacked confidence and was unsure about what she could achieve outside of family life. When she was introduced to time banking, thanks to volunteering at a local clean-up drive by Timeplace Time Credits, she realized its potential. Her confidence grew, and though she had believed she would never be able to start anything of her own thanks to her dyslexia, she started a project called Community Mothers, using a time credit currency system run by Spice (now Tempo), a social enterprise. At coffee meet-ups, people could cash in their time credits to attend, access book and toy libraries and more.[18]

Many time banks work as a skill-swapping forum, where, for example, an IT professional earns a time credit for helping someone set up a digital network, and he later uses that credit to have someone do his gardening.

In this way, time banking could also create new job opportunities for some, while providing an additional/parallel earning source for others, without the actual exchange of money.

TIME BANKING AND WEB3

And in conclusion, if we're able to imagine time-based cryptocurrency, why not time-related NFTs? Or in keeping with the concept of decentralization, why not soulbound tokens (SBTs)?

One of the trending Web 3.0 (Web3) innovations of 2022, soulbound tokens (proposed by Ethereum creator Vitalik Buterin, economist and social technologist E. Glen Weyl and lawyer Puja Ohlhaver) are non-transferable, non-financialized, publicly verifiable digital tokens that together can act as a type of CV for Web3 users, showing an individual's memberships, credentials, achievements and affiliations.[19, 20]

Inspired by items of the same name that are awarded to users on the popular video game World of Warcraft, which they cannot sell to or trade with other players, SBTs add, to the anonymous and impersonalized world of Web3, the element of trust and integrity.

Like NFTs, they can be publicly verified, but unlike NFTs they do not have a market value and are bound to one host account (called a Soul) for their entire lifespan. So, for example, a company could be a Soul that issues SBTs to its shareholders, or an educational institution could be a Soul that issues SBTs to those who graduate.

SBTs are the building blocks of Decentralized Society (DeSoc), another emerging Web3 trend.

'DeSoc sits at the intersection of politics and markets and, much like the wider Web3 context into which it fits, is based around principles of composability, bottom-up community, cooperation, and emergent networks that are owned and governed by network users. It aims to augment Web3's trajectory toward hyper-financialization to something more inclusive, democratic, and decentralized.'[21]

In keeping with this idea, in the future a time bank could issue SBTs as well. Every time someone spends 'x' amount of time helping someone, they could be rewarded with a token, as a badge of recognition that adds value to their list of credentials.

DEVELOPING AN EXPROVEMENT OUTLOOK

What are the types of questions that could have let to making the connection between the ancient system of bartering and modern banking facilities?

- What needs of the future is one able to fulfil today?
- Looking at banking as an industry that caters to fulfilling needs at a later date (for example via fixed deposits or bank insurance schemes), what other parallels can be drawn?
- The barter system was the original form of exchanging goods and services. In today's context, what parallel transaction ideas can be drawn with the barter system?

- Can there be a 'good deeds time bank' in the Web 3.0 space as well, for various forms of social service? What could that look like?
- Can Web 3.0 help decentralize the exprovement of time banking?

17

The Exprovement Mindset

Through the several stories covered in this book, we have seen various ways in which companies from varied industries have bridged the delta to achieve exprovement, by directly or inadvertently drawing a parallel with a process or idea from unrelated industries or phenomena.

We have seen companies draw parallels in several ways, a few examples being:

- Seeing similarities between a Formula One pit crew and how an emergency room could be set up
- Using inspiration from the design of a toy that babies cannot hurt themselves with to design a space component that can land safely in unpredictable terrain
- Applying a combination of behavioural economics and technology from the gaming industry to physiotherapy
- Drawing a parallel between the concept of banking money and developing a way to bank the most precious commodity a human being possesses
- Using the basic design of a centuries' old pastime to create a game-changing alternative to power generation

In some cases, the organizations have looked to 'who does it best' and adapted the process or technology into their own business (Formula One). In some, they have viewed their entire business from a parallel perspective (El Bulli as a laboratory). In some, the marvels of nature have inspired parallel processes and designs (Eastgate Centre). In others it has been a series of improvements on a basic idea that has led to an exprovement (ice stupa).

And now, after having witnessed exprovement in a diverse set of industries through multiple stories, let's summarize how the steps to exprovement can be applied to your own context. These are a combination of:

- Asking the right questions
- Drawing parallels
- Engaging the right team

EXPROVEMENT: TOOLS AND KEY TAKEAWAYS

Given that there are several case studies and tools talked about in this book, as a conclusion, it is prudent to bring them together to give context and to emphasize the key takeaways.

The Delta Graph

While the delta graph in the first chapter helped us understand the difference between improvement and exprovement and which part of the organization they happen in vis-à-vis the important factors of an organization's current position, its goals, the feasibility of achieving those goals and the demographic, political, technological and environmental conditions prevailing at the time, it also brought into focus the following key points:

The Importance of Defining 'What Could Be'

In Chapter 9, we saw how Chef Ferran Adrià, imbibing the 'creating is not copying' mantra, was very clear from the beginning that his 'what could be' had to be something that he created, not a new version of something that had been done before. He might not have had a clear picture of what it would eventually turn out to be, but he knew he wanted it to be something that hadn't been done before. All his experiments with food were based on this principle, which eventually led to some of the most ground-breaking gastronomical exprovements.

On the other hand, had he adopted an improvement mindset, he would likely have developed better or different versions of what the master chefs who came before him had developed—but they would still be considered 'food' as we generally know it, as opposed to completely changing our concept of what food is, as he did.

Exproving and Improving: Very Different Paths

Exprovements are primarily strategic in nature and the operations of a business follow from the strategies so set. Improvements, on the other hand, are generally born out of keeping the users' needs in mind and are more operational in nature.

As a result, exprovements take much more time, effort, persistence and resources to come to fruition than improvements. Chef Adrià's vision called for him to take drastic and investment-heavy measures— such as shutting down his restaurant for half the year and building a lab for food experiments—in order to bring his exprovement to life.

Asking the Right Questions

Along with clearly defining the 'what could be', once one has chosen the path of exprovement, asking the right questions at every point becomes important. We have already covered this in detail in Chapter 1, but here are a few points that are worth re-emphasizing.

Ask Questions that Make the Team Ponder

As shown in the Sony Walkman example in Chapter 1, it is important that the team working on the exprovement be given clear guidelines but be allowed the freedom to be creative at the same time. By asking his team to make a device of a particular size, but leaving everything else up to them, without micromanaging or setting too many constraints, Nobutoshi Kihara was able to get the best out of his team.

Frame Questions Based on the Desired Outcome

Goals and strategy need to be framed depending on whether one is choosing to improve or exprove.

For example, in Chapter 4, Mick Pearce would have achieved an incremental improvement if his question was something like, 'What are all the ways we could cut energy consumption in a commercial building?' He would have worked within the boundaries of what was already being done in architecture.

But since his question was more on the lines of, 'How would termites build this commercial complex?' he was able to come up with something that had never been achieved before.

Use Parallels to Form the Right Question

For example, asking, 'Can injections be made as painless as a leech bite?' can help form the right question for exprovement.

With the example of the voltmeter in Chapter 10, we can see how it became the basis for EEGs, MRIs and CT scans, and ultimately today's cutting-edge concepts, such as neural hardware and sensory substitution.

This was born out of questioning how a device used to measure the flow of electric current could be used to measure the electrical activity in human brains.

Ask 'What could Be' Questions

By focusing on what could be, rather than what is, perspective and context change, allowing for creativity to take centre stage.

For example, in Chapter 15, improvements in wind harvesting technology have come about from focusing only on the 'what is', in this case the windmill design, which hasn't really changed since 644 AD. Improvements have been developed in terms of blade design, lighter material etc. But focusing on what could be—realizing that a kite that is in contact with wind could hold the answer to an entirely new way of harvesting wind—is what resulted in the exprovement of power kites.

Drawing Parallels

The exciting thing about drawing parallels is that it opens up endless possibilities, without constraints. A parallel can be drawn with almost anything—from an ant to the milky way—if one is able to see how things are similar, rather than how they differ.

Vastly Dissimilar Parallels have a Higher Potential for Exprovement

If we consider the Formula One example in Chapter 5, we can see that when parallels are drawn with ER room protocol, auditing and advisory services or sustainable refrigeration—all vastly different contexts—the potential for exprovement is high, i.e., causing radical improvement in those industries.

In the context of drawing a parallel between Formula One and mass production cars, though—a similar context—the potential for exprovement decreases, while the potential for improvement greatly increases.

A Single Exprovement Leads to Diverse Parallel Applications

Almost every chapter has shown us that once an exprovement has been developed, it can find further parallel applications in a variety of diverse industries.

For example, in Chapter 6, we have seen how an exprovement in mountain agriculture has found parallel applications in disaster management, wastewater management, water desalination and tourism, and in Chapter 16 we have seen how the exprovement of time banking has found applications in eldercare management, disaster management, repairs and maintenance, business development and potentially the creation of a parallel economy in the future.

Parallels Can Be Conceptual or Operational

As the stories in this book have shown us, sometimes a parallel can be drawn in the form of an idea or concept borrowed, such as the case of time banking in Chapter 16, where the concept was borrowed from the banking industry. In other scenarios it could be the technology that finds a parallel application, such as in the physiotherapy example in Chapter 13 where gaming technology was applied to exprove the experience of physiotherapy. Sometimes it can be both, as in the football example in Chapter 2, where conceptually we have drawn a parallel with microprocessors, but in its execution it was the application of scientific methods to the sports context that enabled the exprovement to happen.

The Right Attitude to Exprovement

Exprovement can be likened to a chaotic journey with an ambiguous destination.

It thus calls for a certain kind of leadership, outlook and way of thinking—one that can comfortably embrace both chaos and ambiguity.

Be Optimistic

While looking at parallels it is important to look for similarities, rather than differences. It is this mindset that allowed NASA scientists to see that a parallel did exist with an infant's toy, Stephan Wrange to realize that a kite that was in constant contact with wind could probably harness its energy and Jeffrey D. Turner to realize that genetic modification could also be used to create material, not just items intended for human consumption.

The focus needs to remain on what *can* happen, rather than what can't, and why something *could* work, rather than why it can't.

Engage the Right Team

While putting together a team to work on an exprovement or consulting with someone, it is important to remember that while experts in your company's field of work can come up with the best improvements, exprovements often come about from people unrelated to the field. In Chapter 11, for example, we've seen how methodology from the unrelated field of orthopaedics led to an exprovement in the field of construction.

It is important to have people on the team with a mindset that is able to incorporate the points laid out in this chapter.

Encourage Sounding Stupid

The exprovement team should be encouraged to be unafraid of sounding stupid. Many of the world's most important inventions and exprovements have stemmed from something that initially sounded far-fetched or even silly, and while initial versions may have failed, still held a lot of potential. Someone might have once wanted to jump off a cliff and sail through the air using a bedsheet, but today we have the paraglider.

On the surface, calling on inputs from the Batmobile designer to help design a lunar rover (Chapter 3) might sound silly, or believing one could create something that could mind-read (Chapter 10) might sound ridiculous—but as these respective examples have shown us in this book, both have led to exprovement.

Don't be Afraid of Mistakes

It should be accepted that 'mistakes' go hand in hand with chaos and ambiguity and could often more accurately be described as the stepping-stones, or stages of learning on the journey to something better.

Be Persistent

While working on developing an exprovement, one must keep in mind that an exprovement is something that has never been done before and is something being created in an entirely new context. Thus, setbacks, mistakes and obstacles are bound to be a part of the process. Had efforts not been made over the centuries to harvest spider silk despite the numerous difficulties and setbacks as brought out in Chapter 14, today we might not have found ourselves in the position where we're looking at mass scale production of one of the most remarkable materials the world has seen yet!

WHERE IT ALL BEGAN

At the end of the book it is perhaps significant to narrate two parallel stories from the early years of both authors of this book:

When I was a child, I was in the habit of taking apart everything I could lay my hands on to examine what was inside.

More often than not, the object of my investigations was a new toy I had been given. So in general, I never really had a lot of toys to play with; just plenty of parts of toys.

I distinctly remember a particular incident when I was about ten years old, and my parents—after much pestering and convincing—had finally bought me the expensive remote control toy car I had been eyeing for a while.

Much to their exasperation, this toy became the next victim of my investigations, and try as hard as I could, I simply could not put the toy back together again, once I realized how annoyed they were.

Needless to say, the atmosphere at home was tense, and I couldn't wait to escape to school the next day where (probably as a subconscious attempt to appease my parents) I paid extra attention in each and every class.

When I returned from school, I was excited to see a carpenter at home working on a remodelling project in the kitchen—a carpenter at home meant more tools for me to play with!

It was my first introduction to a drill (the manual, not the motorized version) and of course, I had to experiment.

While I was drilling a hole through every centimetre mark of my wooden ruler, wondering what to do with it once I had finished, I suddenly remembered the new gadget we had been taught about earlier that day in geometry class at school.

Like the teeth of gears suddenly falling into place perfectly, I was able, in a lightbulb moment, to see a connection between my broken toy car and the compass I had learnt about at school.

I rushed to find the motor from my broken car, inserted the shaft of the motor into the '0 cm' hole I had drilled and put it through a piece of paper. I switched on the motor, and my invention was able to automatically draw a circle. Next, I moved it to the '1 cm' hole and drew another automated circle.

I was over the moon! I had just invented the next big thing—I had just automated the compass.

That was my first-ever invention, and it drove me to continue the breaking, and in some cases, the making of things.

It was only much later in life, on introspection, that I was able to identify my thought process as one of drawing parallels. I had been able to draw a parallel between something from my geometry class and something from my remote-controlled car to create, what was for a grade five student, a new and exponentially improved way of drawing a circle. I had created the electric compass, one of my first personal exprovements.

As I began my professional life, one of the questions born out of this thought process was: What if parallels could be drawn between the seemingly unrelated to create unparalleled breakthroughs?'

—Hersh Haladkar

There are some 'wow' moments that change the course of one's life. I had one such moment as a young boy in a school. Here is the story.

I was born in a poor family. I did my primary schooling in a municipal school until the seventh standard. I then had to take admission in a secondary school. My mother could not gather the admission fee for a secondary school in time. I missed the admissions for the top schools in the area. I went to the school where most of the resource-poor children from our area went. But that poor school had rich teachers. One of them was my physics teacher, Mr Narahari Bhave. He did not believe in 'chalk and talk' but in seeing, experiencing and learning.

One day he wanted to show us how to find the focal length of a convex lens. He took us out into the sun. He held the lens in one hand and a piece of paper in the other. He moved the lens up and down, and when the brightest spot appeared on the piece of paper, he said the distance between the lens and the paper was the focal length. Then he waited for a few seconds and the paper burnt. When that happened, for some reason, he turned to me and said, 'If you can focus your energies like this, you can burn anything, you can achieve anything'. This magical moment did two things for me. First, I said to myself, 'Science is so powerful—I have to become a scientist.' Second, it gave me the philosophy of my life—focus, and you can achieve great things.

But as I grew older, I saw a much greater meaning in that experiment.

The sun's rays are parallel and the property of parallel lines is that they never meet. The convex lens makes them converge and meet. That gave me the idea for what I termed as 'convex lens leadership', which makes people with divergent views and beliefs meet. Take national leadership, for instance. The nation gets divided on the basis of race, religion, language. A good national leader brings these diverse groups together.

I used this analogy while leading research institutions. The National Chemical Laboratory (NCL) had different divisions, unconnected to each other, like parallel lines. As director of NCL, I provided convex lens leadership to create 'One NCL', 'Team NCL'. I was director general of the Council of Scientific and Industrial Research (CSIR), a chain of forty laboratories, again unconnected to each other, like parallel lines. I provided convex lens leadership to create 'One CSIR', 'Team CSIR'. In fact, the result of this convex lens leadership was so powerful that the CSIR transformation in the 1990s was ranked as being among the top ten achievements of Indian science and technology in the twentieth century.

While engaged in convex lens leadership, my own scientific research led me to explore trans-disciplinary frontiers and has continued to do so for almost four decades. In fact, I brought together several diverse disciplines in my research on stimuli-responsive polymers.

When I was invited to give the Danckwerts Memorial oration in London in 1995, I spoke on the emerging paradigm of seamless or borderless engineering science, emphasizing the need to create engineers with borderless minds.

Later, I extended this parallel lines analogy to ideas from diverse domains, which appear completely unrelated, and therefore are like parallel lines. But a 'convex lens mindset' makes them converge.

And sometimes the result is an astonishing 1+1=11, not just 1+1=2!

In this book, we have focused on the challenge of building a convex lens mindset, which is capable of bringing together the parallel, connecting the seemingly unconnectable. We show how such a convex lens mindset creates the magic of exprovement, going well beyond incremental improvement.

—Raghunath Mashelkar

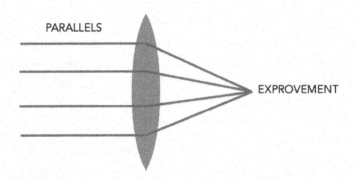

It is the coming together of these ideas—drawing parallels from unrelated industries or realms to bring about unparalleled breakthroughs, the concept of the convex-lens mindset, which is the ability to bring together seemingly unconnected streams of thoughts and ideas with focus, and the paradigm of borderless minds—that we believe is the bedrock of the concept of exprovement.

If the two young children in these stories could figure out exprovement, why not anyone else?

> 'The useful or interesting combinations are those which reveal to us unsuspected kinship between facts long known, but wrongly believed to be strangers to one another ... among chosen combinations, the most fertile will often be those formed of elements drawn from domains which are far apart.'
>
> —*Henri Poincaré*

Bonus Chapter

The Banyan Tree Analysis

Where does one begin on the journey to exprovement once the basic question of whether to improve or exprove has been answered?

It is here that we propose the use of the banyan tree analysis, which views the journey of exprovement as a parallel to the growth and expansion of a banyan tree.

THE BANYAN TREE PARALLEL

Using the analogy of a banyan tree's growth to understand a company's exprovement journey helps identify which stage a company is at and how it can begin to look at potential new areas of growth.

The Banyan Tree

A banyan tree starts to expand by focusing all its energies on growing from its trunk. After achieving a certain point of stability, the tree begins to look for multiple points of potential parallel to its trunk, in order to spread and grow further, while ensuring that its current stability endures.

While most of the tree's energy remains focused on embedding the roots of the main trunk deeper, it begins to spend some of its energy nurturing and incubating the new-found points of potential into aerial roots.

The aerial roots can be largely categorized into two sets:
The first set—closer to the trunk—helps the main trunk grow taller
and maintain its stability.
The second set—further away from the trunk—helps the tree grow
wider and aids with future growth.

While the first set of aerial roots helps the tree grow stronger using
the same/similar sources of energy/nutrients, the second set is on
the lookout for new sources of energy.

Soon these roots hit the ground and start fending for themselves,
using new sources of energy—some successfully and some not so
successfully. Those that are successful dig deeper and then begin
to grow in girth in order to support their own growth and to even
support the tree as a whole.

Some new roots develop so much potential that they eventually
become the main trunk, as over time, the old, aged trunk exhausts
all its resources.

This is how the banyan tree is able to successfully and sustainably
last over hundreds of years (in one case 700 years) and is able to
spread over massive areas (even up to a few acres).

The Organization

The trunk of the tree can be viewed as a parallel to the core
business of the organization. It is what helps the organization
flourish and reach a point of stability after which it can begin to
consider expanding.

On attaining a certain point of stability, organizations need to start
looking for potential ideas (parallel to their core business) to enable
further growth of the core business and to support future growth.

While the core business of the company continues to run, some
resources are allocated to exploring and investing in new potential
areas of expansion.

This is the point where companies need to start investing in ideas of
two kinds:

Improvements, which help the core business grow further (taller).

Exprovements, which aid with the future growth of the
business (wider).

Improvements help answer the question: 'If we could build a
business to this point, so can someone else. What can help us stay
here and grow further?'

Exprovements help achieve exponential growth of the core business
as well as diversification and future growth of the organization.

Soon these new ideas hit the ground running. Some of them succeed
to become verticals of their own, or even independent organizations,
whereas some don't.

Those that are successful are soon not only able to sustain
themselves, but also support the organization as a whole.

In some cases, the newly formed verticals of exprovements grow
so much that they become the core business of the organization,
as the primary business has become outdated and has exhausted all
its resources.

This is how organizations can evolve and sustain growth and
expansion over extended periods of time and eliminate the danger of
becoming redundant.

An organization familiar to all of us that is a good example of the
banyan tree parallel is Amazon. Founded by Jeff Bezos from his garage
in Bellevue, Washington, on 5 July 1994, the company began as an
online marketplace for books—its main trunk. It has expanded into
a multitude of product categories: a strategy that has earned it the
moniker *The Everything Store*.[1] Today, books form just 10 per cent of
its revenues.[2]

The following diagram is representative of the banyan tree analogy:

The height and width of the core represents the maturity of the company (the vertical centre).

The width of the tree is representative of the company's diversification (the horizontal top).

The aerial roots closer to the centre represent improvements.

The aerial roots farther away from the centre represent exprovements.

The length of each of the aerial roots represents the stage the respective improvement or exprovement is at.

The width/girth of each of the aerial roots represents the potential of that particular improvement or exprovement.

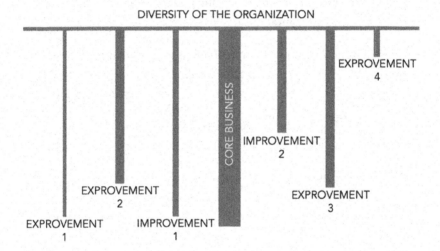

In this particular example:

- Improvement 1 is a parallel that has hit the ground running and has shown some potential.
- Improvement 2 is halfway through the development process but shows a lot of potential.
- Exprovement 1 is radically diverse from its core business, has been fully developed and is yet to show potential.
- Exprovement 2 is a diverse parallel from the organization's core business, with large potential and still has some way to go before becoming operational.

- Exprovement 3 is at a similar stage, potential and level of diversity to exprovement 2.
- Exprovement 4 is a far-fetched bet that shows a large amount of potential but is at a nascent stage of development.

BREAKING DOWN THE FOOTBALL CHAPTER

Let's use one of the case studies from this book to put what we've spoken about into practice:

Looking for Parallels

While Ranieri executed his strategy of conserving and expending his players' energy optimally by integrating methodologies from parallel industries, as explained in the chapter, it is important to note that the development of an exprovement also relies on exploring parallel industries.

In the case of the football example, a starting point or core question could be: 'Who or what else, or which industry, looks to optimize energy for better performance and how do they approach it?'

Exploring how other industries have tackled similar problems could generate ideas, such as:

a. What can footballers learn from microprocessor manufacturers about energy optimization?

Which could lead to more in-depth questions like:

- How has the microprocessor evolved? What lessons does it have for a football club?
- What are the strategies used by microprocessor manufacturers to improve efficiency?
- What are the strategies used by them to reduce power consumption?
- What can football clubs learn from the various phases of microprocessor optimization through its evolution?
- Miniaturization: Can footballers cover a really small area but create a really high impact like the miniaturization of transistors in microprocessors has achieved?

- How can fewer players create a bigger impact, while the others conserve energy, to mimic a multi-core processor?

A strategy developed around these questions could be: Get maximum output from minimum energy usage.

b. What can footballers learn from the automotive industry about fuel management?

Such a question would lead to an exploration of how fuel management systems work,[3] and an understanding of how telematics has combined 'telecommunications, informatics, computer science, electrical engineering, and vehicular technologies to create a vehicle telematics system that functions to collect and derive insight from vehicle telematics data and ultimately improve the efficiency and safety of the overall driver experience.'[4]

Going deeper into the questioning:

- What strategy do automotive manufacturers use to increase energy efficiency?
- How do they get vehicles to achieve peak performance when needed?
- How do they conserve energy?
- Can footballers conserve energy when not active, similar to Volkswagen's Bluemotion technology?
- Can footballers recover unused energy like the kinetic energy recovery system in cars?
- Can footballers get to peak performance just when needed?

Resulting strategy: To preserve when not in use.

c. How do birds manage their energy while flying long distances?

This could have led them to study research conducted by the Royal Veterinary College in England, which suggests that the 'V' formation that birds fly in is what helps them collectively manage their energy most efficiently while flying over long distances.[5]

Perhaps a tweak in the way footballers are positioned on the field could make a difference?

- How do birds maximize the results of the effort they put in?
- How does one bird's movement aid that of the others?
- Can footballers maximize their outcome with minimum effort like birds flying in a 'V' formation do?
- Can one player's actions aid the others, like a group of birds flying together?
- Can the clothes of footballers aid their movement, in the same manner a bird's feathers do?

Resulting strategy: Formations for least energy usage.

d.   How do misers manage their wealth?

Studying the thought process behind how misers function and live could have led to the realization that it is possible to get by on less. An interesting article at moneywizard.com suggests that people living in today's culture of excessive spending might view their grandparents, who lived in the 1940s and 50s, as 'misers'.[6]

With a focus shift from spending (energy) to conserving (energy), could there be a lesson for a football club somewhere in there?

- How do misers decide where they will and won't spend their money?
- How do misers get the most out of every penny spent?
- Can footballers spend their energy the way misers spend their money?
- How can footballers get the most out of every ounce of energy they spend?

Resulting strategy: Use only what's absolutely necessary.

e.   Do all racing cars use the same strategy to win a race?

This question could have brought them to the work of Colin Chapman, founder of Lotus cars and one of motor racing's most influential engineers, who followed a philosophy of 'simplify, then add lightness'.

"'A stripped-down, featherweight car might be slower on the straights than a beefy muscle-machine," he reasoned. But it would be faster everywhere else. Between 1962 and 1978 Lotus won seven Formula One constructors championships.'[7]

- How do racing cars go about stripping down to the bare minimum?
- How do they decide what to shed and what to keep?
- Can the kits of footballers be made lighter, drawing a parallel to how carbon fibre is used in sports cars?
- Can players strip off what's not absolutely needed?
- What can football clubs learn from the decision-making used in race cars regarding what to shed and what to keep?

Resulting strategy: Strip down to the bare minimum for maximum efficiency.

This exploration of parallels that have already achieved what the football club was looking to achieve could have helped LCFC search for 'off the beaten track' solutions.

While most football coaches were looking at pushing their players to achieve maximum performance, what different approach could they take to arrive at the same goal?

One, or a combination, of the parallel paths similar to the four just described would help arrive at a strategy like Ranieri's.

Solutions can be found through parallel paths with other industries, ways of thinking or even observing natural phenomena—the possibilities are limitless.

Of course, some parallels may not lead to feasible or even plausible solutions, but wherever a link is found, it is always worth exploring, even if only to consider later as a further improvement, or at the very least to eliminate it and similar possibilities from the realm of solutions, thus helping to bring further focus to the process.

Ranieri may not have set out to discover parallel pathways but observing his unparalleled results and breaking down the solutions the club eventually chose to adopt suggests that seeking parallel pathways can lead to exprovement.

THE BANYAN TREE IN ACTION

The Exprovements

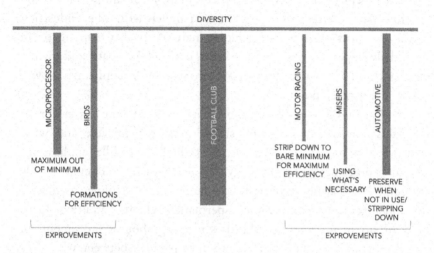

The Improvements
(Refer to Chapter 2)

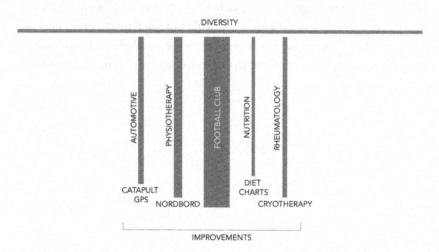

THE BANYAN TREE—KEY TAKEAWAYS

The banyan tree parallel helps an organization that has reached a certain level of stability begin the process of exploring improvement and exprovement alternatives by looking for parallels with other industries, ideas, concepts or systems (including nature). It also helps map out the likely impact of pursuing a particular parallel or path and gives a strategic bird's-eye view of the overall progress of the company's growth plans at any given point.

In Chapter 5, we see how Formula One companies from Ferrari to McLaren, which are amongst the most recognizable and well-positioned brands in the world, began to look for parallel applications for their processes and technology in other industries. They were able to enter into partnerships with companies and disciplines as diverse as manufacturing companies, supermarket chains, auditing firms and airport management, authorities to bring about exprovements in those areas because they were able to draw parallels between what they were excellent at and how their expertise could bring about radical improvement elsewhere, which at the same time allowed them to diversify their revenue streams.

The banyan tree parallel thus can be as an effective starting-point tool for a company beginning its journey to exprovement – to understand where it currently stands as a business, what potential routes of expansion it could take through the concept of drawing parallels and how likely each of these routes are to result in either improvement or exprovement.

Acknowledgements

People often speak about how innovative ideas have led to breakthroughs for businesses and industries. Not too many people, however, speak about how to come up with these ideas.

While working on various innovation projects and consulting with experts to seek solutions, one of the authors of this book, Hersh Haladker, observed that exceptional solutions were often inspired by a completely different industry. The idea for *Exprovement* was born when he realised that anyone could come up with innovative ideas if they just knew how to draw parallels—and a book seemed like the best way to make the concept accessible to all.

About ten years before this, after completing his post-graduation in London, Haladker visited India in the hope of meeting a few people in the innovation space. He read about one of India's foremost innovation and science leaders, Dr Raghunath Mashelkar, and how passionate he was about innovation.

After a lot of research on the Internet, he found Dr Mashelkar's email address and requested an appointment to seek advice on what his career options could be.

'He was gracious enough to give me his time. I travelled to Pune and was extremely nervous, but he was the most encouraging and passionate person I had ever met. This has not changed since.'

Mashelkar's advice was to work in the innovation space in India. *'I will support you in doing so.'* This was all the encouragement Haladker

219

needed, especially motivated by the fact that Mashelkar had shown an incredible amount of faith in someone he had only just met.

Ever since the two have met at every possible opportunity and spoken endlessly about how innovation can change the world. The synergy grew rapidly, as Dr Mashelkar spoke about innovation at a visionary and policy level and Haladker spoke about it from the perspective of a practitioner.

'We connected on how our thought processes were very similar. I guess I saw how much I could achieve in forty years when I spoke to him and he saw how he was 40 years ago in me.'

When the idea of *Exprovement* struck, Haladker knew that Mashelkar would be the ideal person to offer invaluable inputs and guidance, and help develop the concept of *Exprovement* further.

As Sir Louis Matheson, a distinguished professor for the past fifteen years at Monash University, Australia, Mashelkar has been conducting lectures on disruptive game-changing innovation, especially the factors that trigger them and the transformative impact that they have.

A lot of the thoughts that form the subject matter of these lectures—such as serendipity, which is accidental experimental findings, discoveries of unexpected connections by connecting the unconnected dots or the oxymoronic concept of 'organising' serendipity—can be seen flowing through this book, which has drawn parallels between and created exponential improvement from:

- The diversity of a forty-year age difference between the two authors.
- The diversity between a 50,000-ft view and a 5-ft view.
- The diversity between a scientist and an innovator

As Dr Mashelkar observes, *'In a sense, the two of us were ourselves converging parallels.'*

Many people have helped us at the various stages of this book, from its conception as a mere thought to its execution into a completed book.

Hersh would especially like to thank Vijay Nadkarni for seeding the idea of writing a book, his wife Ramya for pushing him to write the book and his parents Prabhu and Ranjana for not only supporting an experimental profession but also for believing in him through his journey of parallels, even though they often did not understand what he was doing.

He would also like to thank his team at InstillMotion, for time and again drawing parallels that have pushed the boundaries of imagination and everyone who has graciously made space to enable him to break a loft of his own perceptions to welcome fresh ones.

The authors are grateful to Sushil Borde, whose insightful critical comments on the first draft helped with early course correction.

We would also like to thank Amya Madan and Omkar Patil, whose new and unobvious thinking helped add some inspiring content and Ramesh Talada for his ingenuity in creating the unique book cover design.

Words are inadequate to thank Gitanjali Singh Cherian, who stayed the course patiently for three years with us. She has been the very soul of this book, with every line in the book having the imprint of her magical touch in some way.

Our special thanks to Radhika Marwah and her colleagues at Penguin for their commitment, perseverance and patience through the painstaking process of the original draft transforming into the final manuscript that it now is.

Hersh Haladker
Raghunath Mashelkar

Notes

INTRODUCTION

1. https://www.uschamber.com/co/good-company/growth-studio/
   successful-companies-that-reinvented-their-business#:~:text=
   Corning%2C%20a%20world%20leader%20in,it%20could%20do%20
   with%20glass
2. https://corporate.ford.com/articles/history/moving-assembly-line.html
3. https://www.history.com/this-day-in-history/fords-assembly-line-
   startsrolling
4. See note 1

CHAPTER 1: Exprovement

1. https://www.exploratorium.edu/cycling/frames1.
   html#:~:text=German%20Inventor%20Karl%20von%20Drais,hit%20
   the%20road%20in%201817
2. https://research.gold.ac.uk/id/eprint/27573/1/49_KRISTENSEN_
   Walkman_FinalEdit.pdf
3. https://www.leadershipnow.com/leadingblog/2009/01/the_block_of_
   wood_that_became.html
4. https://www.researchgate.net/publication/245387767_A_woodpecker_
   hammer
5. https://www.boxfactory.com.au/news/bubble-wrap-a-history-of-the-
   accidental-invention-that-changed-the-shipping-industry/
6. https://www.aarp.org/politics-society/environment/info-07 2010/a_hairy_
   way_to_clean_up_the_gulf_oil_spill.html

7.   ttps://www.chegg.com/homework-help/questions-and-answers/
     associating-great-innovative-entrepreneur-walt-disney-described-role-
     company-founded-creat-q61250651
8.   https://www.azom.com/article.aspx?ArticleID=8307#:~:text=In%20
     1913%2C%20Harry%20Brearley%20of,metal%20that%20did%20
     not%20rust
9.   See note 8
10. https://www.worldstainless.org/Files/issf/non-image-files/PDF/ISSF_
     History_of_Stainless_Steel.pdf
11. https://www.grandviewresearch.com/industry-analysis/stainless-steel-market

CHAPTER 2: How to Make a Footballer as Efficient as a Microprocessor

1.   This data was calculated from information available at: https://www.
     premierinjuries.com/injury-table.php
2.   https://www.ncbi.nlm.nih.gov/pmc/articles/PMC3476519/#b16-
     ccmbm-107-111
3.   https://www.intechopen.com/books/muscle-injuries-in-sport-medicine/
     prevention-of-muscle-injuries-the-soccer-model
4.   https://ne-np.facebook.com/SCIENCESPORT/
     posts/1044383232304950
5.   https://one.catapultsports.com/blog/why-do-soccer-players-wear-
     gps-vests/#:~:text=The%20vest%20holds%20the%20pod,accurate%20
     and%20reliable%20as%20possible
6.   https://www.wareable.com/sport/myontec-mbody-janne-
     pylvasinterview-8668
7.   See note 6
8.   https://youtu.be/KXuLbBdhmts
9.   https://www.myontec.com/ergonomics#:~:text=Myontec%20
     ErgoAnalysis%E2%84%A2%20can%20be,possible%20pain%20and%20
     extreme%20positions
10. https://www.idtechex.com/en/research-report/e-textiles-2019-2029-
     technologies-markets-and-players/671
11. https://www.labmanager.com/news/researchers-develop-a-
     softstretchable-thermometer-27437

ADDITIONAL REFERENCES

Leicester case study:

•   https://premierskillsenglish.britishcouncil.org/skills/read/stories/
     leicestercity-champions-england
•   https://www.premierleague.com/history/2015-16

- https://www.bloomberg.com/news/articles/2016-04-28/leicester-city-defieslong-odds-much-to-bookmakers-chagrin
- https://www.bbc.com/sport/football/36189778
- https://www.theguardian.com/football/2016/apr/29/claudio-ranieri-gentleman-leicester-city-premier-league
- https://www.online-betting.me.uk/injuries/english-premier-league-injuriesand-suspensions
- https://ne-np.facebook.com/SCIENCESPORT/posts/1044383232304950

Myontec:

- https://www.myontec.com/benefits/occupational_health_and_ergonomics/
- https://www.myontec.com/ergonomics#:~:text=Myontec%20ErgoAnalysis%E2%84%A2%20can%20be,possible%20pain%20and%20extreme%20positions
- https://www.myontec.com/products__trashed/muscle_monitor/

Nordbord:

- https://simplifaster.com/articles/review-nordbord-hamstring-testing-system/
- https://valdperformance.com/nordbord/#forceframe

- *Quote, credit: Peter Drucker https://www.growthink.com/content/twomost-important-quotes-business

CHAPTER 3: What's the Link between Babies and Space Exploration?

1. https://www.nasa.gov/content/super-ball-bot
2. https://www.bbc.com/future/article/20130201-nasas-crazy-robot-lab
3. https://www.smithsonianmag.com/smart-news/nasas-next-space-robot-was-inspired-babys-toy-180954479/
4. https://www.manhattantoy.com/collections/skwis
5. See note 2
6. See note 2
7. See note 3
8. https://spectrum.ieee.org/nasa-super-ball-bot
9. https://www.forbes.com/sites/jamiecartereurope/2021/08/24/revealed-exactly-why-nasa-is-sending-a-1-billion-drone-to-saturns-utopian-moon-titan/?sh=783e4b1e44a0
10. See note 2

11. https://www.nasa.gov/directorates/spacetech/niac/2012_phase_I_fellows_agogino.html#.VBBX4STVWlY
12. https://www.nasa.gov/feature/not-child-s-play-toys-that-inspired-nasa-innovations
13. https://www.astroglobefoundation.org/blog/astronomy/nasa-inspired-by-toys/
14. See note 12
15. https://www.bbc.co.uk/newsround/58089325#:~:text=The%20Blob%20will%20begin%20its,slime%20mould%20on%20the%20ISS.
16. https://www.bbc.co.uk/newsround/42960487
17. https://nerdfighteria.info/v/w7n8PWGtzbA/
18. https://earthsky.org/space/landing-on-mars-is-still-hard/
19. https://en.wikipedia.org/wiki/Low-arth_Orbit_Flight_Test_of_an_Inflatable_Decelerator
20. https://in.mashable.com/space/33614/nasa-just-inflated-its-new-age-spaceship-heat-shield-for-mars
21. https://www.sciencedirect.com/topics/materials-science/microfluidics#:~:text=Microfluidics%20is%20the%20science%20and,Food%3A%20Techniques%20and%20Applications%2C%202012
22. https://en.wikipedia.org/wiki/Microfluidics
23. https://www.scientificamerican.com/article/a-chip-against-cancer/
24. https://www.dovepress.com/recent-advances-of-microfluidic-platforms-for-controlled-drug-delivery-peer-reviewed-fulltext-article-DDDT
25. https://www.scientificamerican.com/article/toy-box-tech/
26. https://www.aa.com.tr/en/world/landmines-killed-7-073-in-2020-says-un-institute/2417253
27. https://edition.cnn.com/2012/11/29/tech/innovation/mine-kafon-tumbleweed-minesweeper/index.html
28. https://www.habausa.com/blog/inventions-inspired-by-toys/
29. See note 27
30. See note 25
31. https://www.nanowerk.com/nanotechnology-in-displays.php
32. https://www.nanowerk.com/nanoelectronics.php
33. https://www.zdnet.com/article/scientists-create-a-single-electron-transistor-a-big-step-for-quantum-computing/
34. https://www.techopedia.com/definition/32895/soft-robotics
35. https://www.hackster.io/news/inspired-by-rubber-popper-toy-harvard-researchers-create-a-fast-moving-jumping-soft-robot-actuator-61fe27e024a4
36. See note 35
37. https://news.stanford.edu/2017/01/10/whirligig-toy-bioengineers-develop-20-cent-hand-powered-blood-centrifuge/
38. https://youtu.be/w7n8PWGtzbA

39. https://en.wikipedia.org/wiki/Fischertechnik
40. https://www.fischertechnik.de/en/simulating/industry-4-0
41. https://www.fischertechnik.de/en/simulating/references
42. https://www.fischertechnik.de/en/simulating/references/accso-accelerated-solutions-gmbh-anomaly-detection
43. https://www.fischertechnik.de/en/simulating/references/bmw

CHAPTER 4: How Would an Insect Build a Commercial Complex?

1. https://youtu.be/VIKYjriWgiY
2. www.mickpearce.com
3. See note 1
4. https://www.terminix.com/termites/identification/what-does-a-termite-look-like/#:~:text=Termites%20range%20in%20size%20from,both%20have%20wings%20and%20antennae.
5. https://india.mongabay.com/2020/10/architectural-secrets-of-termite-mounds/
6. https://nautil.us/the-termite-and-the-architect-1483/
7. https://youtu.be/Brl_a4I6qqc
8. See note 6
9. https://www.mickpearce.com/Eastgate.html
10. See note 9
11. https://constructionreviewonline.com/people/mick-pearce/
12. https://www.nytimes.com/2019/03/26/science/termite-nest-ventilation.html
13. https://www.sciencedirect.com/science/article/pii/S1364032117300102
14. https://stories.clintonfoundation.org/four-reasons-why-the-empire-state-building-retrofit-model-works-1e4d9ebdbe9
15. https://www.theenergymix.com/2020/06/02/empire-state-building-retrofits-cut-10-year-emissions-by-40/
16. https://asknature.org/innovation/passively-cooled-building-inspired-by-termite-mounds/
17. https://en.wikipedia.org/wiki/Council_House_2
18. https://youtu.be/JlDR3yNk-0s
19. See note 17
20. https://www.mickpearce.com/CH2.html
21. https://youtu.be/Brl_a4I6qqc
22. https://www.archdaily.com/954004/what-is-biomimetic-architecture
23. https://youtu.be/H0jb-fT6tz0
24. https://asknature.org/innovation/building-materials-inspired-by-marine-sponges/
25. https://design-middleeast.com/patterns-of-life-designing-with-nature/

26. https://psci.princeton.edu/tips/2020/11/3/cement-and-concrete-the-environmental-impact
27. See note 25
28. https://en.wikipedia.org/wiki/Biorock#:~:text=Compressive%20strength%20has%20been%20measured,atmosphere%20rather%20than%20sequestering%20it.
29. https://www.dezeen.com/2020/10/22/michael-pawlyn-exploration-architecture-dassault-systemes-video/
30. https://www.dezeen.com/2020/10/22/michael-pawlyn-exploration-architecture-dassault-systemes-video/
31. https://indiandefencenews.info/650574/news/self-healing-concrete-market-size-share-trends-analysis-growth-and-forecast-2021-2030/
32. https://www.smithsonianmag.com/innovation/with-this-self-healing-concrete-buildings-repair-themselves-180955474/?no-ist
33. https://www.fastcompany.com/90645903/this-self-healing-concrete-automatically-fills-in-cracks
34. https://mashable.com/archive/traffic-signals-bugs
35. https://www.autoblog.com/2012/11/12/how-insects-might-help-make-traffic-lights-smarter-and-more-effi/
36. https://cen.acs.org/materials/adhesives/Mussel-inspired-polymer-glue-sticks/98/web/2020/07
37. https://www.musselpolymers.com/
38. https://www.sciencedaily.com/releases/2015/07/150721111211.htm
39. https://en.wikipedia.org/wiki/Diatom
40. https://en.wikipedia.org/wiki/Aquaporin
41. https://www.learnbiomimicry.com/blog/top-10-biomimicry-examples-2021
42. See note 41
43. See note 16
44. See note 6
45. https://greendreamer.com/podcast/mick-pearce-biomimicry-architect-eastgate-mall
46. See note 6
47. See note 6

CHAPTER 5: What Does Formula One Have in Common with Clean Teeth?

1. https://www.wired.co.uk/article/mclaren-technology-innovation
2. See note 1
3. See note 1
4. See note 1

5. https://ctekleansolutions.com/blog/importance-reducing-cycle-time/
6. https://princemanufacturing.com/reasons-reduce-production-cycle-times/
7. https://www.wsj.com/articles/SB116346916169622261
8. See note 7
9. https://www.weforum.org/agenda/2020/11/formula-one-f1-innovation-ventilators-fridges/
10. https://en.wikipedia.org/wiki/DHL_Fastest_Pit_Stop_Award#:~:text=in%20Abu%20Dhabi.-,2016,the%202016%20European%20Grand%20Prix.
11. https://www.clustre.net/driving-innovation-motorsport-empowers-industries/
12. https://www.reuters.com/article/motor-f1-neonatal-idINKCN0Y11K0
13. See note 12
14. See note 12
15. See note 9
16. https://www.bbc.com/news/business-41998802
17. See note 11
18. https://www.autoevolution.com/news/formula-one-aerodynamics-will-make-grocery-stores-save-energy-94832.html
19. See note 16
20. See note 16
21. See note 16
22. https://www.talkingretail.com/news/industry-news/sainsburys-completes-installation-f1-technology-uk-stores-05-03-2020/
23. See note 16
24. See note 1
25. See note 1
26. See note 1
27. https://www.formula1.com/en/latest/article.how-f1-technology-has-supercharged-the-world.6Gtk3hBxGyUGbNH0q8vDQK.html
28. https://motorsport.tech/formula-1/f1-technology-beyond-motorsport
29. https://www.accountancydaily.co/kpmg-accelerates-audit-analytics-fast-lane-mclaren-deal
30. See note 11
31. https://news.sky.com/story/mclaren-puts-brakes-on-kpmg-and-revs-up-deloitte-partnership-10878675
32. https://www.motorsportmagazine.com/archive/article/december-2001/69/active-suspension
33. https://www.edmunds.com/car-technology/suspension-iii-active-suspension-systems.html
34. https://www.budgetdirect.com.au/interactives/special-feature/f1-trickle-down-effect.php

35. https://www.bbc.com/news/technology-12691062
36. https://www.makeuseof.com/f1-tech-in-road-car/
37. https://f1chronicle.com/how-advanced-technology-gets-transferred-from-formula-1-to-production-cars/#:~:text=of%20road%20cars.-,Enhanced%20Efficiency%20and%20Battery%20Technology,significantly%20contributed%20to%20battery%20technology.
38. https://www.formula1.com/en/latest/article.watch-how-formula-1-is-striving-to-create-a-100-sustainable-fuel.1ENHVTjKDbXNOIidEJ8okc.html
39. https://www.formula1.com/en/latest/article.how-formula-1-will-lead-the-charge-to-use-biofuels.lxWqy8GilwwMBsjKyPiFf.html
40. See note 1
41. See note 1
42. https://www.redbulladvancedtechnologies.com/advancing-development-cycle/
43. See note 27
44. https://www.railway-technology.com/news/smrt-and-mclaren-to-test-formula-1-technology-on-mrt-trains/
45. See note 28

CHAPTER 6: Can a Popsicle Ease Global Warming Problems?

1. https://www.huffpost.com/archive/in/entry/this-ladakh-village-is-using-an-artificial-glacier-to-solve-its-water-woes_a_23192520
2. https://economictimes.indiatimes.com/industry/miscellaneous/chewang-norphel-how-a-crazy-engineer-solved-ladakhs-water-crisis/idea/slideshow/63265622.cms
3. https://scroll.in/article/724624/as-himalayan-glaciers-disappear-ladakhi-farmers-search-for-the-ideal-artificial-substitute
4. See note 3
5. https://kinder.world/articles/solutions/the-ice-man-of-india-is-solving-water-scarcity-with-artificial-glaciers-16726
6. https://ideas.ted.com/no-theyre-not-a-mirage-learn-how-these-ingenious-ice-towers-are-helping-communities-preserve-water-for-dry-times/
7. See note 6
8. See note 6
9. https://timesofindia.indiatimes.com/travel/destinations/the-innovative-ice-stupas-of-ladakh-solving-water-crisis-in-the-himalayas/as78315648.cms
10. https://www.newyorker.com/magazine/2019/05/20/the-art-of-building-artificial-glaciers
11. https://globalpressjournal.com/asia/indian-administered_kashmir/kashmir-ancient-solution-solves-modern-problem/

12. https://edition.cnn.com/style/article/ice-stupa-sonam-wangchuk/index.html
13. See note 6
14. https://www.nationalgeographic.com/magazine/2017/04/explore-desert-glaciers/
15. https://littleindia.com/winter-soldiers-ice-stupa-team-saving-glaciers-world/

OTHER SOURCES:

Websites:

• https://www.nationalgeographic.com/magazine/2020/07/one-way-to-fightclimate-change-make-your-own-glaciers-perpetual-feature/
• https://www.sulzer.com/en/shared/products/freeze-concentration
• https://www.thebetterindia.com/113860/artificial-glaciers-help-mitigatingrural-water-crisis-ladakh/
• https://www.theguardian.com/environment/2017/apr/22/the-ice-stupas-ofladakh-solving-water-crisis-in-the-high-desert-of-himalaya
• https://kashmirlife.net/ice-stupas-were-copied-in-switzerland-skardu-peruand-sikkim-issue-16-vol-11-215342/
• https://www.firstpost.com/long-reads/in-ladakhs-phyang-villagecommunity-driven-initiatives-tackle-climate-change-7349771.html
• https://geographyandyou.com/ladakh-water-security-and-climate-change/
• https://staycoolguide.com/do-misting-fans-really-work-what-they-dont-tellyou/
• https://www.britannica.com/science/hydroelectric-power
• https://en.wikipedia.org/wiki/Alexander_Zarchin
• https://en.wikipedia.org/wiki/Desalination#Freeze%E2%80%93thaw
• https://www.gea.com/en/binaries/crystallization-wastewater-concentrationfreeze-zld-gea_tcm11-34868.pdf
• https://www.scientific.net/KEM.797.55
• https://docs.lib.purdue.edu/alspub/55/

YouTube Videos:

• https://youtu.be/2xuBvI98-n4 Al Jazeera
• https://youtu.be/kptgonELj00 BBC

Books:

• Brown, Tim. *Change by Design.* (2009) Harper Collins

CHAPTER 7: What Do a Pizza Box and Cancer Detection Have in Common?

1. https://www.everydayhealth.com/cancer/breast-cancer/four-time-olympian-and-triple-negative-breast-cancer-survivor-chaunt%C3%A9-lowe-has-a-message-for-you-if-in-doubt-get-screened/
2. https://www.glamour.com/story/high-jumper-chaunte-lowe-conquered-four-olympics-now-shes-training-for-tokyo-through-breast-cancer
3. https://pubmed.ncbi.nlm.nih.gov/25916019/#:~:text=Results%3A%20 14.8%25%20of%20women%20carried,it%20on%20a%20regular% 20basis
4. https://www.who.int/news-room/fact-sheets/detail/breast-cancer
5. https://www.cancer.gov/news-events/cancer-currents-blog/2021/cancer-screening-decreases-coronavirus-pandemic
6. https://www.everydayhealth.com/cancer/breast-cancer/four-time-olympian-and-triple-negative-breast-cancer-survivor-chaunt%C3%A9-lowe-has-a-message-for-you-if-in-doubt-get-screened/
7. https://www.medicalnewstoday.com/articles/316632#mammography
8. https://www.everydayhealth.com/cancer/breast-cancer/four-time-olympian-and-triple-negative-breast-cancer-survivor-chaunt%C3%A9-lowe-has-a-message-for-you-if-in-doubt-get-screened/
9. https://pubmed.ncbi.nlm.nih.gov/18440273/
10. https://pubmed.ncbi.nlm.nih.gov/25916019/#:~:text=Results%3A%20 14.8%25%20of%20women%20carried,it%20on%20a%20regular%20 basis
11. https://www.medicalnewstoday.com/articles/316632
12. https://decemberlabs.com/work/celbrea
13. https://decemberlabs.com/work/wearables#celbrea
14. https://celbrea.com/product/
15. https://www.wsj.com/articles/temperature-tracking-tools-take-center-stage-in-covid-19-vaccine-rollout-11608585973
16. https://www.healthcarepackaging.com/issues/regulatory/press-release/13293798/cti-heatactivated-tamperevident-ink
17. https://www.allaboutvision.com/eyeglasses/photochromic-lenses-good-computer-glasses/
18. https://www.sciencedirect.com/topics/engineering/thermochromic-material
19. https://www.sciencedirect.com/science/article/pii/S1369702108702268
20. https://eandt.theiet.org/content/articles/2022/02/ultrafast-heat-sensor-gives-robots-human-reaction-times-to-heat-extremes/
21. See note 20
22. https://technology.nasa.gov/patent/LEW-TOPS-28

ADDITIONAL REFERENCES

CELBREA

- https://www.startuphealth.com/welwaze
- https://insight.openexo.com/revolutionizing-the-mammogram-the-celbreadisruption-to-breast-cancer-detection/
- https://medpick.in/product/celbrea-breast-health-monitoring-system/
- https://uspto.report/patent/app/20190209019

COLD CHAIN TRACKING

- https://ksusentinel.com/2021/03/30/analysis-of-covid-19-crisis-drivengrowth-opportunities-in-thermochromic-pigments-market/
- https://www.supplychaindive.com/news/coronavirus-vaccine-cold-chaintracking-iot-sensor-technology/583168/
- https://www.tiptemp.com/Products/Cold-Chain-Temperature-Indicators/

TUMOUR AND ELEVATED TEMPERATURE

- https://link.springer.com/article/10.1007/s10147-021-02044-1

CHAUNTÉ LOWE

- https://www.everydayhealth.com/cancer/breast-cancer/four-time-olympianand-triple-negative-breast-cancer-survivor-chaunt%C3%A9-lowe-hasa-message-for-you-if-in-doubt-get-screened/
- https://www.komen.org/share-your-story/chaunte-lowe/
- https://www.glamour.com/story/high-jumper-chaunte-lowe-conqueredfour-olympics-now-shes-training-for-tokyo-through-breast-cancer

HISTORY OF THERMOCHROMIC MATERIAL

- https://www.sciencedirect.com/science/article/pii/S1369702108702268

THERMOCHROMIC INKS

- https://veritech.in/security-inks/#:~:text=Secure%20inks%20are%20used%20as,environment%2C%20required%20level%20of%20security
- https://www.labelandnarrowweb.com/contents/view_onlineexclusives/2019-11-12/labels-to-help-combat-counterfeiting/
https://en.wikipedia.org/wiki/Thermal_printing

CHAPTER 8: A '70s Fashion Fad That Saves Lives

1. https://lancasteronline.com/opinion/don-t-be-glum-mood-rings-are-making-a-comeback-the-scribbler/article_ea42f6c6-3656-11eb-8605-5b6702d2945d.html
2. https://www.mayoclinic.org/tests-procedures/biofeedback/about/pac-20384664
3. https://www.sciencedirect.com/science/article/pii/S1369702108702268
4. https://cfjctoday.com/2022/04/06/mood-rings-from-70s-fad-and-90s-nostalgia-to-lcds-and-nfts/
5. https://www.newscientist.com/article/mg13017684-900-technology-clothes-that-change-colour-in-the-heat-of-the-moment/
6. https://www.latimes.com/style/la-ig-hypercolor6-2008jul06-story.html
7. https://www.vogue.co.uk/news/article/nikolas-ajagu-dior-1s
8. https://news.ncsu.edu/2021/02/more-than-just-shoes-what-you-need-to-know-about-sneakerhead-sub-culture/
9. https://www.fastcompany.com/90637534/how-sneakers-became-a-79-billion-business-and-an-undisputed-cultural-symbol-for-our-times
10. https://www.motor1.com/news/483180/temperature-sensitive-paint-audi-a4/
11. https://www.tandfonline.com/doi/abs/10.1080/17569370.2016.1216990?journalCode=rffp20
12. https://journals.sagepub.com/doi/abs/10.1177/0040517520910217
13. K. R. Karpagam, K. S. Saranya, J. Gopinathan & Amitava Bhattacharyya (2017) Development of smart clothing for military applications using thermochromic colorants, The Journal of The Textile Institute, 108:7, 1122-1127, DOI: 10.1080/00405000.2016.1220818; https://www.tandfonline.com/doi/abs/10.1080/00405000.2016.1220818
14. https://www.wsj.com/articles/a-tattoo-that-knows-when-youre-drunk-1470939713
15. https://www.darkdaily.com/2021/09/22/proof-of-concept-study-at-university-of-colorado-boulder-shows-dynamic-tattoos-can-help-detect-and-track-health-issues/
16. See note 14
17. https://www.sciencealert.com/there-is-now-an-actual-tattoo-that-can-change-colour-based-on-glucose-levels
18. https://www.npr.org/sections/goatsandsoda/2015/06/11/412862651/how-bindis-could-help-women-and-their-babies-stay-healthy#:~:text=The%20mark%20is%20known%20as,ages%2C%20as%20a%20beauty%20mark.
19. https://time.com/3989379/iodine-deficiency-bindi/

MOOD RING

- https://www.encyclopedia.com/fashion/encyclopedias-almanacs-transcriptsand-maps/mood-rings
- https://wonderopolis.org/wonder/how-do-mood-rings-work
- https://www.venly.io/post/the-original-mood-ring-will-drop-on-the-venlymarket

THERMOCHROMIC INKS

- https://veritech.in/security-inks/#:~:text=Secure%20inks%20are%20used%20as,environment%2C%20required%20level%20of%20security
- https://www.labelandnarrowweb.com/contents/view_onlineexclusives/2019-11-12/labels-to-help-combat-counterfeiting/
- https://en.wikipedia.org/wiki/Thermal_printing

OTHERS

- https://www.prnewswire.com/news-releases/the-mood-ring---a-culturalicon-re-emerges-as-smart-wearable-nfts-301414759.html
- https://entertainment.howstuffworks.com/question443.htm
- https://www.ncbi.nlm.nih.gov/pmc/articles/PMC8541014/

CHAPTER 9: What's a Bicycle Pump Doing in a Michelin-Star Restaurant?

1. https://www.foodtimeline.org/foodeggs.html#abouteggs
2. https://www.alcoholprofessor.com/blog-posts/blog/2016/03/24/the-history-of-egg-cocktails-unscrambled
3. https://www.lhf.org/2014/03/beyond-sauerkraut-a-brief-history-of-fermented-foods/
4. See note 3
5. https://www.independent.co.uk/life-style/food-and-drink/features/bulli-for-him-ferran-adria-on-why-he-s-the-world-s-greatest-chef-395311.html
6. https://artsandculture.google.com/story/twenty-five-creations-that-changed-the-world-of-cooking-real-academia-de-gastronomia-espa%C3%B1ola/xwVR2-z5ZGiPKw?hl=en
7. https://artsandculture.google.com/story/the-story-of-elbulli-real-academia-de-gastronomia-espa%C3%B1ola/qwURzFLVhm19LQ?hl=en
8. https://www.britannica.com/biography/Ferran-Adria
9. See note 5

10. See note 7
11. https://en.wikipedia.org/wiki/The_World%27s_50_Best_Restaurants
12. https://archive.nytimes.com/dinersjournal.blogs.nytimes.
    com/2010/02/12/el-bulli-to-close-permanently/
13. See note 8
14. See note 7
15. See note 8
16. https://www.theworlds50best.com/stories/News/12-iconic-dishes-el-
    bulli-ferran-adria.html
17. See note 7
18. See note 7
19. https://www.theworlds50best.com/stories/News/12-iconic-dishes-el-
    bulli-ferran-adria.html
20. https://www.youtube.com/watch?v=Qglfsp_pfF8 (translated into English
    from Spanish)
21. See note 20
22. See note 20
23. See note 20
24. https://archive.nytimes.com/dinersjournal.blogs.nytimes.
    com/2010/02/12/el-bulli-to-close-permanently/
25. http://pre.contenidos.icex.es/spanishfoodwine/global/traininq/cooking-
    techniques/cooking-technique-detail/REC2017737077.htm|
26. https://www.dnaindia.com/lifestyle/report-deconstructed-food-done-
    right-2611212
27. https://www.eater.com/2013/7/12/6404927/has-ferran-adria-had-a-
    catastrophic-effect-on-the-younger-generation
28. https://www.cntraveler.com/restaurants/barcelona/disfrutar
29. https://www.gq-magazine.co.uk/lifestyle/article/ferran-adria-interview
30. See note 27
31. See note 29
32. https://www.nytimes.com/2015/01/04/business/ferran-adria-the-
    former-el-bulli-chef-is-now-serving-up-creative-inquiry.html
33. See note 32
34. https://elbullistore.com/en/bullipedia/
35. See note 32
36. https://bullinianos.com/en/what-are-the-bullinianos/

OTHER REFERENCES

• https://elbullifoundation.com/en/
• https://hashtaglegend.com/icons/el-bullis-ferran-adria-thinks-
  moleculargastronomy-myth/
• https://www.sogoodmagazine.com/pastry-chefs/oriol-castro/
• http://elbulli.com/historia/version_imprimible/1961-2006_en.pdf

CHAPTER 10: How Is a Voltmeter Similar to a Mind Reader?

1. Bauby, Jean-Dominique. *The Diving Bell and the Butterfly*. Harper Perennial 2007

2. https://www.aruma.com.au/about-us/blog/the-story-behind-the-diving-bell-and-the-butterfly/

3. https://www.irishtimes.com/sport/in-the-blink-of-an-eye-1.57219

4. https://en.wikipedia.org/wiki/Jean-Dominique_Bauby

5. See note 3

6. https://youtu.be/NhmXaeaHkDc

7. http://www.edisontc.org/ui/home/course/unit-i/voltmeters/

8. https://youtu.be/hlCHpkkmBdo

9. https://cosmosmagazine.com/health/medicine/hans-berger-has-a-real-brainstorm/

10. https://www.britannica.com/science/electroencephalography

11. http://www.sinhaclinic.com

12. https://choosemuse.com/how-it-works/

13. https://www.frontiersin.orq/articles/10.3389/fpsyg.2017.01657/full

14. https://news.sap.com/2019/09/emotiv-sap-personalizing-workplace-learning/

15. https://youtu.be/aIpbEQZlgk8

16. https://www.theguardian.com/film/2008/jan/27/features.review4

17. https://newatlas.com/neurable-brain-control-interface-vr/50817/

18. https://venturebeat.com/2020/12/07/nextmind-real-time-brain-computer-interface-dev-kit/

19. https://www.youtube.com/watch?v=693m2ufstls

20. https://youtu.be/fs2GDSYYCoA

21. https://www.neurolutions.com/device

22. https://capgemini-engineering.com/cz/en/news_press_release/altran-presents-use-mind-control-technology-aircraft-manufacturing-paris-air-show/

23. https://youtu.be/Gv_XB6Hf6gM

24. https://www.businesswire.com/news/home/20220329005986/en/Synchron-Announces-Long-Term-Safety-Results-from-Fully-Implanted-Endovascular-Brain-Computer-Interface-Stentrode%E2%84%A2-for-Severe-Paralysis

25. https://youtu.be/693m2ufstls

26. https://massivesci.com/articles/bmi-brain-machine-interface-burkhart-paralyzed-touch-motion/

27. https://eagleman.com/science/sensory-substitution/

28. See note 27

29. https://www.smithsonianmag.com/innovation/could-this-futuristic-vest-give-us-sixth-sense-180968852/

ADDITIONAL REFERENCES

- https://www.youtube.com/watch?v=qnqLh32bGBM
- https://neuralink.com/applications/
- https://www.neurable.com/
- https://www.youtube.com/watch?v=Rae6NzMWTRo
- https://www.kernel.com/products - brain reader for behavioural change and impulse control
- https://www.youtube.com/watch?v=c8Dna8Lk_jM
- https://www.next-mind.com/?cn-reloaded=1 - brain controlled IOT
- https://www.youtube.com/watch?v=4c1lqFXHvqI
- https://www.youtube.com/watch?v=0YlBl4VeIiY
- checko.ai
- https://imotions.com/blog/top-6-common-applications-human-eeg-research/ -
- https://en.wikipedia.org/wiki/Electric_battery
- https://en.wikipedia.org/wiki/Hans_Berger
- https://mayfieldclinic.com/pe-eeg.htm
- https://youtu.be/HqtpMDEwiyM
- https://youtu.be/-CUWZk3fNlo
- https://youtu.be/aIpbEQZlgk8
- https://www.vice.com/en/article/wx88yw/device-paralyzed-people-controlcomputers-brain-thoughts
- https://choosemuse.com/muse-research/

CHAPTER 11: Broken Bones Fix Disaster Zones

1. https://www.concretecanvas.com/uploads/CC-Shelters-Brochure-1.pdf
2. https://specialtyfabricsreview.com/2008/07/01/concrete-cloth-applications-may-save-lives/
3. https://www.newsweek.com/tech-tents-made-cement-85967
4. See note 1
5. See note 2
6. https://www.unhcr.org/refugee-statistics/
7. https://www.vox.com/2014/5/14/5717526/33-million-people-are-refugees-in-their-own-countries
8. See note 1
9. https://www.concretecanvas.com/blog-concrete-canvas-the-company-behind-the-inflatable-concrete-shelter/
10. See note 2
11. https://www.concretecanvas.com/concretecanvas/
12. https://www.nbmcw.com/product-technology/construction-chemicals-waterproofing/concrete-admixtures/concrete-cloth-its-uses-and-application-in-civil-engineering.html

13. See note 2
14. https://buildabroad.org/2016/09/29/concrete-canvas-ltd/
15. See note 3
16. https://www.youtube.com/watch?v=a63S8ZxVu4A&ab_channel=ConcreteCanvasLtd
17. https://youtu.be/VyuJLe1WIOw
18. https://www.concretecanvas.com/uploads/CC-Channel-Lining-Coalcleugh-Northumberland-UK.pdf
19. See note 12
20. https://www.designboom.com/design/rug-n-roll-stools-concrete-canvas-organic-forms-johannes-budde-09-09-2022/
21. https://theconstructor.org/concrete/concrete-cloth-properties-applications-process/17070/
22. https://www.ncbi.nlm.nih.gov/pmc/articles/PMC5420179/
23. https://youtu.be/Vb1pdvvoVoQ
24. https://www.concretecanvas.com/concrete-canvas-just-got-better/

CHAPTER 12: Can Human Beings Become Electronic Circuits?

1. https://www.theguardian.com/technology/2014/apr/27/electric-paint-bare-conductive-paintable-wire
2. https://cdm.link/2009/08/human-synthesizer-with-calvin-harris-lots-of-girls-electric-ink-behind-the-scenes/
3. https://www.gov.uk/government/case-studies/bare-conductive-original-paint-technology-opens-a-digital-world
4. See note 1
5. https://www.bareconductive.com/pages/what-is-bare-conductive
6. https://www.bareconductive.com/collections/electric-paint
7. https://www.prnewswire.com/news-releases/global-printed-circuit-boards-pcbs-market-to-reach-72-7-billion-by-2026--301505577.html
8. See note 7
9. https://onboardcircuits.com/how-global-shortages-are-impacting-printed-circuit-boards/
10. https://luxury-pianos.com/the-most-expensive-pianos-in-the-world/
11. https://www.bareconductive.com/blogs/community/liquid-midi-ejtech
12. https://www.prnewswire.com/news-releases/global-greeting-cards-market-2022-rising-popularity-of-digital-cards-continues-to-negatively-impact-sales-of-traditional-greeting-cards-301500897.html
13. https://www.instructables.com/Festive-electronic-greeting-cards-using-conductive/
14. https://www.bareconductive.com/blogs/community/adding-interactivity-into-an-exhibition-stand-with-the-interactive-wall-kit
15. https://www.bareconductive.com/blogs/community/creating-a-smart-retail-experience-with-the-interactive-wall-kit

16. https://www.bareconductive.com/blogs/community/vitamin-creating-an-interactive-wall-for-a-car-company
17. https://www.idtechex.com/portal.v2/pages/company-profile.asp?articleid=24937&portaltopicid=all
18. https://www.laiier.io/
19. https://www.laiier.io/use-cases/detergent-levels-for-commercial-washers
20. https://www.alliedmarketresearch.com/liquid-detergent-market

CHAPTER 13: A Gamer's Take on Physiotherapy

1. https://www.physio-pedia.com/The_emerging_role_of_Microsoft_Kinect_in_physiotherapy_rehabilitation_for_stroke_patients#cite_note-Fitness_Gaming-21
2. https://themontrealeronline.com/2013/02/virtual-rehab-for-stroke-victims/
3. https://youtu.be/5rsyr8oS_xs
4. See note 2
5. https://www.who.int/initiatives/rehabilitation-2030
6. https://www.physiospot.com/2019/07/11/rehabilitation-2030-2-4-billion-people-are-in-need-of-rehabilitation-services/
7. https://jintronix.com/clinical-overview/
8. https://youtu.be/2Aewor16erA
9. https://jintronix.com/wp-content/uploads/2020/02/Jintronix_Clinical-Research-Summary.pdf
10. See note 9
11. https://pubmed.ncbi.nlm.nih.gov/32326849/
12. https://www.ncbi.nlm.nih.gov/pmc/articles/PMC6981843/
13. https://www.who.int/initiatives/rehabilitation-2030
14. https://www.thehealthsite.com/diseases-conditions/world-physical-therapy-day-2021-what-is-telerehabilitation-and-why-it-matters-836478/
15. https://archivesphysiotherapy.biomedcentral.com/articles/10.1186/s40945-020-00089-5
16. https://www.thegoodbody.com/physical-therapy-statistics-and-facts/
17. See note 3
18. See note 8
19. https://www.cbc.ca/news/canada/british-columbia/physiotherapy-graduates-licensing-failure-covid-19-1.5759855
20. https://www.gonzaga.edu/news-events/stories/2020/4/17/dancing-at-a-distance_pedagogy-in-the-pandemic-series
21. https://researchmatters.in/ta/node/141
22. https://www.tandfonline.com/doi/abs/10.1080/14647893.2021.1980524?src=&journalCode=crid20

23. https://www.auganix.org/how-augmented-reality-can-be-used-for-industrial-skills-training/
24. https://www.webmd.com/fitness-exercise/features/can-you-get-really-fit-with-wii-exercise-games
25. https://systematicreviewsjournal.biomedcentral.com/articles/10.1186/s13643-020-01421-7
26. https://en.wikipedia.org/wiki/Gerontechnology
27. https://www.sciencedaily.com/releases/2014/01/140114102457.htm
28. https://www.straitstimes.com/asia/as-japans-population-greys-video-games-now-target-silver-generation
29. https://www.sciencedirect.com/science/article/pii/S2666691X22000136
30. https://www.analog.com/en/applications/technology/3d-time-of-flight.html
31. http://pervasivecomputing.se/M7012E_2014/papers/P09-S02-Martin-Developing%20a%20gesture-based%20game.pdf
32. https://www.irjet.net/archives/V3/i11/IRJET-V3I1155.pdf
33. https://www.ibm.com/in-en/topics/what-is-a-digital-twin#:~:text=A%20digital%20twin%20is%20a,Twin%20Exchange%20(01%3A41)

OTHER REFERENCES

- https://www.neuro-concept.ca/en/technologies/interactive-games/
- https://www.new-startups.com/jintronix-kinect-based-physicalrehabilitation/
- https://www.looper.com/301470/this-is-why-microsoft-kinect-was-acomplete-failure/

CHAPTER 14: Spiderman, Goats and Haute Couture: What's the Link?

1. https://www.scienceabc.com/humans/movies/can-spiderman-really-stop-a-train-with-his-web-spider-silk.html
2. See note 1
3. https://www.newyorker.com/tech/annals-of-technology/in-the-future-well-all-wear-spider-silk
4. See note 1
5. https://daily.jstor.org/the-tangled-history-of-weaving-with-spider-silk/
6. https://www.theguardian.com/artanddesign/gallery/2012/jan/23/golden-silk-cape-spiders-in-pictures
7. https://www.vam.ac.uk/articles/golden-spider-silk
8. See note 5

9. https://books.google.co.in/books?id=_
   03QAAAAMAAJ&dq=spider+silk+machines&as_
   brr=1&pg=PA697&redir_esc=y#v=onepage&q&f=false

10. See note 5

11. See note 5

12. https://www.fda.gov/food/agricultural-biotechnology/
    science-and-history-gmos-and-other-food-modification-
    processes#:~:text=1973%3A%20Biochemists%20Herbert%20Boyer%20
    and,human%20insulin%20to%20treat%20diabetes

13. See note 12

14. https://www.bbc.com/news/av/science-environment-16554357

15. https://www.nytimes.com/2002/06/16/magazine/got-silk.html

16. See note 15

17. https://bechtel.colorado.edu/~crimaldi/publications/press/2001/
    smithsonian_july_2002.pdf

18. https://www.treehugger.com/bizarre-examples-of-genetic-
    engineering-4869360

19. https://modernfarmer.com/2013/09/saga-spidergoat/

20. https://www.smithsonianmag.com/innovation/new-artificial-spider-silk-
    stronger-steel-and-98-percent-water-180964176/

21. https://futurebrh.com/news/spider-silk-a-biodegradable-alternative-to-
    traditional-glue/#:~:text=Synthetic%20Spider%20Silk%3A%20A%20
    Biodegradable%20Alternative%20to%20Traditional%20Glue,-by%20
    Future%20BRH

22. https://interestingengineering.com/science/artificial-spider-silk-is-
    stronger-than-the-real-thing

23. See note 14

24. https://www.globenewswire.com/news-release/2022/05/02/2433669/0/
    en/Global-Sports-Fishing-Equipment-Market-to-Reach-16-Billion-
    by-2027.html

25. https://www.prnewswire.com/news-releases/global-synthetic-fibres-
    market-report-2022-2026-frequent-fluctuations-in-raw-material-
    prices--health-and-environmental-risks-of-synthetic-fibres-restraining-
    growth-301534528.html

26. https://www.startus-insights.com/innovators-guide/5-top-synthetic-
    spider-silk-startups-impacting-the-materials-industry/

27. https://www.prestigeonline.com/hk/style/spider-silk-is-the-future-of-
    fashion/

28. See note 27

29. https://www.startus-insights.com/innovators-guide/5-top-synthetic-
    spider-silk-startups-impacting-the-materials-industry/

30. https://www.scmp.com/lifestyle/fashion-luxury/article/2113819/spider-
    silk-bullet-stopping-plane-catching-fabric-thats-got

31. See note 3

32. https://vegnews.com/2021/6/vegan-spider-silk-replace-single-use-plastics
33. https://www.ingredientsnetwork.com/cambridge-university-invents-vegan-spider-silk-to-news113156.html
34. https://idstch.com/technology/materials/emerging-new-field-bionicomposites-researchers-created-one-strongest-materials-earth-silk-spun-graphene-fed-spiders/
35. https://en.wikipedia.org/wiki/Dragon_silk
36. See note 32
37. https://www.wearethemighty.com/mighty-trending/body-armor-spider-silk/
38. https://www.sciencealert.com/researchers-have-created-an-antibiotic-spider-silk-that-can-heal-wounds
39. See note 36
40. https://www.seevix.com/medical/
41. https://www.genengnews.com/topics/translational-medicine/spider-silk-proteins-developed-into-gel-for-biomedical-applications/
42. https://www.labiotech.eu/trends-news/airbus-amsilk-spider-silk-planes/
43. See note 42

CHAPTER 15: A Fifth-Century Invention Helps Solve a Twenty-First-Century Problem

1. https://en.wikipedia.org/wiki/Energy_crisis#2020s
2. https://www.nytimes.com/2022/03/18/climate/global-energy-crisis-conserve.html
3. https://en.wikipedia.org/wiki/2021%E2%80%932022_global_energy_crisis#cite_note-10
4. https://www.bloomberg.com/news/articles/2021-10-07/china-s-energy-crisis-envelops-an-already-slowing-global-economy
5. https://timesofindia.indiatimes.com/who-invented-the-kite-and-when/articleshow/6211967.cms#:~:text=It%20is%20thought%20that%20the,message%20for%20a%20rescue%20mission.
6. https://skysails-power.com/about-us/
7. https://www.bbc.com/future/article/20220309-the-kites-flying-to-harness-the-worlds-strongest-winds
8. See note 7
9. https://www.britannica.com/technology/windmill
10. https://thekitepower.com/product/
11. https://www.smithsonianmag.com/innovation/could-high-flying-kites-power-your-home-180979894/
12. See note 10
13. See note 7
14. https://thekitepower.com/kitepower-in-aruba/

15. See note 11
16. https://thekitepower.com/
17. See note 7
18. See note 7
19. https://e360.yale.edu/features/after-a-shaky-start-airborne-wind-energy-is-slowly-taking-off
20. A Short History of Kites: History of Flying – The Kites Role in Aviation and the Airplane. Author Paul R. Wonning. Publisher Mossy Feet Books
21. https://en.wikipedia.org/wiki/Kite#cite_note-Murphy-27
22. See note 14
23. https://www.future-islands.org/projects/20220512-aruba-as-successful-test-case-for-global-wind-energy-innovation
24. https://www.choicesmagazine.orq/2006-1/biofuels/2006-1-05.htm
25. https://www.ship-technology.com/analysis/feature-skysails-bringing-wind-back-ship-propulsion/
26. https://www.nytimes.com/2008/01/20/business/worldbusiness/20iht-ship.1.9349041.html
27. https://archive.fortune.com/galleries/2008/fortune/0810/gallery.tech_windpower.fortune/index.html
28. https://www.nature.com/articles/news.2008.564
29. See note 25
30. https://skysails-power.com/offshore-units/
31. https://skysails-power.com/airborne-wind-applications/
32. See note 11
33. https://www.fastcompany.com/90710052/this-giant-kite-helps-power-cargo-ships-and-reduces-greenhouse-gas-emissions-by-20
34. https://thenextweb.com/news/can-airseas-make-cargo-ships-more-sustainable
35. https://www.airseas.com/seawing
36. https://allthingskites.com/what-is-the-easiest-type-of-kite-to-fly/
37. https://www.canadiankitecompany.com/blogs/tie-to-the-sky/what-is-a-parafoil-kite
38. See note 33
39. https://www.bbc.com/news/business-59401199
40. https://minesto.com/projects/faroe-islands
41. https://minesto.com/projects/holyhead-deep
42. https://innovationorigins.com/en/kitepowers-kite-generates-energy-by-spinning-in-figures-of-8-at-high-altitude/

CHAPTER 16: Can Banks Borrow and Lend Time?

1. https://youtu.be/UIvnJJWyUuQ
2. https://www.wionews.com/world/watch-time-is-money-people-in-switzerland-can-actually-deposit-their-time-in-banks-442315

3. https://www.chinadaily.com.cn/a/202201/25/
    WS61ef4befa310cdd39bc82ff0.html
4. https://www.who.int/docs/default-source/documents/
    decade-of-health-ageing/decade-ageing-proposal-en.
    pdf?Status=Temp&sfvrsn=b0a7b5b1_12#:~:text=By%20the%20end%20
    of%20this,than%20double%20to%202.1%20billion.
5. https://magazine.wharton.upenn.edu/digital/challenges-and-solutions-
    for-elder-care/
6. https://www.homecareassistancearlingtontx.com/advantages-of-home-
    care-for-seniors/
7. http://www.bjreview.com/Nation/202101/t20210104_800231674.html
8. See note 7
9. http://www.transitsocialinnovation.eu/sii/ctp/tb-japan-1
10. https://ssir.org/articles/entry/the_time_bank_solution#
11. See note 10
12. See note 10
13. See note 10
14. https://timebanks.org/day-3-disaster-preparedness-and-response/
15. https://www.investopedia.com/terms/t/time-banking.
    asp#:~:text=The%20term%20%E2%80%9CTime%20
    Banking%E2%80%9D%20was,to%20supplement%20government%20
    social%20services.
16. https://www.downtoearth.org.in/news/economy/why-time-banking-is-
    a-crucial-tool-to-empower-women-82369
17. https://nonprofitquarterly.org/time-banking-a-community-path-to-
    addressing-social-exclusion/
18. https://www.theguardian.com/voluntary-sector-network/community-
    action-blog/2015/mar/30/time-banking-encouraging-new-volunteers
19. https://www.axi.com/au/blog/education/blockchain/soulbound-tokens
20. https://decrypt.co/resources/what-are-soulbound-tokens-building-
    blocks-for-a-web3-decentralized-society
21. See note 20

OTHER REFERENCES

• https://www.weforum.org/videos/what-is-time-banking

BONUS CHAPTER: The Banyan Tree Analysis

1. https://en.wikipedia.org/wiki/Amazon_(company)
2. https://www.techtarget.com/searchaws/feature/Amazons-impact-
    onpublishing-transforms-the-book-industry#:~:text=During%20the%20
    past%2015%20years,%2D%2D%20%24280%20billion%20and%20
    climbing.

3.   https://www.simform.com/blog/fuel-management-system/
4.   https://www.omnisci.com/technical-glossary/vehicle-telematics
5.   https://www.nytimes.com/2014/01/21/science/bird-data-confirms-that-vs-help-save-energy.html
6.   https://mymoneywizard.com/learning-about-money-from-mr-mrs-miser/
7.   https://www.economist.com/science-and-technology/2021/04/14/why-people-forget-that-less-is-often-more